SADOMASOCHISM

Etiology and Treatment

Susanne P. Schad-Somers

JASON ARONSON INC.
Northvale, New Jersey
London

THE MASTER WORK SERIES

First softcover edition 1996

Library of Congress Cataloging-in-Publication Data

Schad-Somers, Susanne P. (Susanne Petra), 1939–
    Sadomasochism : etiology and treatment / Susanne P. Schad-Somers.
        p.   cm.
    Originally published: New York : Human Sciences Press, 1982.
    Includes bibliographical references and index.
    ISBN 1-56821-789-7 (alk. paper)
    1. Sadomasochism.   I. Title.
    RC560.S23S3   1996
    616.85'835 — dc20   95-52080

Manufactured in the United States of America. Jason Aronson Inc. offers books and cassettes. For information and catalog write to Jason Aronson Inc., 230 Livingston Street, Northvale, New Jersey 07647.

This book is for Bill with love,
for my patients with admiration,
and for Giulietta with gratitude.

CONTENTS

ACKNOWLEDGEMENTS

Some debts can never be repaid, they can only be acknowledged with gratitude. The gifts of our mentors rank highly among them. It has been my experience, that no amount of evidence to the contrary will deter a determined mentor from the steadfast—if not stubborn—belief in the perfectibility of the human mind. Since this conviction is usually coupled with a passionate and infectious involvement with ideas, these individuals must be responsible for the majority of books ever written. Since this book addresses the subject of gratitude at length, it seems only fitting to thank the following individuals: Elisabeth Wöhler, Rosemarie Stein, Walter Schäfer, Heinz Edelstein, Max Horkheimer, Theodore W. Adorno, E. Belvin Williams and Paul F. Lazarsfeld.

Helga Aschaffenburg taught me most of what I know about the *art* of psychotherapy; the vital importance as well as the limitations of empathy and compassion, and a healthy respect for human perversity. Besides, she always appreciated my sense of humor.

I am grateful to Ned Polsky for having been the first person to point out that my papers were beginning to add up to a book and for his skillful nudging to do something that would obligate me to actually write it.

3

The following colleagues read the manuscript in its various stages and offered invaluable advice and encouragement: Shirley Panken, John Gagnon, Morris Stein, Elizabeth Hauser, Larry Hauser, Jay Jacobs and Regi Goldberg. I am deeply indebted to all of them. I owe special thanks to Morris Stein for extending himself over and beyond the call of duty.

I also want to thank all my friends for bearing with a writer so disinclined to do her suffering in silence, and for trusting that one day this too would be over. However, none of this would have been written without the trust and commitment on the part of my patients who risked so much in endeavoring long–term psychotherapy, an enterprise which probably constitutes one of the profoundest exercises in courage. Thus, it is ultimately my patients to whom I owe the greatest amount of gratitude.

Susanne P. Schad-Somers
East Hampton, N.Y.
June, 1981

INTRODUCTION TO
THE SOFTCOVER EDITION

Anticipating how this volume will be received in the age of Oprah and past-life regressions simply exceeds the powers of my imagination. It was never politically correct, even when it was first written, and it is by now fatally flawed politically and probably hopelessly quaint.

Back in the good old days of the '60s and '70s, when we were riding high on a crest of moral and political self-righteousness at an altitude never to be attained again, the vague term "liberation" encompassed many diverse populations and social institutions. What is more, it seemed to be clearly within our reach.

In that spirit in 1971–1972, with some like-minded colleagues, we set up two psychotherapy referral services that were to be free of homophobia and sexism. One was the Homosexual Community Counseling Center (H.C.C.C.); the other was the Psychology and Psychotherapy Committee of NOW (National Organization for Women), out of which evolved the Women's Psychotherapy Referral Service (W.P.R.S.). Then, of course, we had to figure out what a nonsexist psychology of women should entail. Pretty heady stuff. We talked a lot, fought with passion, and held innumerable workshops. Coming up with new paradigms for our work proved to be much more difficult than anybody had thought. The tension between the ideological blue-print and the private reality seemed insurmountable.

Specifically, the vast discrepancy between our notion of how "liberated women" ought to act in all spheres of life and the actual behaviors of just about every woman we knew suggested that perhaps the troublesome concept of female masochism we had just buried had to be exhumed in order to be examined critically. Clearly, "liberation" has not even begun to eradicate any, let alone all, of those self-defeating behavior patterns that in our culture are typically female. However, instead of assuming a biological origin, it made more sense to look at it as a psychosocial phenomenon, a way of being in the world that the little girl learned from her parents.

While nobody enjoys suffering per se, it can become a learned response in the face of rejection and persecution. Understood as a child's adaptive response to the sadism of another person, one that is retained in the form of internalized self- and object representations (with all the staying power of a genuine character armor or structure), it explained the self-defeating behavior patterns sufficiently as a social rather than constitutional phenomenon. Furthermore, conceptualized in this way it also means that sadism and masochism are invariably covariants, differing only in their relative distribution within any given individual and changing over time. As such, the syndrome assumed quite recognizable and human dimensions, familiar and certainly treatable. "Female Masochism: The Anatomy of an Ideology" (1976) was my attempt to articulate this dialectic and to show that it was in no way in conflict with feminism. Judging from some of the responses, the latter thought proved to be a major error in judgment.

Given the social structures and norms that characterize Western patriarchal societies, it seemed logical to assume that in such social systems men would be more likely than women to occupy the sadistic end of the sadomasochistic continuum. By that I am referring to observable behavior patterns, not unconscious intent. "Male Sadism: Envy, Hostility and Perversion" (1977) was intended for a conference on sadomasochism given by the National Institute for the Psycho-therapies (N.I.P.). However, shortly before the beginning of the conference the planners decided to restructure our panel in such a way that the professionals on it would be discussants and the actual presentations would be given by twelve representatives of the Eulen-spiegel Society, one of the main voices of the S & M liberation front.

The main thrust of their argument was, and still is, that sexual sadomasochists are essentially an oppressed sexual minority, marginalized and pathologized by the psychiatric profession and denied equal rights. There was to be no argument, according to those speakers, S & M practitioners are a discriminated group of people whose bedroom practices have no bearing whatsoever on the other aspects of their interpersonal relationships or their professional lives. My insistence that sexual sadomasochism as a predominant sexual preference cannot be divorced from its corresponding characterological base was booed loudly by roughly 297 out of 300 participants. Unwilling or unable to shut up, I placed my paper at another conference and proceeded to write *Sadomasochism.*

Now, almost twenty years later, when the categories "masochism," "sadism," and "sadomasochism" have been all but banned from the *DSM-IV,* in a climate that seems to know primarily victims and one that has created an entire and vast industry of survivor therapy services complete with an extensive and rapidly growing literature and lecture circuit, to reissue a volume centered unambiguously around the concept of "self-responsibility"˙ as *the only pragmatically useful and morally defensible therapeutic goal in the treatment of abuse victims* seems quaint indeed for two reasons:

1. One of the basic beliefs of feminist therapy has been that when it comes to the subject of parental brutality, particularly in the case of sexual abuse and incest, we first and foremost start by believing the patient. Lately, however, that resolution may require an almost unilateral suspension not just of disbelief, but also of the basic rules of scientific reasoning and research. In the absence of any empirical proof we are asked to believe in, among other things, the existence of a vast underground of satanic cults that are maiming, killing, and torturing thousands of children. These cults have brainwashed their victims either to deny or to repress the experience. Victims who manage to tell will be killed. We are also expected to take at face value the notion that, again, thousands upon thousands of people all over the world are being abducted by flying saucers and subjected to unspeakable sexual experiments and tortures. The treatment of those who "tell" is similar to that of the cult members.

2. "Survivors" are frequently encouraged to confront their accus-

ers, be it by taking them to court or by revealing their awful deeds on talk shows. Failing that, to denounce them to their families and friends, even when the abusers are lying on their deathbeds or, as a last resort, during their funerals. The underlying assumption is that confrontation empowers and "heals." To question the purpose and the psychic functions of such a powerful need for revenge as a very understandable but ultimately futile expression of the bottled-up rage and as an expression of the victim's own capacity for sadism is considered heresy: we are then blaming the victim. Furthermore, a critical examination of these vengeful impulses would be antithetical to the building up of the victim's self-esteem. *Sadomasochism,* in contrast, argues that ultimately only the patients themselves can make it all good again and that sadomasochism had once been a lifeline, a survival tool in a hostile world that in adult life represents a major handicap. Specifically, it assumes that the intrapsychic function of the self-hatred typical for the masochist is that it retains the illusion of the goodness of the maternal other at the expense of the goodness of the self. Interpersonally, the masochist hopes to trade suffering for love and may use failure as an indictment of the unloving parent. As hope for changing a bad parent or current love object into a good one fades, suffering can take on a sadistic coloration, manifesting itself in self-mutilation and, in the extreme, suicide.

Furthermore, *Sadomasochism* contends that while psychotherapy can offer the patient a great deal of compassion and empathy, eventually it has to aim for the only feasible and effective goal, namely, providing patients with the tools to take charge of their lives by assisting in the development of those psychic structures that make it possible to repair the damage done to them when they were children. What we are treating, after all, are varying degrees and forms of developmental arrests. In order to accept that unpalatable proposition, patients first have to confront their own capacity for sadism, the shocking recognition of some of the aspects of the brutal parent as an integral part of the self. At that point life seems doubly unfair, particularly since it would be so much more in keeping with the spirit of our times—not to mention how potentially lucrative it could be—if this reservoir of sadism could be utilized for extraction of material as well as emotional reparations or the exercise of outright revenge. To make them "quiver in their boots" as the toddler once did.

Finally, in treating patients with a sadomasochistic or self-defeating orientation, the single most difficult variable is shame. Shame is not only the most archaic of emotions, one even animals can experience, but it can also cause more vitriolic, even deadly, rage than any other feeling; it is the axis, the ever-present potential land mine, around which the entire treatment revolves. In fact, success or failure, therapeutic progress or premature termination, will depend on how skillfully patient and therapist together can navigate this treacherous fault line. One way of dealing with one's shame is via "reaction formations" during which the person aggressively and publicly shames him- or herself bigger and better than any opponent could. The person reasons that "if I publicly parade my perversion or affliction, if I do so 'in your face,' I emerge not only triumphant but seemingly invulnerable." Exhibitionism and sadism are, after all, twins. The much more difficult tasks, such as taking control over one's archaic responses, becoming slowly more desensitized to the agents of one's shame reactions, anticipating and circumventing people or situations that are potentially shame provoking, and maintaining dignity in the face of provocation, all take years of work — and what is worse, they *can never be fully attained.*

With a great deal of work and some luck, what we can attain is the "good enough" life, one in which the capacity for love and work has been restored sufficiently for the weight of the past to recede and where the mistakes of the parents can be laid to rest. That, to my mind, is not bad at all.

INTRODUCTION

Sadomasochism, the confusion between love and hate, power and submission, is a uniquely human phenomenon. It is one, though by no means the only one, of the inevitable products of man's prolonged dependency in early childhood, for dependency invariably means inequality. Since the human infant is born several years prematurely, physiological birth and psychological birth are roughly three years apart. During that time, the infant's emerging sense of self, and its external and internal reality are filtered through those of its mother's. And what makes us human, and therefore unique, creative and capable of complex feelings and thought processes is the eventual resolution of the tension between the wish for symbiosis and the need for autonomy. Only a perfect balance between holding on and letting go on the mother's part would permit complete separation and individuation—which is to say that it can never be fully attained. What is more, for childhood to be free of lasting trauma, parents would have to be mind readers and utterly selfless. Finally, since there is no such thing as a compromise between unequals, the subjective experience of oppression is therefore a universal part of childhood. Remnants of symbiotic attachments and corresponding rage over its limitations, impingements and frustrations remain in all of us, experiences that are never

11

fully metabolized. Given the fact that individuation is never complete—mother remaining part of me—the feeling of oppression readily lends itself to its subsequent transformations, namely self oppression and the oppression of others as parts of the self. In other words, even under the best of circumstances, the biological fact of utter physiological and psychological dependency in early infancy leaves us also with, among many other feelings, some vengeful impulses towards the primary caretaker as well as a certain readiness or need for masochistic surrender to symbols of that caretaker. For social order to be possible, all societies have to see to it that this nonmetabolized childhood trauma or sadomasochistic substratum is somehow dealt with. This is done in a number of different ways, which in most societies differ for males and females:

1. The institutions of secondary socialization such as school, church, scouts or the military, etc. are sometimes geared towards helping youngsters to further metabolize and transcend this trauma.
2. Society can offer legitimate or socially valued outlets or avenues into which to channel these impulses. Examples would be professions, careers or social roles that glorify self-sacrifice or violence, submission or power or both. Alternatively, a society may encourage the externalization of these impulses by designating the members of another society or ethnic or political minority as legitimate recipients of oppression or violence, and others as the objects of idealization and subjugation.
3. Containment and social control are regulatory mechanisms which determine how much and what forms of sadism or masochism are permitted when and by whom. For example, in our society boys may fight physically with other boys but not with girls. When fighting, however, boys are not permitted to kill. A middle-class man can slap his wife but he is not allowed to beat her up. Couples can slap each other in the privacy of their homes but not at public events. While the law tries to control violence against other persons, social control agents, such as psychiatry and religion, function also as restraining forces for potential violence against the self (e.g., attempted suicide). We may work ourselves into a heart attack but we are not supposed to immolate ourselves.

4. A certain amount of sadomasochism has been institutional-
    ized in the traditional relationship between the sexes, particu-
    larly in the rules governing the nuclear family. In fact, sexism
    represents a culturally-valued sadomasochistic arrangement,
    based on complimentary needs and fears; it is socially sanc-
    tioned, and has been in evidence in all known societies.

While by and large this sadomasochistic substratum does not
seriously interfere with normal living, its pathological forms—or
rather those that society deems pathological—are the subject of this
book. However, like most clinical literature on the subject, it deals with
masochistic behavior more extensively than it does with overt sadism.
Even though in terms of observable behavior and unconscious intent—
sadism and masochism are but two sides of the same coin—it is the
masochist who typically comes to the attention of the psychotherapist.
This explains the commonly encountered clinical bias which assumes
that under less than optimal conditions, masochism is the more typical—though by no means the only possible—outcome of man's prolonged dependency in infancy. Sadomasochism as the *predominant*
adaptive defensive feature in the relationship between the child and
the parental other arises in response to a very specific emotional
climate. It has the following components: parental sadism, narcissism,
rejection and persecution of the child. Since these parental attitudes
are usually present at birth, sadomasochism is by definition a preoedipal condition. Consequently its sexual manifestations are really symptoms of pregenital conflicts, masquerading as oedipal problems. Put
differently, sadomasochistic sexual practices are an example *par excellence* of the reenactment of—or defense against—the power struggle
between the toddler and its preoedipal caretaker. While I have seen
patients who have claimed that their sadism or their masochism pertained to their sex lives only, I have never found this to be so. To the
contrary, sadomasochism as a sexual perversion is a particular constellation of sadomasochistic impulses and narcissistic defenses in
which the partner serves at least in part as a transitional object, one
which embodies all the threatening aspects of the preoedipal mother.
Depending on the pervasiveness and depth of the parental pathology, the resulting sadomasochistic stance or life style, as defined here,
cuts across and overlaps with other diagnostic categories, ranging from
the most severe and debilitating pathologies to normalcy. It is thought
of as an interpersonal orientation, or a form of object relationships,

differing in extent and range, i.e. the degree to which it affects a person's being in the world and being with others, and how many vectors of a person's life are affected by it. The spouse who subtly undermines a partner clearly differs from the one who habitually batters his wife or child. The person who sabotages career, personal relationships and his or her sex life is obviously more sadomasochistic than the one who confines the undermining to one or the other area of his or her life.

If sadomasochism is defined this broadly, the question could be raised how does sadomasochism differ from other nosological entities? The answer to this question is twofold:

1. The sadomasochistic syndrome, as conceptualized in this book, is characterized by a specific, though usually unconscious *interpersonal intent,* a particular adaptation to an early environment that continues to persist into and dominate adult life. For example, Masterson's (1976) typical borderline patient, some pathological narcissists and the sadomasochistic patient described here, may all consistently jeopardize their careers. But they do so for different reasons. The Masterson patient must fail because independent mastery spells separateness from mother which is experienced as a rendezvous with death. Many narcissistic patients cannot risk truly testing the possible discrepancy between their grandiose fantasies and their actual accomplishments. The sadomasochistic patient, on the other hand, fails in order to indict and punish a significant other—alive or dead—who was or is experienced as unloving. In other words, the suffering of the masochist has to be seen at times as being quite vengeful in its intention—if not outright sadistic—aiming at victory through self-defeat, control through submission.

2. It is hoped that the overlap with some of the other diagnostic entities, notably depression and pathological narcissism will be a fruitful one, for it invites the clinician to perhaps more sharply focus on the adaptive interactive function of all pathology, even if the final product is seemingly devoid of interpersonal purpose. While it goes without saying that a proper diagnosis always has to determine on what levels a patient's development has been arrested, and what the var-

ious structural defects are, it is also true that within each of those diagnostic categories there is also always to be found a passionate involvement with a parental object or part object. To the extent that this passionate involvement is sadomasochistic in its orientation it is the focus of this book.

The treatment plan proposed here is developmental, long-term, and aimed at as complete a rehabilitation of structural defects as a patient will commit him or herself to. However, the therapeutic course described here differs from other developmental models in the following way: It assumes, in the case of the sadomasochistic patient, that before the crucial issues of separation and individuation can be approached, a great deal of reparative work, duplicating the earlier developmental phases, has to be accomplished. This decision rests on two conclusions. One, sadomasochism is, among other things, essentially an emotional "deficiency disease" of earliest childhood. Secondly, given the fact that the famous "negative therapeutic reaction" induces so many sadomasochistic patients to terminate therapy prematurely, we have to offer these patients a great deal of hope in order to seduce them into wanting to truly live.

The case material presented here, has not been chosen for its "neatness," but in order to illustrate the variables that seem to determine the relative chances for therapeutic progress. After all, we learn as much from our therapeutic failures and mistakes as we do from our successes. With that thought in mind, the entire treatment process has been described, warts and all. Four patients are discussed in this book. They will be called Karl, Bob, Larry and Anna. Two of them are homosexuals and two are heterosexual. Diagnostically, one was a schizophrenic, one a borderline patient and the two others were lower-level character disorders. In the course of treatment ranging from six to eight years respectively, this is what happened: Each of the men in this group at first attributed the origin of his difficulties to his father's treatment of him. Karl, who hated his father, reported brutal beatings and not so subtle threats with a butcher knife. Bob, who had also been beaten regularly and rather severely, kept yearning for his father's love since his father had shown considerable affection toward some of the other siblings. Larry, who described his father as cold and distant, had made it his life's ambition to win his father's love and admiration through remarkable artistic accomplishments. Anna, on the other hand, stated that her father had been a very nice and loving, though at times irresponsible, man. Like so many masochistic women, she felt essentially victimized by her mother, to whom she referred as "that unloving, depriving and hysterical shrew." However, if we look at the actual family dynamics, as they emerged in the course of therapy, we get quite a different picture. That does not mean that what the four patients reported with respect to their fathers represents a screen memory—to the contrary, it was true enough—but that their particular relationship with their fathers constitutes the end-product of a faulty or inadequate relationshp with their preoedipal mothers and the concomitant ego and object splitting on the part of the patients. Bob's and Anna's mothers had nine and five children, respectively. Bob's mother wore a surgical mask whenever she handled the infant, lest he catch her germs. Anna's mother, a devout Catholic, had two D&C's prior to Anna's birth which clearly were ill-concealed attempts at birth control. Karl's mother had wanted a girl. Failing at that, she dressed Karl in girl's clothing until the age of twelve. Larry's mother regarded her children not only as unwelcome interruptions of her professional career, but also as interlopers in an extremely symbiotic marriage. It would be fair to state that all four patients in infancy were "house-broken" rather than socialized.

Psychodynamically, all three male patients followed a similar pattern: disappointed in their mothers, or rather unable to deal with her pathology, they turned to their fathers with hope for a more stable kind of mothering and for what Kohut (1971) has termed compensatory structures. They defined themselves in terms of the real but mostly imagined and essentially negative expectations that their fathers had of them. Lacking a stable sense of self and maternal other, the process of ego and object splitting involved, on one hand, the attribution of the most threatening aspects of both the mother and the self to the father, and, on the other hand, their subsequent re-incorporation. Anna, in contrast, had idealized her father and had defined herself primarily by incorporating fully her rejecting mother, whom she reproduced through her choice of sadistic love objects and with the help of her cruel superego.

Given these backgrounds and the adaptation that these patients made, it is hardly surprising that all of them entered therapy with considerable structural defects and with a thoroughly sadomasochistic orientation or lifestyle. However, all four patients have made an enormous amount of progress. In fact, Anna and Karl are presently terminating. Larry will probably do so in another year and Bob has only recently reentered therapy in earnest with a solid wish for genuine change.

Whether or not a different understanding of these people's problems and, correspondingly, a different treatment approach would have resulted in a better and quicker adjustment, is for the reader to decide.

Chapter 1

SADISM AND MASOCHISM:

Metapsychology

The term *sadomasochism,* in what follows, refers to object relations that are characterized by an observable predominance of either sadistic or masochistic features on the one hand and an unconscious though willful sadistic or masochistic interpersonal intent on the other. In other words, overt sadomasochistic behavior and its unconscious purpose—be it sadistic or masochistic or both—are conceptualized as covariants. That means that the term *sadomasochistic* will be applied *only* if the overt masochistic behavior has a covertly sadistic goal or vice versa. Consequently, the distinction between sadism and masochism is essentially an artificial one, since it merely indicates the predominance of one observable behavior pattern over another. The emphasis in the foregoing is on the word *predominance,* however, since I also intend to show that the sadomasochistic syndrome or character formation is usually accompanied by varying degrees of pathological narcissism, or paranoia, or sometimes both. The definition of sadomasochism that I have just given implies a number of separate but interrelated statements regarding the nature of psychopathology in general, and the origins of sadomasochism in particular. These metapsychological assumptions, and their application to the subject matter at hand, will be spelled out in detail, since taken together they entail the rationale for the treatment process discussed in later chapters. The simplest way of doing this would be to simply state my position and leave it to the reader to judge it by its theoretical merits and its usefulness in treating patients.

The subject of sadomasochism, however, occupies a curious position in the history of psychoanalytic theory. Until almost 20 years ago, one can find it regularly discussed in the literature, usually within a framework based on dual-instinct theory. Since then, very few analysts have made an original contribution to the subject. Given the enormous advances in ego psychology, self psychology, developmental psychology, and object relations theory in the last two decades, this is a curious phenomenon. It almost seems that the concept of sadomasochism has been the property of Freudian and neo-Freudian thought and has never really been brought up to date to incorporate the newer ways of conceptualizing psychopathology. Thus, for the purpose of historical continuity alone, a critical, though selective, overview of the literature would be in order. There is a more important reason, however; one which in my opinion is essential for the understanding of the therapeutic approach presented later. To be specific: the subject of sadomasochism, more than any other, forces one to examine critically the origins of the sadistic component in the human psyche, in general, and in the sadomasochistic involvement in particular. After all, since anger, directed either at the self or at others, is the baseline, one wants to know where it originates. Theoretically, one can conceptualize it as coming from the infant, the environment, or both. Either the infant has a biological predisposition to angry reactions not related to frustrations, or one can explain infantile rage as being purely *reactive*. Obviously, the answer to this question is central to any discussion of sadomasochism. My review of the literature, therefore, will address itself essentially to this particular question. Needless to say, no final answers can be given, and none are attempted here. All the practicing clinician can do—and I think must do—is to examine the various metapsychological points of view, and to make choices on the basis of their plausibility and their pragmatic usefulness. This I will attempt to do in a fairly systematic fashion.

Since the beginnings of a fully interpersonal—though not yet developmental—theory of sadomasochism, namely the contributions of Berliner, Menaker, and Guntrip, have been the starting point of my own thinking, I shall show how and where I have attempted to go beyond their ideas and how I have related them to the newer theories. Additionally, since the final product, as I see it, is by no means a "neat" clinical entity but a syndrome that partially overlaps with other known and well-defined entities, the components of the sadomasochistic syndrome will be spelled out not only in relation to the newer concepts but also in relation to the empirical—as distinct from the clinical—evidence supporting them.

Thus, without duplicating the work done so ably by others, notably Panken (1973) and Sack and Miller (1975), the review of the literature will address itself to the following:

1. What model of the psyche is employed?
2. The retrospective approach—what are the psychotoxic elements in the etiology of sadomasochism? Among the psychotoxic elements we will distinguish between the hostile-rejecting parental environment and the narcissistic parental involvement with the child. As the corollary of those last two points, we will examine respectively the intrapsychic and the interpersonal functions of the sadomasochistic adaptation for the child and the future adult, and discuss the relationship between sadomasochism and pathological narcissism or self pathology.
3. An attempt will be made to explain the motivational bond that connects the subject and the object, through one unifying concept that encompasses all the different psychological threads.
4. Finally, the relationship between the sexual and characterological manifestations of sadomasochism will be discussed.

MODELS OF THE MIND

As indicated already, this review of the literature is not intended to be systematic. It will merely explore three positions: human destructiveness as originating essentially in the subject; human destructiveness as an interplay between constitutional disposition and a less than optimal environment; and finally, a view that dispenses with the concepts of drives and primary aggression altogether and explains sadomasochism strictly as an adaptive response to the sadism of *another person*.

The Freudian Model: Eros and Thanatos

The masochism literature which is fully—or partially—based on dual-instinct theory is by far the most common type. This cannot be explained merely by the fact that for so long the Freudian model of the mind was the most prominent one. What seems to be equally important is that the Freudian metapsychology is singularly suited to explain the curious phenomenon of pain becoming pleasure. In fact, it does not only explain it, it suggests it as being a logical possibility as well as constituting part and parcel of the human condition—which in my opinion, it is indeed. I believe this, however, for reasons that differ from those offered by Freud or his followers.

The two facets of Freud's metapsychology particularly suited to the understanding of the puzzle of masochism are 1. his hypothesis of the existence of a death instinct; and 2. his theory pertaining to the vicissitudes of the instincts, and the assumption that one's drives are enormously flexible both as to their aims and their objects. Freud, who unlike many of his disciples never failed to remind his readers that most of his premises were just that, rather than empirically verifiable— let alone tested—hypotheses, stated quite unambiguously that:

> We know two kinds of things about what we call our psyche (or mental life): firstly, its bodily organ and scene of action, the brain (or nervous system) and, on the other hand, our acts of consciousness, which are immediate data and cannot be further explained by any sort of description. Everything that lies between is unknown to us, and the data do not include any direct relation between those two terminal points of our knowledge. (1949, p. 1)

In other words, one can observe people's actions, hear their thoughts, experience feelings and ideas, and draw inferences about the connections between those phenomena and the nature of their physiological substrata. Given this assumption and starting point—that one has to explain the forces that translate the activity of the brain into human behavior and consciousness—Freud started out with a question that could be considered unfortunate and unanswerable, namely, why does the organism move?—instead of simply taking it for granted. It needed no further explanation.

As Becker pointed out, "The organism is active by *definition of organism*. We do not have to explain why animals move, any more than why the universe is in motion; it is a fact we can easily accept—and, indeed, must accept." (1965, p. 110). But Freud, in his search for a motivational force, proposed the existence of drives to explain human activity and motivation. Being also acutely aware of the infinite capacity of the human animal to annihilate its own kind and deliberately to self-destruct, Freud concluded that destructiveness per se is a given in the human psyche and its physiological substratum. It is not my intention here to give either a complete or an historical account of Freud's thinking on the subject of sadomasochism, but rather to extract from his writings the most salient features about the subject. I shall focus primarily, though not exclusively, on Freud's theories pertaining to the vicissitudes of the instincts (1915b) and how they relate to the problem of masochism, and on Freud's paper (1924) on the Economic Problem in Masochism. I shall then examine how useful and how tenable the Freudian framework is for the explanation and the treatment of the sadomasochistic syndrome.

Freud (1920) had concluded that the human organism is governed by two opposing instincts, eros and thanatos, whose expressions are not only in conflict with each other, but also largely in conflict with the demands of civilized life. Civilization is possible only because our instincts are extremely malleable and flexible. Since instincts constitute a constant force, however, rather than act as a momentary impact or event, no escape from instinctual life is ever possible. In the collision between the demands of the reality principle and instinctual forces, what makes human survival possible—albeit at the price of neurosis—is the human ability to subject these instinctual forces to the processes of: reversal into their opposite, both in aims and content; turning round upon the subject; the fusion of opposing instincts; repression; projection; and sublimation. Our inner lives revolve around three antitheses: 1. Subject (ego)-object (external world); 2. Pleasure-pain; and 3. Active-passive. These general principles led Freud, in dealing with sadomasochism, to conclude that human life is a continuous struggle between eros and thanatos, the instincts of life and death, the striving for the ultimate equilibrium—namely the return to an inorganic state and the instinct of love and self preservation. Far from taking the organism's determination for survival for granted, Freud saw it as a tenuous—if not tortuous—mental accomplishment, in constant need of renegotiation since self-destruction is an ever-present possibility.

Freud (1924) distinguished five manifestations of masochism: a. erotogenic or primary masochism (the lust of pain); b. female masochism (to be discussed in the third chapter); c. secondary masochism; d. feminine masochism in men; and, e. moral masochism.

Primary or erotogenic masochism (from which all other forms of masochism derive) and primary sadism are the products of the encounter between eros and thanatos; they are present in all multicellular living organisms. The libido renders a portion of the death instinct harmless by directing it toward objects in the real world, where it manifests itself as the desire for mastery, destruction or the will to power. A section of the instinct is placed directly in the service of the sexual function as "true sadism." Another section, however, is not included in this displacement outward; it remains within the organism and is bound there libidinally with the help of accompanying sexual excitation, and this "we must recognize as the original erotogenic masochism." (p. 260)

Secondary masochism arises if a part of the death instinct which has been directed towards the outer world is introjected, i.e., turned inward again and, thus, supplements the primary masochism. The masochistic substratum of primary erotogenic masochism passes through all developmental stages that give it the various shapes encountered in mental life. The oral stage contributes to the fear of being devoured by the totem animal, the father; the anal stage produces the desire to be beaten; castration fantasies emerge in the phallic phase; and the genital stage adds desires to experience passivity in intercourse and the desire to give birth, characteristic of female sexuality.

Feminine masochism in men is entirely based on this primary erotogenic masochism and its subsequent developmental modifications. This explains the various sexual acts typical of male masochism, such as the males who want to experience themselves passively as castrated females in intercourse or who wish to be treated like a helpless and naughty child.

Moral masochism, though derived from the same substratum (primary erotogenic masochism), differs from feminine masochism by its object choice. The moral masochist typically does not elicit punishment from a loved one, but from fate or his own superego. An unconscious sense of guilt—as distinguished from consciously experienced sadism of the superego—prompts the masochist to act in self-destructive ways. His sadism resides in the ego. Its sexual content, however, and its derivation from erotogenic masochism, though disguised, can, according to Freud, be easily deduced. Excessive renunciation of primary sadism and other instinctual gratifications, result in an intensification of the masochism of the ego that is supplemented by the sadism of the superego. In a regressive move, the oedipus complex becomes resexualized and, with it, the wish for passive sexual relations with the father, and its regressive derivative, the wish to be beaten by the father. Only, the moral masochist has substituted internal forces for the original parent.

Although few of Freud's followers adhered to the concept of a death instinct—notably Franz Alexander (1924) and Karl Menninger (1938)—dual-instinct theory, which assumes that there are inborn drives of an aggressive or sadistic nature, became the bedrock of Freudian and Neo-Freudian psychoanalytic theory; it has been incorporated into many of the newer psychoanalytic theories ranging from ego psychology to object relations theory. Clearly, this Freudian metaphyschology does succeed in explaining the paradox of pain becoming pleasure as a *natural phenomenon*. With its global definition of sexuality, and the assumption that small infants respond to increases in psychic tension with sexual excitement, and that painful tensions could elicit concomitant sexual responses, the physiological substratum for all other forms of masochism, the problem of sadomasochism, is fully explained. Moreover, on a descriptive level, the Freudian theory of sadomasochism is singularly accurate. For example, the sadomasochist is indeed characterized by weak or impaired ego functions and a sadistic superego. But what has to be questioned is how this structural defect developed.

The Intermediary Position: Bernard Berliner

The fact that dual-instinct theory and an object relations theory of masochism can be combined is most clearly exemplified by the work of Berliner (1940; 1942; 1947; 1958), though he is by no means the only one to have done such combining. He is one of the first analytic writers to examine systematically the role of parental rejection and hostility in the etiology of masochism. He defines it as "the sadism of the love object fused with the libido of the subject." (1958, p. 41) Having stated clearly and unambiguously that he strictly adheres to dual-instinct theory, Berliner then, nevertheless, explains the masochistic stance *entirely* in terms of aggressive-sadistic elements in the preoedipal maternal environment, such as maternal hate, mistreatment, non-love, wish for infanticide, etc. The question as to how the "masochistic ball gets rolling," so to speak, is answered by Berliner's assertion that from the beginning the infant meets hostility and sadism, which are experienced *as if* they were love, and the rejecting love object is introjected. The aggressive components in masochism, which Berliner distinguishes from oral and anal sadism, are explained as 1. repressed hostility toward the bad love object; 2. emotional blackmail, the attempt to extort love from the object through suffering; and 3. the indictment of the love object in order to induce guilt that might then motivate the object to give love after all. The primary defense mechanisms employed against the experience of hostility and rejection are denial and the libidinization of suffering. Secondary defenses are the "aggressive defense"—a counter-masochistic attitude, and identification with the aggressor. Berliner further concludes that the incorporation of, or the identification with, the punitive parent operates not only in the masochist but in varying degrees in all of us. Thus, a certain amount of sadism is continuously passed on from one generation to the next, which explains the universality of moral masochism in our culture. And Berliner adds: "No death instinct needs to be postulated to explain masochism." (1958, p. 50)

This short summary is not designed to do justice to Berliner's treatment of the subject, but to raise questions. Beyond stating that the destructive instinct is instrumental but not the driving force in masochism, e.g. Berliner's treatment tells us little about the relationship between aggression as an instinctual force and reactive aggression. Second, masochism, as conceptualized by Berliner, is composed of ego defenses and superego pathology, which are fully accounted for by his analysis of the parental attitude and treatment of the child—the child's attempts to reconcile its love and dependency needs with the non-love on the part of the needed object, and finally the reenactment of that interaction with other—similar—objects in adult life.

Thus, two questions remain: a. What, if any, is the fate of primary aggression in the etiology of masochism? and b. If masochism can be fully explained in interpersonal terms, what other phenomena are there that require the concept of primary aggression in order to be understood?

The Fully Interpersonal Model: Esther Menaker and Harry Guntrip

Menaker (1979), very clearly and deliberately moved from a framework of conflict theory—be it intrapsychic instinctual conflicts or conflicts between instinctual impulses and the demands of civilized life—to a model that has adaptation as its central concept. The ego and its subsystems, such as identity and ego ideal, are seen as adaptive, even creative, agents that aim at survival, mastery, and in the ideal, even social change. According to Menaker, masochism is an adaptive response of the ego that originates during the oral stage when infantile dependence is total. In other words, the emergent ego of the child with an unloving or even hateful mother cannot unfold naturally, since from the beginning, it has to adapt to an object that does not want it to be. The ego, instead of growing with, or from, an accepting nurturing other, has to find ways of surviving through subjugation, surrender, appeasement, and consequently, with a self that is crippled in terms of becoming an autonomous center for willed action. Identity formation under such circumstances proceeds not on the basis of a positive maternal mirror experience but through the incorporation of the negative attitudes that the mother harbors toward the child. Genuine separation and individuation from the mother are not possible since the self is not experienced as a source of pleasure. All goodness for such a child resides in the maternal other.

In other words, the starting point in the masochistic development is the devaluation of the child on the part of the mother. The resulting devaluation of the self on the part of the child and the corresponding view of the mother as the source of all supplies is the center of the masochistic bond. The weaker the ego, the more parasitic the relationship will be. The maternal attitudes are incorporated into the ego, although her judgments constitute the stuff of which a sadistic superego is made. The experience of guilt for its very existence not only prevents the child from taking pleasure in life but also prevents it from expressing the rage that a stronger ego could more easily master. The masochist, as Menaker sees him, lives on hope that someday things will be better, that eventually suffering will be rewarded. Essentially, he is tied to the parental other on the basis of ego weakness and corresponding dependency. This is true enough. Although repressed rage is seen as an important part of the masochistic syndrome, it still seems that the sadistic component is somehow neglected.

Menaker's masochist is basically a weak person, yet experience shows that masochists can be extremely powerful—even ferocious—as ruthless toward others as they are toward themselves. Part of the explanation for the sadism, as will be shown later, lies in the distinction between ego weakness on one hand, and ego impairment coupled with pathological narcissism on the other.

Since the sadomasochist is anything but weak, how can one account for the source of power that characterizes this particular involvement in the world and the stubborn determination to maintain the intrapsychic and interpersonal status quo? Also, the sadistic strain in the sadomasochistic personality formation? Here, Guntrip's (1961) work provides a useful set of concepts to answer some of these questions. He, following Fairbairn, distinguishes between the following sets of object relationships: 1. the libidinal ego that develops in relationship to the exiting object; 2. the antilibidinal ego that responds, and is built in response to the rejecting object; 3. the central ego emerges through the relationship with the ideal object. From these building blocks that designate interactive patterns, Guntrip builds a set of interpersonal relationships ranging from total infantile dependence through the various forms of psychopathology to maturity and mature dependence. Although Guntrip has devoted most of his theoretical and clinical work to schizoid conditions, the sadomasochistic involvement can be found as one of his 13 "basic forms of human relationships." He defines it as: "*Aggressively Rejective.* The *Libidinal Ego* as a needy, frightened, rejected child masochistically suffering under the angry, Rejective Object, the sadistic adult. An unequal relationship giving rise to a child-parent pattern involving great hostility." (1961, p. 376)

What is central to Guntrip's theory is his distinction between the active and the passive aspects of infantile dependency. The infant actively approaches the mother for life-giving supplies (libidinal ego). If the child meets with frustration, the healthy aggressive stance takes on a sadistic tinge that is anxiety provoking. If the child consistently experiences the mother as frustrating and rejecting (rejecting object), three things are going to happen: a. The anxiety caused by the sadistic component of the child's relationship to the mother, transforms the active dependency of the child into a passive one; reactive rage manifests itself only in sadistic fantasies, later to be repressed. b. Through the process of "incorporative identification" the anti-libidinal ego is built up, which functions as a saboteur of the child's libidinal needs.

c. The anti-libidinal ego joins forces with the rejecting object to persecute the child's own needs—the masochistic stance, and later those of
others—the sadistic position. In other words, the repressed sadism of
the oral-dependent stage constitutes the bottom line of the sadomasochistic character formation. The persecuting inner objects are retained as a defense against depersonalization. After all, according to
Guntrip, the deepest fear of a person in such a predicament is that the
sadism could destroy the needed object, and since a bad object is
infinitely preferable to having no object at all, the status quo has to be
maintained. In the case of the sadomasochist, it is the person or the
analyst who tries to *disrupt* this inner arrangement who is likely to
become the target of this destructive rage.

CONCLUSIONS

In the evaluation of a psychoanalytic theory or a model of the
mind, four criteria seem to be of utmost importance: 1. its usefulness in
explaining normal and abnormal psychic phenomena, (Stone, 1971);
2. the degree to which it stands up in light of the *empirical* evidence,
(Gedo and Goldberg, 1973); 3. its applicability to the understanding of
social groups or aggregates, (Guntrip, 1961); and 4. its usefulness in
the treatment of patients. After all, one has to remember that "scientific theories are devised in order to gather together what has been
learned, to give coherence to scientific findings. As such they can never
be considered final versions of the truth; they can at best approximate
validity." (Gedo and Goldberg, p. 3) That means that whenever one
employs an untested and/or untestable theoretical construct—such as
primary aggression—to explain human behavior, it is done because it
seems to make a given phenomenon more intelligible than it otherwise
would be. Consequently, if it were possible to eliminate it altogether, it
would add to the soundness of our discipline. To do so however, is only
possible *if—and only if*—the behavior which is to be understood can,
first, be explained comprehensively and convincingly in terms of other
variables that can be tested empirically; and, second, if on the basis of
this explanation patients can be treated successfully. If both of these
conditions are met, the abstract theoretical construction can, and
should be, eliminated. Thus, if the four criteria listed above are applied
to dual-instinct theory, a number of objections come to mind which,

taken together, suggest that a fully interpersonal model of the mind is far better suited for the understanding of sadomasochism than dual-instinct theory, even though, as Chessick (1977) and Gedo and Goldberg (1973) have pointed out, such a model has the disadvantage of containing a certain degree of terminological ambiguity.

It is hoped that the review of the theories of Berliner, Menaker, and Guntrip have succeeded in illustrating that in order to understand sadism and masochism one need not hypothesize any force in the human organism to account for its self-destructiveness or the compulsion to attack others. This is particularly true, as will be shown later, if one examines the problem of sadomasochism in light of the current knowledge of pathological narcissism. In other words, in terms of the first criterion, namely the capacity to explain normal and abnormal psychic phenomena, dual-instinct theory, or rather the assumption that there is such a thing as primary aggression and the interpersonal model which assumes no such thing, are equally capable of accounting for the phenomenon in question; the explanatory power of both models should be evident.

If one looks at the empirical evidence for the existence of primary aggression, one can only conclude that the final evidence as supplied by anthropology, ethology, ethnology, and academic psychology is not yet in, which is understandable in light of the fact that what is being dealt with is a hypothesis that, at least until now, seems to be untestable. Consequently, one has to look at the evidence at hand, namely the data provided by developmental psychology and clinical practice. In other words, what scientists studying children have actually been able to *observe*. The examination and evaluation of the empirical findings of developmental psychology, and the development of normal children, however, is an extremely difficult task. Paradoxical as it may sound, there is quite a discrepancy between the way Spitz (1965) and Mahler (1975) relate their findings to Freudian theory and the data they actually present as I understand them. Bowlby (1969) on the other hand, is clear and unambiguous:

> In place of psychical energy and its discharge, the central concepts are those of behavioral systems and their control, of information, negative feedback, and a behavioral form of homeostasis.

and he adds:

> . . . the theory of psychical energy remains untested; and until it is
> defined in terms of something that can be observed, and probably
> measured, it must be regarded as still untestable. For a scientific
> theory this is quite a crippling handicap. (p. 18)

Spitz and Mahler, however, whose observations give no indications whatsoever for the existence of primary aggression or the death
instinct—to the contrary—both claim that their findings are quite
compatible with the basic tenets of Freudian metapsychology. Since
this is not the place for a critical examination of the possible internal
contradictions in Spitz's and Mahler's pioneering works, I merely want
to point out that from my point of view, Spitz, Mahler, and Bowlby
present compelling evidence for the contention that the human organism seems to be exclusively geared toward survival, adaptation and
attachment to the primary caretaker. Moreover, it seems to be capable
of an enormous resilience in the face of adverse conditions. This does
not mean that all infants are alike, that they do not show constitutional
differences, but these differences pertain to physiological homeostasis,
more or less diffused tension states, endowment or *Anlagen,* rather
than aim directed drives. In the absence of psychotoxic elements and
gross physiological disturbances, growth and maturation during the
first year of life must be thought of as the unfolding of a set of cognitive
and interactive patterns that emerge *in interaction* with and *in response* to
the primary caretaker. Spitz writes about the "organizers of the psych-
e"; Bowlby (1969) uses the term "attachment behavior". Both phrases
designate behavioral systems that are activated in the mother-child
dyad and mutually reinforce each other. According to Bowlby, the
smiling response of the three-month-old intensifies the attachment of
the *mother,* or, as Menaker puts it: "The infant's smile can thus be
viewed as a *signal* to the mother which is calculated to evoke, or in terms
of ethology, to release motherliness and mothering, both of which are
necessary for physical survival and for the further development of the
ego as well." (1979, p. 125)

Thus, the smiling response is seen as a flattery, an idealization that
elicits and promotes a loving response from the mother. In other
words, what the human infant brings into the world is a rather powerful armament for the extraction of mothering behavior without being
in any way conscious of the meaning of those signals. This only happens at a later point of development. For example, to attribute envy to

the nursing infant, as Klein (1957) has done, i.e. "the angry feeling that another person possesses and enjoys something desirable (i.e. the breast)—the envious impulse being to take it away or spoil it," seems to be a rather absurd adultomorphism, since it presupposes a capacity for self-object differentiation and the development of cognitive capacities that, according to Spitz and Piaget (1966), the nursing infant is entirely incapable of. What appears as aggression in the first year of life, according to most authors, are either attempts to cope with physiological tension states, reactions to frustrations, psychotoxic elements in the mother-child interaction, or separations from the mother. Thus, it seems much more plausible to view all early childhood pathology— short of death by miasma—as an *adaptive and reactive* response to a less than optimal human environment, as a more or less desperate attempt on the part of the infant to *survive,* rather than as an attempt to return to an inorganic state, the expression of the death instinct.

The predictive and discriminatory power of a theoretical construct is measured by its capacity to explain individual differences and differences between social groups and to predict the likelihood of a specific phenomenon to occur in a given environment. For example: which child, in a given family, is likely to show a greater or lesser degree of sadism or masochism? Or: why are certain forms of sadism or masochism more prevalent in one social class than in another? Except for the X-factor, namely constitutional predisposition such as "poor tolerance for anxiety," (Reik, 1941), or excessive amounts of aggressive energy (Freud, 1924; Gero, 1962; Kernberg, 1976) dual-instinct theory offers very little in terms of either explaining or predicting individual or group differences. For example, Bromberg (1959) has shown that among siblings those children "are candidates for the development of moral masochism who are unconsciously identified, by the type of mother to be described, with that one of her own parents toward whom she showed the most ambivalence, with a preponderance of hostile feelings." (p. 803)

In my own professional experience, I have seen the same dynamic operate with respect to the singling out of one child who is seen as being most like the husband with whom the mother lives in a more or less stable sadomasochistic balance. Wolberg (1973) has made the same observation and a similar pattern has been observed with respect to those children who are singled out for child abuse. (Helfer and Kempe, 1968; Steinmetz, 1977) Furthermore, the incidence of rape, the epitome of sexual sadism, correlates with low socioeconomic status more than with any other sociological or psychological variable. Unless one assumes that those particular aggressive or sadistic drives that predispose a male toward rape are a genetic characteristic of the lower class, and somehow vanish as a result of upward social mobility, dual-instinct theory is really at a loss in explaining or predicting what kind of boy will grow up to be a potential rapist. On the other hand, if one views this kind of sadism as *one* possible response to a combination of parental neglect and hostility which offers the child no avenues of recourse, and if one takes into account what is known about the subculture of violence, one will probably come quite close to understanding the dynamics of the "police blotter rapist" (Brownmiller, 1975) which, after all, constitutes the majority of all rapists in our society.

In the context of this book though, the most important objections to the hypothesis of primary aggression and a death instinct pertain to their therapeutic implications. To name just a few: stated in the simplest form possible, if survival is seen as the primary goal of the human organism, then the only problem—though a formidable one indeed— is to help the organism to survive with fewer sacrifices. If aggression does not constitute psychological bedrock, then there is at least theoretically no reason why a patient could not learn more constructive ways of getting what he wants. Put differently, if psychopathology is essentially learned behavior, it can be unlearned given sufficient motivation and proper help. Moreover, if, as Menaker (1979) claims, infantile depression and masochistic surrender are seen as appeasement signals to the mother—rather than aggressive drives turned upon the self— then the therapeutic goal is one of undoing an internalized threat, rather than that of taming or rechanneling instinctual drives. Stone (1971), in his discussion of the Oedipus complex, has pointed out that Sophocles version of the tragedy has to be reversed, namely that the abandonment threat *precedes* the parricidal prophecy. "The murderous thrust originally awakened in the earliest experience of helplessness may provide an *Anlage* of hostility, rage and aggression resembling 'drive.' However this cannot be drive in the inborn, constant, autochthonous sense of psychoanalytic usage." (pp. 220-1) If one accepts this interpretation—and I do—this would also considerably alter the therapeutic approach to oedipal conflicts.

In sum, I am in full agreement with Stone (1971) who, in his extensive review of the psychoanalytic literature on aggression concluded that "I do not regard as proved, nor as pragmatically useful the concept of primary or essential aggression. The same is true of the origin of aggression in a death instinct." (p. 238) And "unlike sex, in itself a primary and powerful motivating force, aggression is, with rare pathological exceptions, usually clearly and extrinsically motivated. Motivations are numerous and various." (p. 238). Instead, it seems more desirable to follow the tradition of analysts like Guntrip (1961), Kohut (1977), Bowlby (1969), and Fromm (1973), to name just a few, and to try to conceptualize sadomasochism within a fully interpersonal framework that additionally examines it in developmental terms. It assumes that neither sadism nor masochism are expressions of instinctual drives but, rather, the product of a less than optimal parent-child interaction, i.e. defenses of the ego, superego pathology, and pathological narcissism. Given the truism that there is no such thing as a perfect mother, but only a "good enough" mother who meets her child's needs most of the time, one has to distinguish between a more-or-less universal sadomasochistic substratum in the human psyche, not fully metabolized experiences of infantile helplessness and corresponding rage, that do not seriously interfere with adult functioning (which will be discussed in chapters 3 and 4) and pathological sadomasochism where the masochism or the sadism have become the predominant lifestyle. It is the latter that is the subject of chapter 2. In the case of pathological sadomasochism, one assumes that a variety of specific psychotoxic elements in the early mother-child relationship interfered with the natural growth or unfolding of the child's potential. Specifically, referred to here are arrests in ego development and the establishment of a cohesive self.

Chapter 2

THE ETIOLOGY OF SADOMASOCHISM

In the presentation that follows, it seems useful to present the material in two ways: 1. The retrospective approach that summarizes the elements that clinically have been found to have been instrumental in the etiology of sadomasochism. In other words, here we are approaching the problem from the adult point of view, of how patients and therapists have reconstructed the patient's early history. 2. The developmental approach (presented in chapter 6) that examines, from the standpoint of developmental psychology, how specific acts and attitudes on the part of the primary caretaker would affect the child in the course of its early growth. It tries to determine, as accurately as possible, *how* and at *what point* or stage in infancy the environment failed the infant in terms of meeting its age-appropriate needs. It addresses itself to the question: How does the sadism of the object become the masochism of the subject? After all, it is not enough merely to look at the parental input per se, but to examine its effect on the evolving psychic structures of the child, its ego, self, superego, and ego ideal. Maternal overindulgence for example, as Masterson (1976) and others have demonstrated so convincingly, is hardly harmful during the very early stages of development, but disastrous during the separation and individuation phase. Conversely, aloofness on the mother's part, though not exactly growth-promoting during the separation phase, is less toxic for the child than overindulgence. This very aloofness on the part of the mother during the earlier phases, however, may have retarded the infant's early ego development to such an extent that the separation from the mother is really a pseudo-event. This is the interactive constellation typically found in the history of the sadomasochistic patient.

THE RETROSPECTIVE OR CLINICAL APPROACH

The literature on the subject as well as my own professional experience suggests the following elements as being responsible for the etiology of the sadomasochistic syndrome:

1. Traumatic deprivations on the oral level. (Menaker, 1953)
2. Parental rejection. (Berliner, 1947, 1958; Bromberg, 1955; Bloch, 1965; Millet, 1959; Thompson, 1959; Menaker, 1953; Reich, 1933)
3. Narcissism on the part of the parents and the infliction of nacissistic injuries on the child. (Bernstein, 1957; Eidelberg, 1959; Millet, 1959; Menaker, 1953; Bychowski, 1959)
4. Parental inconsistency, i.e. the promotion of behavior of which the parents disapprove. (Bromberg, 1959)
5. Seductive and sadomasochistic games played by the parents during the oedipal period. (Lowenstein, 1957)
6. Parental persecution. (Eisenbud, 1967)

Even Reik's (1941) assertion that masochists are essentially spoiled children, with the implication that it was excessive love that produced the masochism, rests on the mistaken assumption that "spoiling" is a sign of love, rather than repressed hostility and a lack of empathy. Thus, the composite picture of the parent of the future sadomasochist is of one who does not function primarily as a facilitator of the infant's physiological and psychological development, but rather as an active or passive inhibitor—an incompetent gardener so to speak—who cannot, or will not, supply adequate and age-appropriate nutrients, stimulation, rest periods and positive mirroring to the growing child.

Generally speaking, we can distinguish between two major parental traits as being responsible for the sadomasochistic personality formation: parental hostility and rejection and narcissism on the part of the parent. In what follows, we will—for the clarity of the argument—discuss the hostile and the narcissistic parent separately, even though in reality these two traits often overlap.

The Hostile Rejecting Parent

According to Berliner

> In the history of all masochists there were actual severe traumatic situations in early childhood. In my experience most of them were unloved, or directly hated, mistreated children; all were made to feel that they were in some way unwanted. Hatred on the part of the parents was frequently covered by oversolicitude and possessive demands for love which burdened the child with obligations and with guilt feelings for his very existence. (1940, p. 324)

Since both the symptomatology as well as the etiology of depression and masochism show a great deal of overlap, in fact the predominantly depressed patient may, after some treatment, become less depressed and more masochistic (or vice versa), we shall begin with a comparative note on the difference between the depressive and the masochistic involvement with the hostile rejecting parent. With respect to masochism, Berliner and Menaker are in agreement that one of the major defenses operating is the denial and libidinization of suffering. The actual experience of the ill-treatment is repressed—or rather disavowed—instead it is experienced as if it were love; this illusion allows the child to survive. The price for this adaptation is the introjection or incorporation of the hateful aspects of the parental other. Berliner believes that essentially the same process underlies depression. Although up to a point this is indeed true, it neglects the more passive stance taken by the depressive as compared with the masochist. Bloch (1965), in her paper on the effect of the wish for infanticide in neurotic depression, shows that such an extreme of murderous feelings on the part of the parent will result in a wholesale introjection of the parent's attitude. Such children believe that they are monstrous, unlovable, and do not deserve to live. In order to conceal their murderous wishes (as well as their own homicidal feelings) from themselves, the protection of the illusion that their parents *do* love them becomes the driving force in their lives. It becomes their raison d'être, without which they might feel compelled to commit suicide. Abnegation, self vilification, continuous attempts to prove how horrible they actually are, are attempts to prove that the parents were right in their estimation of their children. In describing such a patient, and the enormous suffering that this young woman created for herself, Bloch explains that this patient faced the almost insurmountable task to survive with the unconscious knowledge that her seemingly loving mother wanted to destroy her. In order to justify her mother's feelings, the patient had to prove to herself over and over again, and beyond a shadow of doubt, that she was, indeed, so bad and so worthless that her mother's feelings were justified. Having established her sense of badness, she could then delude herself into thinking that if she, the patient, changed she might yet obtain her mother's love. As Bloch adds, however: "This self-deception had to be maintained at all cost and demanded that there be *no resolution to the conflict,* because on an unconscious level Norma knew just what the score was. *She had to trick herself into living.*" (1965, p. 63 emphasis mine) In other words, even though the dynamics in masochism and depression are quite similar, the accent is different. The masochist is much more actively involved in obtaining the parent's love, and suffering itself does indeed become libidinized. Although sheer survival through repression or denial of rage and the maintenance of the illusion of parental love are the primary goals of the depressive, the masochist seems to be more inclined to *actively* change the rejecting love object. He seems to be the more optimistic one. This seemingly small difference is well kept in mind when we examine the description given by other authors, because we have to conclude, that no matter how abusive the parent of the future masochist might have been, he also offered the child the element of hope that "one day all will be well" which is so typical of the masochistic involvement.

Although Menaker, Berliner, Millet, and Thompson all emphatically stress parental rejection during the oral stage, the description of the mother-child relationship lacks the unambiguous quality exhibited by Bloch's mothers. Menaker refers to a mother love, which on the oral level, is almost deficient; Millet writes about a highly unsatisfactory relationship with the mother; and Thompson, found "No affection from either parent, parents at war with each other," and she goes on to say, "One of them can be seduced into a show of concern for the child if the child can demonstrate that he has suffered at the hands of the other, or if he can create some other situation of suffering." (1959, p. 34) In other words, it is the parent who hands the child, together with rejection and hostility, also the element of hope, which Reik has so eloquently described as the "element of fantasy." Bromberg (1959) focuses even more sharply on the element of seduction on the part of the parent. "They present themselves as devoted, self-sacrificing, solic-itous and kind, but their high degree of narcissism and hostile attitude towards the selected child results in behavior which belies this at every turn." (p. 805)

These parents elicit overt manifestations of sexual impulses, by being sexually provocative and stimulating, only to punish the child severely for its response. Usually, these mothers are controlling and possessive—mother knows best—and can do no wrong. By undermin-ing the child's attempts to relate to other children, by treating them as a rejection or expression of ingratitude on the child's part, she creates an exclusive bond that effectively cuts off the child from alternate love objects from which it could obtain a modicum of emotional breathing space. The element of seduction has also been noted by Lowenstein in his discussion of the seduction of the aggressor which one can find in all children. . ."the seeking of situations that entail fear and unplea-sure, and their attenuation through loving, erotic complicity of the threatening person." (1957, p. 215) Such rather common childhood games involve throwing the child high up in the air and only catching it in the last moment; rocking in the high chair until the child screams, etc. Reich (1933), who dates the development of masochism during the oedipal phase, also agrees that it is not only the lack of love which is instrumental, but a severe *disappointment* in love. "It started during that phase in childhood in which violent aggression and incipient infantile sexual (as opposed to oral and anal) impulses met with severe frustra-tion and punishment." (p. 249) According to Reich, the child seeks a parental beating in order to forestall a worse punishment, namely castration.

Another element, which seems to be of importance in this context, is that quite often, one child gets singled out for the masochism-producing treatment. As was noted earlier, according to Bromberg, it is the child which the parent identifies with his own parent toward whom he felt most ambivalent with a predominance of hostile feelings. Of equal importance, however, is a situation where the mother's "split off" bad self is attributed to a particular child and then relentlessly persecuted. Alternatively, as will be shown in chapter five in the case of Anna, a parent whose maternal capacities have been overtaxed by the first or second child may scapegoat the third child as the source of all her troubles. In either case, it seems reasonable to assume that the observation on the part of the child, that vis-à-vis its siblings, or vis-à-vis the spouse, the parents seem to be, indeed, capable of the expressions of love—or a reasonable facsimile thereof—will intensify the child's determination to get that love, no matter what the cost. Hostility and rejection, particularly on the part of the parent who identifies a particular child with either a parent, sibling, or a split-off part of his or her own psyche, may not necessarily express itself in the severity of the frustration imposed on the child, but in the style of the attempts to socialize the child. A mother who is uncomfortable with her own animalistic impulses—oral, anal or sexual—will persecute these same impulses in her own child, a process that Eidelberg (1959) noted so astutely is "far more threatening to the self-esteem than mere frustration" (p.564) since its goal is not teaching but *humiliation*. In the extreme, that form of persecution may entail that the child smiles after a severe punishment and—in one case I know of—that the child should first kiss the punishing parent and then kiss the very rod with which the beating has been administered. Even without such pathological forms of persecution, however, a hateful look on the part of the mother may convey, instead of mere displeasure over yet another dirty diaper, a wish to exorcise the child's alimentary canal, its greedy stomach, or its budding sexuality. Usually, this kind of persecution takes place at an age where the child is not yet capable of controlling its physiological functioning and its psychological impulses. Consequently, as Bromberg (1955) noted, "the inevitable failure results not only in further punishment, but in the child's loss of self-esteem." (p. 807)

It is my own conviction that *persecution* coupled with *humiliation* and *shame* are the *key variables* in the formation of the sadomasochistic character formation.

The Narcissistic Parent

As has been pointed out earlier, the narcissistic parent in his actions resembles the hostile-rejecting parent in many ways. The dynamics underlying their reactions to their children, however, are quite different. Also, since narcissistic parents tend to produce pathological narcissism in their children, together with sadomasochism, it seems necessary to untangle these two parental traits. Furthermore, since I have never seen a masochistic patient who did not also show a certain amount of pathological narcissism, and since the treatment of the latter differs from the treatment of the former, it is necessary to trace the impact of the narcissistic parent on the child separately. The central mechanism through which the narcissistic mother relates to her child is to view the infant as an instrument of her own narcissistic needs. The child is not a little person in its own right, but a mere extension of the mother. (Millet, Menaker) Consequently, the child tends to regress to its own narcissistic gratifications whenever the relationship with the mother ceases to be satisfying and becomes frustrating instead. Having been deprived of any sense of autonomy, such children are particularly vulnerable to "introjection of the object and a regressive splitting of the object and self-representations into the idealized good parent-child with all of the love and aggression embodied in the superego and the bad parent-child with all of the hate and devaluation directed toward it as the object embodied in the ego." (Bernstein, 1957, p. 375)

One extreme example of maternal narcissism is best illustrated by studying the dynamics of child abuse. In this case, the mother aims at complete role reversal, where the child is expected to play the comforting reassuring mother. According to Steele and Pollock (1968), "the child is not perceived as a child, but as some symbolic or delusional figure," and "may be perceived as the psychotic portion of the parent which the parent wishes to control and destroy." (p.96) A statement from an abusive mother makes this point painfully clear: "I have never felt loved all my life, when the baby was born, I thought he would love me; but when he cried all the time, it meant he did not love me, so I hit him." (ibid. p.96) The amount of narcissistic rage on the part of this particular mother is evidenced by the fact that at the age of three weeks the baby had to be hospitalized because of bilaternal subdural hematomas. Since abusing parents typically have been abused children themselves, however, their sadistic assaults on their children must be understood as the end product of a lifetime of a very masochistic adaptation to their own parents. Having been all their life a poor parent substitute to their parents, and—predictably failed at this impossible task—the crying of their own children is interpreted as a criticism, identical with the criticism received from their own parents. Thus, the pent-up rage against the parents breaks through and is displaced at the child. That means that at the moment of abuse the infant combines to the mother the monstrous aspects of *her* own mother as well as the split-off monstrous aspects of herself. Self- other differentiation crumbles and the abusive parent does, indeed, treat the infant as if it were a delusional figure.

The pervasiveness of the symbiotic tie between abusing parents and their children, their sense of helplessness and distrust, and consequently their inability to constructively relate to people other than their families, is illustrated by the observation made by Davoren (1968) and other social workers, namely that a house with drawn shades, unrepaired cars in the driveway, an unlisted phone and a total lack of involvement with neighbors and the community at large represents as good a set of indicators as any not only for the presence of child abuse but also for that of the battered wife syndrome.

Although the physically abusive parent may represent an extreme of a totally narcissistic-sadomasochistic involvement, it exemplifies the essential psychotoxic element inherent in the interaction between the narcissistic mother and her child, namely the expectation that it is the child's job to keep the mother happy, rather than the other way around. The physically abusive parent is but one variant—though an extreme one of this general principle of role reversal, which also operates in a rather common phenomenon, which at least on the surface, may seem to be anything but malignant but contributes to both the narcissism and the masochism of the child. The extremely devoted mother, whose child is her raison d'être, usually has a very clear idea as to what that child should be like, namely a helpless creature that cannot exist without her continuous assistance, and, at the same time, should be an instrument for the attainment of glory, that she, the mother, was deprived of. The stage mother is a very good example. By doing everything for the child, she severely injures the child's self-esteem. The message that is conveyed is: you can't do anything right, unless I do it for you. No genuine sense of mastery and pride are possible, and its very absence, according to Bernstein (1957), constitutes a potential source of narcissistic mortification which, in turn, strengthens the sadomasochistic bond between the child and its mother. The child has to deal with the fact that it is not being loved for any of its intrinsic qualities, i.e. for just being, but for what it might *do* for the mother. Its place in the world is never secure or taken for granted. This mother should not be confused, however, with the consistently overindulging mother of Masterson's patients. Her doing for the child is usually quite selective and entails many frustrations and impingements. One such mother, for example, who was abandoned by her husband after her second child was born, habitually ignored her children when *they* asked for attention. As soon as an eligible male appeared at the house, however, the children were wakened or interrupted in their meal or play so that the mother could arrange a tableau of devoted mother-hood for the benefit of her date. The message "Look at my pretty baby," though directed at an audience, stays with the child. As a result, the grandoise self (Kohut, 1971), instead of being slowly integrated, remains unconsciously intact, particularly if the parent provides vi-sions of great future accomplishments. Furthermore, since maternal narcissism precludes the capacity for empathy—the child gets fed when the mother is hungry—the child will lack a necessary survival tool for coping with inner tensions in its primary narcissistic equilibrium, namely the capacity to internalize the soothing functions provided by an empathic mother. Without these "transmuting internalizations" (Kohut, 1971), the child will show a "hypersensitivity to disturbances in the narcissistic equilibrium with a tendency to react to sources of narcissistic disturbance by a mixture of wholesale withdrawal and unforgiving rage." (ibid, p.65) Thus, what we called the stage mother promotes masochism by her message that as an autonomous person, the child is a perpetual failure. On the other hand, her consistently unempathic responses will prevent the infant from outgrowing its own age-appropriate exhibitionism and grandiosity.

THE INTRAPSYCHIC AND THE INTERPERSONAL FUNCTIONS OF THE SADOMASOCHISTIC SYNDROME

Having stated that sadomasochism is a response to hostile, reject-ing and/or narcissistic parental objects, we will now examine the re-sponses of the child to such a hostile and difficult environment—in other words, the *adaptive* functions of the syndrome. We will do this at first in a rather global fashion, where degrees of parental rejection and hostility are not yet accounted. Consequently, the *relative* effect on the child's psychic structures is not yet discussed. Obviously, depending on the severity of the environmental failure, the corresponding develop-

mental arrests can range from schizophrenia to a nearly normal adjustment and cover all the stages in between. This will be examined in
chapter five. For the moment, we will merely look at the sadomasochistic response as a specific survival mechanism within a particular environment. For the sake of clarity, we will temporarily distinguish
between 1. the predominantly intrapsychic, and 2. the predominantly
interpersonal functions of the sadomasochistic position.

The Intrapsychic Picture

For the infant, survival is only possible if it can maintain at least the
illusion of maternal love. Without it, life is literally not possible. The
price that has to be paid for this illusion is a rather steep one if the
reality of the parental environment spells hostility and deprivation. It
means that from the very beginning, the child experiences itself increasingly as the sole source of its own and its mother's displeasure,
unhappiness, and rejection. Her hostile, bad, and frustrating aspects
are attributed to the self, while the good and safe experiences are
perceived as pertaining to the parental other. These mechanisms cor-
respond to what Winnicott (1965) and Modell (1968) have described as
transitional object relationships. The object—the mother—is distorted
to fit an inner need, namely survival. The child, who in this fashion
locates all the feelings of badness in the self, thus, trades self love, the
prerequisite for the development of a strong and healthy ego and the
establishment of a cohesive sense of self, for the semblance of maternal
love and thus security. This is, indeed, a desperate bargain, but one
which at least allows for survival as long as the symbiotic tie with the
mother is not severed. This does not mean that later in life the symbiotic tie has to remain with the actual mother; in fact in adult life it is often
transferred to another—usually sadistic—love object. Reich's (1940)
study of extreme submissiveness in women is a case in point. The
German term *Hörigkeit,* which she employs, conveys much more than
submissiveness. It describes a state of virtual non-being, of abject
slavery, where the subject experiences itself as immobile and as direc-
tionless as a well-trained dog in the circus. But even for the circus dog,
walking on its hind legs is better than being sent to the pound. The
relationship between many prostitutes and their pimps constitutes a
typical example for this type of interaction. The internal dialogue goes
as follows: "I am terrible, I am worthless, but they (mother, lover,

pimp, slavemaster) are perfect, wonderful, omnipotent and, thus, my only hope for survival." Unless the surrender is more-or-less total and results in autism or other forms of severe childhood pathology, however, the disavowed recognition of parental abuse and rejection produces rage. In order to keep the rage from conscious awareness and expression, it is transformed into guilt which has to be perpetually exorcised. (Eidelberg and Eisenbud) Thus, a sadistic superego can be found in almost all masochistic patients.

The son of one of my patients made this point painfully clear. Having been born just when the mother started to rejoice because all her older children were in their teens, he exorcised his guilt for his very existence most symbolically. Until the age of 13, at each of his birthdays after he had received his presents, but before the actual birthday party with the much longed-for treats of ice cream and cake, he developed an upset stomach and threw up. In other words, he acknowledged his "sin" of having been born by always being the only child at his own birthday parties who was deprived of all food and sweets. Needless to say, his parents attributed this odd symptom to overstimulation and too much excitement. Concealed in his guilty acknowledgment of feeling like a burden whose birthday was not a day of rejoicing, however, we can also already detect a slightly sadistic element. The orderly progression of the day was disrupted, the "good clothes" intended for the party ended up soiled, and he looked less than picture-perfect. In examining the guilt so commonly encountered in the sadomasochistic patient, we have to distinguish between two separate sources of guilt: 1. the guilt already mentioned that arises in response to the angry feelings prompted by parental rejection or ill-treatment and can be easily transformed into a sadistic position such as juvenile delinquency or perpetual underachievement; and 2. the parental *attribution* of guilt. In the case of the boy just mentioned the problem was compounded by the fact that since his mother's displeasure at being again homebound and tied to a husband she did not love was ill-concealed by a facade of overindulgence and the attribution of extreme specialness, the young boy was quite aware of the fact that his birth in more ways than one had drastically altered his mother's plans. Thus, a seemingly exalted position in the family easily can be conflictual and a major source of guilt. Other examples are tales of a "difficult birth," "mother's ruined career," "endless nights" where the child's crying kept the parents awake, ingratitude on the part of the small child, illnesses that cost a fortune, etc., all of which leave memory traces of having done wrong, having somehow injured the parents, and are, thus, acts which demand self-punishment.

The attribution of guilt can have a particularly pernicious effect on the child because it is often faced with "proof" of seemingly real misdeeds in the past. For example, mother has, indeed, been sickly ever since its birth, and the evidence is ever-present while the child is clearly powerless "to make it all good again." This kind of guilt, unlike the one which results from rage over mistreatment, never can be exorcised or alleviated by turning it into its opposite, namely sadism. Like a gigantic unpayable debt, it resides in the child's psyche, a psyche not yet capable of detecting the hostile, manipulative intent of mother's tales. All the child can see is that it has done something injurious to the parents that it is powerless to change. The situation can be compounded if shame and guilt become intertwined. If, for example, the standards of proper behavior that can be expected from a six-year-old are applied to a three-year-old, or if a broken dinner plate is treated like a major tragedy, the child—out of fear of excessive punishment, shaming, ridicule, or moral condemnation—may well resort to lying about its "misdeeds." In that case, the child is trapped between the guilt over the deed—after all, the mother did not break the dish, the child did and the presence of the broken china is incontestable evidence—and the wish to attribute the accident to the cat. The experience of shame and guilt over the accident, compounded with dishonesty, is bound to produce on one hand the continuous fear of discovery, and on the other, the need for self-punishment, particularly if honesty ranks very highly in the parental set of values. This guilt cannot be easily externalized but has to be borne. Even though the difference between the two types of guilt is never clear-cut (in fact they are often intertwined); the distinction is, nevertheless, an important one because it determines the possibility of turning into anger at the parental objects, either in the course of growing up or through therapy, while in the case of the second type the anger is forever redirected at the self and, thus, represents the more difficult therapeutic problem. This difficulty is particularly acute with patients from large families, where the mother was clearly overworked and a victim of cultural or religious pressure; an example is the Catholic prohibition of birth control that can, indeed, produce unwanted children who are a very real burden on the mother without household help. As will be shown later in the case of Anna, it was precisely the mixture of her mother's very real feeling of being overworked and her expressed resentment directed at her third child, which produced in Anna a life-time pattern of trying to redeem herself for her very existence. Whenever Anna felt resentment toward her mother, she would shortcircuit her angry feelings with the statement that she, herself, would not have been able to care for five children either, and that she, Anna, was, indeed, a difficult child given to temper tantrums (or so she was told). Finally, among the intrapsychic functions of the sadomasochistic syndrome, the element of control has to be mentioned, i.e. the attempt to be in control of the punishment, which is experienced as being both inevitable and unpredictable. The self-punitive measures represent an attempt of setting up a system of internal moral bookkeeping. In an almost ritualistic fashion, the illusion of inner peace is "bought" by the regular infliction of pain or deprivation.

The Interpersonal Picture

I am in full agreement with Berliner, who stated that "masochism is a defensive reaction, motivated by libidinal needs, to the sadism of another person." (1958, p.44) That means that the quest for love (or the illusion of it) is the central mechanism operating in the psychic economy of the masochist. The rejecting, hateful unloving behavior of the preoedipal parent is experienced "as if" it were love; a fateful misunderstanding that is contingent on the child's ability to repress the rage that such a treatment would evoke in a more mature ego. If one conceptualizes the sadomasochism of the subject—in relation to the object—as a continuum ranging from the meekly saint to the sadistic self-mutilator, then one has to account for the variables that determine where on this continuum a given subject has settled at any given point in his or her life. The two endpoints of this continuum, as it is seen, are on one hand the quest for survival by eliciting love from an unloving object, and on the other, the attempt to inflict a maximum of punishment on the object for having failed to give love. The choice of location on this continuum, on the part of the subject, seems to be contingent on two variables: 1. The element of hope that may persist or deteriorate; and 2. The narcissistic injuries that resulted from the humiliating parental treatment of the child. We shall examine the element of hope and its deterioration and the vicissitudes of narcissistic injuries separately. Since sexual sadomasochism correlates most closely—though not exclusively—with narcissistic mortifications, it will be discussed in that context.

As has been stated earlier, the parents of the future masochist, together with rejection and guilt, also leave the child with the notion that there is always the possibility of redemption through suffering. The child, having introjected the bad aspects of the parental objects, is faced with the challenge of turning the bad love object into a good one. Depending on the extent to which this attempt appears to be successful in warding off depression, the search for love through suffering, compliance, seduction of, and identification with, the aggressor, i.e. the predominantly masochistic end of the sadomasochistic continuum, is occupied. The substitution of power for love could be seen as the midpoint, and revenge and outright sadism as the goal for which the suffering is employed the sadistic end of the continuum. Unfortunately, the inability on the part of many writers on the subject to see the move toward the sadistic position as a product of demoralization—the loss of hope—has robbed them of the compassion that is necessary in order to understand and properly treat the sadomasochistic syndrome. When Reik (1941) claims that "the masochist is a person of a strongly sadistic disposition, who has been diverted from its instinctual aim by the vision of punishment," (p.191) he is really missing the essential point, namely that the sadistic component arises as a *reaction* to an all powerful and sadistic object, and that the original aim of *any* human infant is always survival and consequently love. The battered child is a case in point. Having no alternate love objects, they are fiercely attached to their parents; consequently, social workers have always found it extremely difficult, if not impossible, to persuade these children to testify against their abusers. (Wolberg, 1973; Helfer and Kempe, 1968)

A similar mechanism and interpersonal arrangement very often operates in the battered wife and her relationship with her spouse. The key variable is dependency. The battered wife rationalizes the physical assault with the notion that she provoked it by her nagging, complaints, or her inability to keep the kids quiet. Alternatively, she may reason that her husband was drunk and that she should have known better than to ask him just then for money to buy the kids sneakers. In other words, the anatomy of wife battery serves as an excellent example for both the intrapsychic as well as the interpersonal elements in sadomasochism: husband and wife are equally dependent on each other, each projecting their disavowed self-representations onto the other. Since from the husband's point of view, children distract from this symbiosis, pregnancy increases the violence, very often with the conscious intent to produce a miscarriage. The inner stance taken by the chronically battered wife resembles that of an isolated, demoralized infant. Almost invariably, they are also socially isolated; friendships with the extended family and with neighbors are forbidden and their relationships with their husbands truly mirror the relationship between a helpless infant and a monstrously sadistic mother. The repressed rage on the part of the wife may break through, however, and, in the extreme, can result in homicide. The examples below will illustrate this point: One, a victim of "habitual assault"—as opposed to the "Saturday night brawl"—and the other, a former victim of habitual assault who in the process of breaking away, shot and killed her ex-husband. According to the court record,

> The woman, six months pregnant is repeatedly beaten in the stomach. Her husband keeps screaming 'Bitch, you are going to lose that baby,' and then beats her in the stomach again. After the assault . . ., accused told victim to cook dinner. Victim stated that the accused picked up a butcher knife and put it to the victim's throat and told victim, 'I am going to kill you and you know I can do it, too, don't you?' Victim answered 'yes' and accused laid butcher knife on the table and turned around and hit victim in the face with his fist and knocked victim to floor. Then the accused sat down on the victim's stomach and put his knees on victim's arms so victim could not block any kicks from accused. Then accused started beating victim in the head, face, and stomach." (Steinmetz, 1977 pp. 28–9)

This victim explained to the interviewer: "You put up with six days of beating because there is *one good day* to have someone to share things with." (Steinmetz, pp. 28–9, *emphasis mine*) The second woman, (State vs. Guido; Supreme Court of New Jersey 1963) had succeeded in separating from her husband, although he continued to harrass and follow her around. Occasionally, he beat and threatened her at her place of employment. Finally, he abducted her and their young daughter to a cottage in the country with the intent of taking the child to another state. While her ex-husband was sleeping the woman took his gun in order to shoot herself. It was only when she saw her tormentor "sleep like a contented baby," that in a split-second decision she diverted the gun from her own head to that of the ex-husband. It is interesting to note that in reading the entire court record there was nothing that either the prosecutor or the defense could produce from her life history, the testimony of the psychiatric experts and the entire parade of character witnesses that could provide the court with evidence for a single sadistic trait or act prior to the murder.

Since for obvious ethical reasons longitudinal observations of mistreated children are not possible and available, one has to rely on ex post facto explanations of how the behavior of the two women just mentioned, came about. Clearly in both instances, the attachment to one powerful figure and the fear of loss and abandonment were the overriding factors that necessitated the tolerance of extreme cruelty. In Guido's case, even a legal separation did not sever the symbiotic ties sufficiently to allow her to disobey her husband's commands. Since she had also found some rudimentary sense of survival through some tenuous attachments to her co-workers in her job, however, the threat of losing her fragile sense of autonomy suddenly brought the pent-up rage to the surface. The same was not true for the woman interviewed by Steinmetz. She had no alternative attachment figures. Her hopes for survival were pinned exclusively on her husband and that *one* day out of seven when she was not beaten and had someone with whom to share things. It does not seem too farfetched to assume that as a child she endured an enormous amount of parental abuse to earn an occasional benign smile. These two women both occupy the almost exclusively masochistic end of the sadomasochistic continuum: enraged but compliant children with a sense of utter worthlessness, presumably feeling guilty for their very existence and symbiotically tied to a sadistic parental other. They are children, who in terms of what Maslow has called the "hierarchy of needs," never progressed beyond the level of physical survival.

Compliance with an unloving parent, one of the key mechanisms operating on the masochistic end of the continuum, is not restricted to physical abuse. The competitive and overprotective mother conveys the message that she will love the child *only* if it remains a helpless, dependent failure; an insight which one of my patients with such a mother once wistfully acknowledged when she stated: "Success is really the best revenge, isn't it?" The element of compliance in these cases is not a conjecture because when such patients recall all the prohibitions and warnings pertaining to simple physical mastery of the environment, such as running, jumping, climbing on things, riding a tricycle or swimming, they also remember that whenever they attempted to accomplish these things in spite of the warnings, they almost invariably did so in such a way that an accident was inevitable, thus proving mother right. A woman patient of mine who had been labeled too fragile for almost any normal task in life, including childbirth, remained childless for the first ten years of her marriage and chose to adopt a child instead. The adoption of the baby was never a source of real joy, however, since she saw it as a constant reminder of her failure as a woman. She worried about this child incessantly; every cold was seen as a potentially fatal illness that would only compound her sense of personal failure. It was only after she had achieved a modicum of separateness from her mother in therapy, that she became pregnant and, despite her mother's dire predictions, carried the child to term and delivered a healthy baby. Although in the past her mother's fussing produced fear in her, it now produced rage and a fierce determination to *be* healthy and to *have* a healthy baby. Though she did not exactly become an athlete, she learned how to swim, ride a bike, and most important, she ceased to be sickly and overweight.

The seduction of the aggressor is another predominantly masochistic response to an unloving parent. Unlike the compliant child described above, which is given a blueprint for its behavior by an everpresent, overprotective mother, the seductive child is trying to get an emotionally absent parent to pay attention. These mothers, typically don't want to be bothered by their children, but will make themselves available when the child is dangerously ill, injured, or otherwise deeply and visibly troubled. Thus, in the child's mind, suffering buys love—or at least attention—and it nourishes the secret hope that "if I suffer enough, she will become the good mother forever." The accident-prone daredevil who attempts to gain admiration by its daring and courage and tries to insure continued attention and care by its accidents falls into that category. This particular defense has the additional advantage of eliciting genuine concern and care from the doctors and nurses who are called on to treat the injured child. Additional rewards may be obtained for "bearing the pain so bravely" and for acting so maturely in the doctor's office or the hospital. In the extreme, such children can become almost immune to physical pain through a process resembling self-hypnosis.

The three patterns just described, share several important features: 1. the firm conviction, based on experience, that just being does not entitle the child to be loved; 2. the conclusion that the child must be bad or have committed some more or less obscure crime or crimes; 3. the willingness to settle for attention—including a negative one—in lieu of genuine love and concern; and 4. a semblance of intrapsychic equilibrium, which means that on one hand the child receives enough attention to "get by," i.e. to ward off depression, and on the other, manages to retain the hope that in relationship with the parents it is "on the right track," so to speak, that it has indeed found a tool to make things better, and that maybe, one day, it "can make it all good again." In other words, in terms of sheer emotional survival, the system "works," as long as all the actors involved stick to their agreed on parts. If suffering ceases to bring its minimal rewards, the child may lose hope and withdraw, or alternatively move toward the more sadistic end of the continuum. Conversely, an unexpected display of parental affection may produce a reaction similar to what has been called the "revolution of rising expectations," a forceful quest for more love and corresponding expressions of rage if this quest is not met.

The exchange of power for love is approximately the midpoint of the sadomasochistic continuum, and, therefore, might be considered sadomasochism proper, since the sadistic and the masochistic impulses are equally strong. The internal bargain that is struck is still basically adaptive, i.e. life-affirming, since it aims at survival through manipulation of the human environment. Although power in this context means primarily negative power, it is, nevertheless, quite effective. If being pathetic, helpless, incompetent, sickly, and passive evokes in the parental other the willingness to do for the child, it may gladly forfeit the joy of mastery, exploration, and autonomy for the sake of being taken care of and depriving the parents of their freedom. Bowlby's (1969) description of the child who is school-phobic is a case in point. Also, the mother whose child has just injured itself cannot go out and play bridge. The child who keeps failing in school may get the mother to tutor it, or at least supervise the homework. Allergies may severely limit the choice of vacation places, household items, pets, etc. Extra care will have to be given to housecleaning should the allergic agent be just plain dust or cigarette smoke. Asthma attacks require instant attention; they necessitate that the parents interrupt whatever they are doing, whether it is entertaining company, taking care of other children, work, or sex. Needless to say, the maintenance of this system is also contingent on the fact that the parental other is responsive, either out of a sense of duty or guilt or on the basis of the child's masochistic needs. For example, the obese child, with two cold and withdrawn parents who are, nevertheless, concerned about his weight, may learn from experience that with a simple request for a cola he can instigate a prolonged fight between them over the question whether the child should be given a regular cola or diet soda. The child may wind up with either or none, but for the duration of the battle, he is a very thirsty but mighty powerful little person. Although obesity in children can be a symptom of a very wide range of pathological conditions, even on the sadomasochistic continuum, for example, it can be the result of compliance with a hostile overfeeding mother or a powerplay. In this instance, since the child has a nutritionist as a parent, it is a form of revenge, an indictment of the parent, an embarrassment for all the world to see.

To the extent that revenge becomes the dominant motivation, we are approaching the predominantly sadistic end of the sadomasochistic continuum where the life-affirming stance begins to corrode. The internal dialogue now goes as follows: "If I cannot obtain love or power, I can at least punish the unloving object with my suffering." But even the question, "After all my mother has done to me, how can I be anything but a roaring failure in life?", still contains a minute element of hope, that the parents may yet see the light, that the intended punishment has its desired effect of turning the unloving object into a loving one. Many of the self-destructive or delinquent acts of adolescents fall into that category. The daughter of an upper-class, highly conventional family who clumsily shoplifts,—aside from crying for help—is also attempting to disgrace her parents in the community. The fourteen-year-old son of an alcoholic father, who stole a bottle of Scotch from a neighbor and drank the entire quart in the course of one afternoon accomplished three goals simultaneously: he called attention to the problem of alcoholism in the family ("Like father like son") he demonstrated the inadequacy of the parental supervision and—most important—he made a rather serious suicidal gesture, designed to test the ability of his environment to hear his despair and to provide help. When this desperate act resulted in nothing further than a pumped stomach, horrendous hangover, and solid beating, this youngster turned to not-so-petty theft that was deliberately designed to be discovered by his father, who promptly called the police. When again the cry for help went unheard, and the boy got off with a judicial warning, he resorted to a full-time career of drinking. When he discovered in his mid-20's that the family was secretly pleased with his alcoholism, he weaned himself rather quickly and effectively, started therapy, and put all his energy into work and school. This last example, far from representing a spontaneous cure, illustrates rather clearly what can happen if there is absolutely *no* response to the indictment, but if, on the contrary, the object is secretly pleased. In most instances, the love object toward whom the delinquency or the suicide attempts are aimed, shows some facsimile of a response, and the pattern becomes set. It can culminate in either a slow or a sudden suicide if the response of the love object becomes increasingly negative or, if the "black sheep" is finally disowned by the family. Pure sadism emerges when a person has found that all else has failed, and will now do unto others what was done unto him.

The Relationshiop Between Sadomasochism and Narcissism

I have found degrees of narcissistic disturbances in all sadomasochistic patients I have treated and reached the tentative conclusion that the extent of the narcissistic disturbance determines, or rather correlates, with the speed with which the sadomasochistic syndrome can be treated. In the usage of the term "narcissism," we are following Kohut's (1977) conceptualizations. Two of his theoretical premises are of particular importance in this context:

1. His view of the self not as an agency of the mind, but as a structure within the mind and his claim that there are two psychologies of the self that complement each other; "A psychology in which the self is seen as the center of the psychological universe, and a psychology in which the self is seen as a content of a mental apparatus." (p. xv)
2. His distinction between horizontally and vertically split-off sectors of the narcissistic energies, since it is the latter that poses particularly difficult obstacles in the treatment of the sadomasochistic syndrome. The therapist dealing with such a

patient will have to be continuously alert to the distinction
between a narcissistic disturbance of the transference and a
masochistic distortion of a therapeutic interpretation.

In light of what has been said about the parents of sadomasochistic
patients, it is hardly surprising that they also failed to provide their
children with a stable and cohesive sense of self, and that they were
unable to allow the age-appropriate display of their children's grandiose and exhibitionistic self. According to Kohut, the unempathic
mother does not function appropriately as a stimulus barrier; her
presence does not have enough of a soothing function to relieve the
infant's internal tensions in order to allow it to sleep peacefully and
gradually internalize the soothing functions of the mother and thus,
soothe itself. Thus, a necessary psychic structure does not develop,
which leaves the child with an intense "object hunger" representing an
attempt to supply this missing segment of the psyche from the outside.
The objects that are pursued for this purpose are not recognized as
proper persons with specific personalities or attributes; what is longed
for are specific qualities in the relationship, namely its soothing functions and uncritical acceptance and mirroring. Every maternal kindergarten and grade-school teacher will attract a group of children who
seem to have an intense need to bask in their teacher's presence, who
eagerly gobble up every bit of affection that comes their way, and who
will wait for hours on end for a chance to hold the teacher's hand on the
way from school to the school bus. What distinguishes these children
from others is their bottomless adulation of the teacher, who in the
child's eyes can do no wrong. The wise teacher does not interfere or
curb this idealization because, on the child's part, this idealization
represents a belated attempt to deal with a disappointing parent whose
shortcomings were such that the child's development remained fixated
on the level of archaic self-objects. The child, unable to cope with a
sudden or too severe disillusionment in the idealized parent, cannot
internalize the good aspects of the parent and strives to recreate them
in another person, a mother substitute, in order to fill the urgent need
to be part of something omnipotent and glorious. This is a function
which in adult life is only too willingly supplied by the various self-
appointed gurus and other saviors of the world. Conversely, the suppression or persecution of the child's grandiose and exhibitionistic self,
inhibits the gradual integration of these strivings into the ego and,

thus, the development of healthy self-esteem. Instead, much of the narcissistic energy will flow into the superego, in the form of perfectionistic standards.

If the superego due to parental hostility also shows sadistic traits, the combination of these two components will set the child on a course of enormous internal suffering. The grandiose self, which was deprived of appropriate mirroring, will undergo almost complete repression; a horizontal split results which requires a great deal of psychic energy to keep the grandoise self from breaking through and overwhelming the reality ego. The ego in this case is characterized by low self-esteem and a propensity toward shame and hypochondria. A vertical split of the narcissistic energies, however, will result in openly-displayed infantile grandiosity that is related to the mother's narcissistic use of the child's performance. The stage-mother, described earlier, is a perfect and obvious example for such a pernicious development. Yet, the narcissistic use of a child by the parent can be much more subtle. To wit: allusions to the child's potential for greatness coupled with the implication that the child's lack of effort, laziness, or perversity keep it from performing on the expected level which, in effect, is the level on which the parents would have liked to have functioned. This message will have these interrelated effects: 1. it will stimulate the child's grandiosity; 2. it will inhibit a realistic level of performance; and 3. it will induce a chronic sense of shame and inadequacy. It is the vertical split which, in the case of the sadomasochistic patient, will most seriously interfere with the establishment of a sound therapeutic alliance and the working through of the sadomasochistic qualities in the patient's object relations. A patient, who over the slightest frustration of his overt exhibitionism and grandiosity, flies into attacks of unforgiving rage—often with a paranoid tinge—will be unable to utilize any expression of empathy on the part of the therapist. Furthermore, any attempts at providing insights into the origins of the narcissistic injury will not only be essentially wasted, but deepen the rage and include the therapist as one of the targets of that rage. Patients who cannot handle any form of criticism in school or at work and who then proceed to attack all those friends and group-members, including the therapist, who do not support them 100 percent in their victimized interpretation of the event, are perhaps the most difficult of all sadomasochistic patients to treat because of their compulsion to cut themselves off from any kind of help.

Bob, whose case will be discussed in detail later, and who epitomized this toxic combination for many years, may serve as an example. He experienced any interpretation of his behavior as so shameprovoking and consequently enraging that he felt he had to interrupt his individual therapy for several years—though he stayed in group—until he had acquired some external psychological coating to protect him. He could only begin to accept helpful interpretations when he had reached a position of professional accomplishment, which not only exceeded that of all other group members, but also significantly reduced direct supervision by his superiors in his job to the point where he had enough "time off" from his encounters with seemingly disapproving authority figures, who in the past had been the main source of his narcissistic injuries and reactive rages. In many such cases, the therapist may have to stand-by patiently, working on some changes in the real-life situation, such as the attainment of a graduate degree that can function as an emotional scaffold and allows the patient to feel secure enough to resume therapy in earnest. With patients of this kind, two separate psychotherapeutic approaches will have to be employed, one that is purely supportive and one that is insight-oriented. Any ill-timed contamination of the two approaches can result in losing the patient altogether.

Narcissistic rage is essentially a shame reaction, and it derives its enormous intensity from the fact that it is a threat to the cohesiveness of the self that can spell psychosis. Since this shame is inflicted by all-powerful others, no escape from it is ever possible, and, subjectively, it is experienced as a fate literally worse than death. Pure sadism, then, should be conceptualized as an attempt at repairing a narcissistic humiliation through role reversal. Hitler was not content with having the perpetrators of the July 20 insurgence torn from limb to limb; he had the event filmed and often had the filmstrip replayed to lift his spirits. The sadistic satisfaction does not primarily derive from the infliction of injuries, but at least in equal measure from the pleasure of having the subjects plead and beg for mercy and watching them divesting themselves of any sense of internal integrity. The actual killing, then, is in fact a mere *coup de grace*. Sexual sadomasochism is a continuous attempt at redressing grievances that have to do with power and shame, but without the aim of eliminating the other. After all, if this were done, the game would be over.

It seems reasonable to conclude, then, that the strength of the sadistic component in sadomasochism is fully accounted for if one sees it as repressed rage over mistreatment, combined with varying degrees of narcissistic rage—a powerful shame reaction resulting from persecution and humiliation.

Willing as a Unifying Concept

Since, at times, it is also of importance to articulate the central dynamic of sadomasochism *to the patient* so that he or she has a better tool to work through the resistance, a minor switch in conceptual framework seems helpful. Although it is perfectly accurate to view sadomasochism as an ego-defense, as the incorporation of sadistic object relationships, the expressions of the "anti-libidinal ego," self pathology and narcissistic rage, these concepts are not very helpful for a patient who wants to understand what the whole battle is all about. In order to articulate the problems of resistance to the patient, to arrive at a commonly shared language which also does justice to the powerful investment in the sadomasochistic behavior pattern, the concept of the "unconscious fantasy" or "the hidden agenda" is extremely useful. In order to define its precise meaning in this context, we shall utilize a much neglected psychoanalytic concept, namely that of *willing* (Rank, 1978), which has the enormous advantage of providing a theoretical bridge between the concepts of ego-impairment and self pathology. If one assumes that from birth on there is a "real drive to life" (Schilder, 1951), which during the individuation and separation phase, is increasingly felt as a force that exists *in opposition* to the will of another object or person, then one may ask what happens to the capacity for willing under less than optimal circumstances. Menaker (1979) points out that masochism is the subjugation of the child's will to that of the parental other. In the case of the extremely hostile and controlling mother, a child may survive only by sending out a non-verbal message of total surrender and self-loathing—the equivalent of an appeasement gesture among animals. In that way, the child keeps the mother all-good at the expense of self-humiliation and self-loathing. On the surface "willing," on the part of the child, seems to be totally absent when in fact the opposite is true. It is what I shall call, "negative willing," which is powerfully aimed at establishing and maintaining a symbiotic bond with the other by substituting the other's will for one's own. Its goal is the maintenance of the status quo, the unconscious fantasy that self humiliation will ensure survival and maternal love. Alternatively, a child whose early training consisted of a humiliating subjugation of its autonomous will will probably soon cease to struggle overtly. A "counter-will," comprised of wishes for revenge and indictment of the parents, together with sadistic fantasies of role reversals will emerge, however, and it will co-exist with the overt behavior pattern of obedience and subjugation. The unconscious fantasy is that if the parents have been sufficiently indicted and punished, they will repent and then offer the child the love that they did not offer before.

Positive willing, i.e. the desire for a less-troubled and more rewarding life, is what brings our patients into therapy. As will be shown in chapters 5 and 6, this capacity is strengthened during phase one and two of the treatment process. During Phase three, the separation and individuation phase, it is the balance between positive willing on one hand and negative and counterwilling on the other that determines the quality of the working-through process. Moreover, one can conceptualize the balance between the masochistic and the sadistic components as roughly corresponding to the distribution of negative and counterwilling, respectively. Taken together, they determine the content of the "hidden agenda," i.e. the unconscious fantasy of what kinds of behavior will ensure love and admiration that is in direct conflict with positive willing, which in the case of our sadomasochistic patient at the beginning of Phase three, consists of the conscious agenda to take care of himself in order to lead a more rewarding life. Consequently, one of the most important concepts that patients will have to be taught is that all behavior is purposeful in that whatever goal is pursued—no matter how self-destructive it may appear—it is on some level more desirable or less frightening than a seemingly more constructive goal. Failure, for example, can be pursued in the service of negative willing as well as counterwilling. The hidden agenda can either spell the equation Failure equals Subjugation that equals Survival; or Failure equals Indictment that leads to parental repentance resulting in love.

The most important treatment objective, then, is to slowly make the unconscious hidden agenda conscious. The choice to slowly abandon the hidden agenda in favor of positive willing must be presented as a choice or option that only the patient can exercise, but one for which he will get all the emotional and therapeutic support possible. Thus, one has to sort out the origins of the various components that make up the complex script that constitutes the hidden agenda. The patient will have to be encouraged to re-experience the pain and the rage that the child must have felt each time its attempts at autonomy were interfered with, natural inquisitiveness was punished, and self-assertion was ridiculed. At the same time, the patient has to be encouraged to risk mastery in the real world without a sadomasochistic pricetag. For example, Lillian, a young woman who had both a study block and a weight problem, slowly came to realize that she responded with a compulsive eating binge after each successful day in the library. Being both smart *and* attractive meant competition with her older brother and pleasing her mother simultaneously; it, thus, constituted too much of a threat to her customary sense of self. But eventually she did learn to head off the eating binges by phoning a young man who, in group, had come to represent her brother. Thus, by reassuring herself with a "transitional brother," she could "risk" being bright. Since her weight also constituted an indictment of her mother's narcissistic display of her as the "cute little girl" in childhood, she compromised her desire for beauty for many years by being neither slim nor overweight, but simply "chubby."

This example neatly summarizes all the treatment elements that are of importance;

1. *Conscious agenda:* Encouragement by the therapist to learn a marketable skill during phase two had seen Lillian through college; her wish for a serious career motivated her to go to graduate school.

2. *Ego impairment:* Her sense that her intellect did not function properly, since she had a hard time paying attention to what she read, and the experience of going blank during an exam, produced shame and activated her low self esteem, which further impaired her intellectual functioning.

3. *Negative willing:* Questions as to what would happen if she successfully competed with her brother revealed her enormous fear of losing his protection, which she had insured in childhood by being his adoring, but incompetent, one-person audience.

4. *Transitional object and the exercise of mastery:* Once she had "adopted" a group member as her brother, her intellectual performance improved markedly, but was offset by her eat-

ing binges, which most of the time, ended in her vomiting all the junk food she had eaten.

5. *Self-Pathology:* Since throwing up constituted, in Lillian's view, her "real craziness" it provided on one hand an additional source of shame and at the same time a sense of specialness.

6. *Counterwilling:* Questions as to what would happen if she allowed herself to be slim and pretty revealed that this would make her mother very happy and proud, and Lillian was far too angry with her mother, for having treated her like a pretty little doll rather than a person, to give her that satisfaction.

7. *Individuation:* The rage against her mother needed ventilation, resulting in gradual disillusionment with her mother and allowed Lillian to separate step-by-step.

8. *Reapproachment maneuvers:* Increasing demands and hypochondriacal exaggeration of her problems in individual and group therapy, when examined, revealed her enormous fear of being ignored if she performed too well. She needed to play the cranky baby after each successful exam.

The Relationship Between Sexual and Characteriological Manifestations of Sadomasochism

As has been stated earlier, one of the principal misunderstandings concerning the nature of sexual sadomasochism pertains to the notion that it has anything whatsoever to do with genital sexuality or oedipal problems, when in fact it represents the sexualization of pre-oedipal and pre-genital conflicts. It does not really matter whether one thinks of this fusion of sex with non-sexual aims as a premature sexualization of oral and anal conflicts or whether one sees it as a carry over of these earlier problems into the oedipal period, since these two processes usually overlap. It will be shown in chapters three and four that a certain preoedipally based sadomasochistic substratum persists in the sexuality of the average American male, and to a lesser extent in that of the female. The difference between that substratum and the dynamics operating in the members of the S&M subculture, is essentially one of degree. Although the average reader of *Playboy* or *Screw* can alleviate his preoedipal anxieties away from the sex act by reading the same joke in a different version over and over again without necessarily understanding its real meaning, the sexual sadomasochist needs the reenact-ment of oral, anal, and phallic conflicts as an integral part of the sex act and as a prerequisite for orgasm. It is as if the person were saying: "I cannot relate to another person intimately and sexually unless I have first redressed some grievances with the mother of earliest infancy—defused her so to speak—and until I have created a scenario that guarantees the illusion of utter safety. I will recreate these early power struggles and shame experiences, but this time I will be in charge of it all."

The typical scenarios include: 1. spanking (punishment of the naughty child); 2. bondage and domination (B&D) 3. undinism,* and 4. enemas including coprophilia (watersports). These, however, are very broad categories. Most S&M scenarios are mixtures, and they range from the simple combination of sex and spanking to the more elaborate arrangements that include elements of almost all parent-child conflicts and can last up to 10 hours. For the full understanding of the underlying dynamics and their relationship to non-sexualized sadomasochism, I shall also include in this discussion the usage of any form of sexual deviance for the purpose of dealing with current interpersonal and intrapsychic conflicts such as pseudo-homosex-uality, the pursuit of depravity, etc.

A successful S&M scenario has to include the following elements: illusion, power, pain, humiliation, mirroring, and shame. These sce-narios are usually very carefully orchestrated in order to duplicate the original childhood trauma as closely as possible. That means that the paraphernalia have to resemble as much as possible those instruments or garments that are meaningful to the participant and his or her childhood memories. The literature put out by the S&M liberation front devotes a great deal of effort to letting its audience know which stores in the various cities—knowingly or unwittingly—carry the neces-sary ingredients for the scene (riding supply stores usually carry the best assortment of whips) or, alternatively, instructions on how to build one's own equipment. The theatrical aspect is so essential because it serves the purpose of maintaining the illusion. The element of power expresses itself in the script. The scenes are usually very carefully designed in such a way that the masochistic partner is in full control

---

*The term undinism refers to a wide variety of sexual practices employing liquids that range from the wearing of wet clothing during the sex act to the act of urinating on one's sexual partner.

over the sadist's actions. Although on the surface the masochist pleads and begs for mercy, the sadist knows *precisely* how far he or she can go. In that way, both the masochist and the sadist split themselves—and identify with—the parent and the child, with the masochist having the upper hand. Through projective identification, the powerlessness of both partners is reversed. The fact that the masochist has the greater power, however, explains why sadists are so rare, and that the supply never meets the demand.

Another important element which serves both the maintenance of the illusion and the effectiveness of the game, is the aspect of mirroring. By that it is meant the verbal and non-verbal acknowledgment of the victim's fear, humiliation, and pain, preferably in an exaggerated form. The masochist is encouraged to exaggerate his responses through writhing, clutching, gasps, and moans. Conversely, the sadist should be as threatening and as contemptuous as possible. The experience of shame thus becomes diffused and turned into its opposite since the masochistic partner ultimately calls all the shots. To quote Greene and Greene, perhaps the most articulate advocates of the S&M liberation movement: "For the submissive to have to lie, say, in a bath and to be urinated on by a beloved can provoke a feeling of total humiliation and, accordingly, *delicious shame*." (1974, p. 195, *emphasis mine*) In other words, the attempt to turn shame into a delicious experience, via denial, disavowal, splitting and role reversal, lies at the heart of the S&M scenario. What, then, are the main traumas or intrapsychic dangers that the S&M participant constantly has to defend himself against? If the threat to the bodily cohesiveness of the self spells fear of psychosis, then parental invasiveness, coupled with parental persecution, must be one of the main elements. Greene and Greene, (1974) in their chapter on watersports, quote from a treatise on family medicine, dealing with the subject of toilet training that bears quoting in full:

Just as the child's volition to eliminate must be scrupulously supervised, so also must his refusal to eliminate on command be remorselessly rectified. The problem will inevitably arise, at one time or another, that the subject being commanded to function, will protest his 'inability' to do so. To meet this contingency, the parent can either inspect the toilet after each 'visit', or—better yet—stand over the child throughout it, with a switch. When the subject pretends an inability to pass solid waste, then the author com-

mends the use of an *enema*. Two quarts of soapy water, administered on the spot as painfully as possible (for the property of the
anus as a sexually responsive area cannot be too vigorously prohibited), should suffice to correct the most recalcitrant bowel, and a
diet of bran and prunes at each meal for a week afterward will
effectively prevent a recurrence of this phenomenon. Toilet paper, needless to say, should be as abrasive as possible, and in
abundant supply. (p. 200)

Here, the persecutory element is quite pronounced, and the fusion of oral, anal, and phallic elements is clear and unambiguous.
Thus, a recommendation by one of the authors on how to build a
perfect enema nozzle, namely "a cigar holder-designed for the mouth,
to be inserted into the other end of the human being's inner tube" (p.
203), makes perfect sense.

Fears of loss of ego boundaries are defended against counterpho-
bically, by deliberate merging with, and splitting of self, and other in
sequential role reversals and finally in the experience of mutual or
simultaneous orgasm. In other words, control is being taken over that
which the sadomasochist fears the most, namely loss of self. If one
accepts the re-analysis of the Schreber case (Schatzman, 1973) as being
the result of paternal persecution and intrusiveness of the boy's bodily
integrity and its subsequent paranoid projection and reintrojection—
and I do—then it prompts one to hypothesize that if Schreber had been
able to become a sexual sadomasochist, he might not have become
psychotic.

In order to see the connection between sexual sadomasochism and
the sadomasochistic personality formation, the sadomasochistic utilization of sexual deviance can serve as a good illustration. The following
example also shows how complex and multi-layered sexual expressions
of sadomasochism can be. Fred, a very personable male homosexual
patient of mine, had for most of his adult life been quite attracted to the
concept of depravity. Genet's *Our Lady of the Flowers* was one of his
favorite novels. At the very point in treatment when we were working
through Fred's grandiosity he experienced the overwhelming compulsion to visit public bathrooms for quick impersonal sexual encounters,
"tea room sex." In the past, he had frequented the warehouses on the
waterfront in New York for the same purpose. On one level, this
highly-cultured young man was quite aware of the fact that he was
counteracting an anticipated humiliation in therapy by one that he

himself inflicted, since his sense of shame after each visit was pronounced. But this did not yet explain three other questions: 1. Why
would he risk exposure (the exhibitionistic element)? 2. Why had he
switched from the warehouses to the public toilets?, and 3. Why had he
felt so compelled to talk about the subject with me? When questioned
whether he was not afraid of meeting someone from his professional
life, he responded gleefully that anyone encountered under such circumstances would hardly be in a position to talk about the experience;
in other words, finding "partners in crime" was seen as acquiring
siblings that reduced my imagined powers to control and prohibit.
Furthermore, it turned out that he switched from the warehouses to
the public toilets *after* he had accidentally learned from an acquaint-
ance that, in the course of doing research for this book, I had taken
several trips to the warehouses. Suddenly, the switch of locale and his
compulsive discussion of the subject matter made perfect sense: a
public male toilet is *one* place which even the most inquisitive female
social scientist cannot invade. Thus, his "shame-producing confes-
sions" were really an expression of triumph (delicious shame) for they
proclaimed: "Your power is limited. I have the power to get away from
you and you cannot follow me into my secret hiding place, no matter
how badly you may want to." This example brings together almost all
the important elements that are responsible for this pathological
formation: 1. infantile phallic exhibitionism; 2. defenses against invasiveness on the part of a controlling mother in order to preserve the
cohesiveness of the self; 3. a reaction formation against "passively
endured intrusions" inflicted on the infant by a nonloving mother
during the oral stage (Heimann, 1966); and 4. the reestablishment of
active *willing* since "for the deeply masochistic individual, bound in a
symbiotic relationship to the mother, an act of will is forbidden, un-
allowable. It is as if the mother had said: 'you dare not be yourself; you
have not the ability to be yourself; you need me to exist.' " (Menaker,
1979, p. 93) Since these experiences of utter impotence were never
metabolized or integrated by the sexual sadomasochist, however, they
have to be re-enacted over and over again through a transitional object
relationship where the partner is distorted in such a way that he
represents the most threatening aspects of the preoedipal mother.
Triumph over the persecuting and anxiety-provoking mother, rees-
tablishes his belief in his potency and autonomy and active willing
is—at least for the time being—possible again. This precarious inner
balance, however, has to be renegotiated prior to each sexual encounter.

Chapter 3

FEMALE MASOCHISM:

The Anatomy of an Ideology*

The assumption that women are by *nature* masochistic has provoked more anger among modern feminists than any other idea in psychoanalytic theory. It has been debunked as a particularly cruel joke in the history of female oppression and rightfully so. Yet this controversy, which supposedly has been laid to rest, merits serious attention—even at this time—for three reasons.

1. The relative distribution of observable masochistic and sadistic character traits or behavior patterns among men and women, respectively, needs examining, particularly since it is my contention that the traditional relationship between the sexes is, among other things, a reified and institutionalized sadomasochistic arrangement.
2. Even though the debunking of female masochism as a natural biological phenomenon was an important and necessary step, we are still left with the reality of the existence of female masochism as a fairly common observable interactive stance.

*An earlier version of this chapter was presented at the 28th Annual Meeting of the New York Society of Clinical Psychologists; New York City, Sept. 1976.

There may be less of it today than 100, or 200, even 20 years ago, but there is certainly enough of it to make it necessary to re-examine the problem of female masochism.

3. To state that there is no empirical evidence to support the underlying assumptions for a prevailing theoretical proposition is necessary, but not sufficient as long as the behavior that the theory purports to explain is still in evidence.

If female masochism is not a natural-biological phenomenon, then what is it? I believe that a content analysis of what I shall call the "psychoanalytic myth of female masochism" might hold the key to the understanding of the problem. In other words, I propose to approach the analysis of the subject matter through its myth. After all, it was Freud, more than anybody else, who suggested that the myth is an attempt to cope with a fear-inspiring reality.

First, however, the concept of female masochism should be defined, or rather that of masochistic behavior which is typically female. In the previous chapter, the term "masochistic" was applied to any behavior that has as its *goal*, directly or indirectly, injury to the self, attempts to jeopardize what is supposedly one's own best interest, the choice of the self as the main target for one's anger, and the need to deprecate the self. Subjugation, martyrdom, self-abuse, and passivity all characterize the masochistic life-style. Although masochistic women today no longer faint from corsets designed to produce a wasp-waist, spike heels, which are an invitation to permanent disalignments of the spine are back in style according to the fashion supplement of the *New York Times* (Aug. 24, 1980). Masochistic women today still tend to become overworked, underpaid, and self-deprecating members of the helping professions, graduate students who have work-blocks and hopeless affairs with their professors, or working-their-fingers-to-the-bone housewives with too many children. Any perusal of college catalogues and their adult education section are filled with courses on assertiveness training for women although no such courses seem to be necessary for men. Among the approximately 1,000 adult female students I have taught on the very subject of masochism versus self-responsibility during the last five years (in the adult education program of the New School for Social Research) only a tiny fraction have chosen to take themselves seriously enough to learn a marketable skill that would enable them to become economically self-sufficient rather than to depend on a real—or hoped for—male other. Put differently, what the feminists have identified as male oppression, from an objective point of view, certainly entails suffering on the part of women, and its continued existence is clearly evidenced by the troubled history of the E.R.A. Although suffering is real enough, and although true oppression has in fact been clearly in evidence, and still is, it is also, in my view, only half the story.

The association of femaleness and suffering is an ancient one indeed. It can be found in varying degrees in almost all cultures and all ages. It is as old as patriarchial society; that means as old as recorded history. "In sorrow thou shalt bring forth children" God informs Eve, and, as if this were not good enough, He goes on: "and thy desire shall be to thy husband. And he shall rule over thee." Eve is condemned to suffering ostensibly because she succumbed to temptation and because she succeeded in getting her man to do likewise. In other words, her *sexuality* is the source and the focus of her pain. It instigated her to disobey, and in its reproductive functions it spells sorrow. Even though Adam did not put up much resistance to her temptation—in fact he cooperated rather nicely—he is made the master over her. He becomes the parent; she, the more adventurous of the two, becomes the child. This little fable contains the two key elements that can be found in almost all ideologies advocating the necessity for female suffering: Woman's sexuality is dangerous unless it is severely restricted; and woman equals child who needs and wants a master. She fits what the authors of the *Authoritarian Personality* (Adorno et al., 1964) have referred to as the "dangerous little person" category: something that is contemptible because it is weak, small and inferior and, which at the same time, is also the source of terribly destructive powers. In the course of history, ideological justifications for the oppression of women have varied greatly, stressing either the destructiveness or the fragility of female sexuality. For example, although the witch-hunters of the Middle Ages focused primarily on the evils and the wantonness of woman's sexuality, psychoanalysts such as Freud, Bonaparte (1953), and Deutsch (1944) present a view of female sexuality that is purely passive and receptive and that is experienced by the woman as a rather mixed blessing. Women are no longer seen as lustful creatures; their sexuality is about as robust as a mimosa. To contrast the two views: *The Malleus Maleficarum* (1928) the official guide to witch-hunting states:

"All witchcraft comes from carnal lust, which in women is insatiable. . . . wherefore for the sake of fulfilling their lusts they consort even with devils." Bonaparte, in contrast, states: "Now, whether or not it will please women to hear it, the feminine organism, quantitatively speaking, is in general more poorly endowed with libido than the male, a fact true of all animal species. Doubtless this is because the more dynamic activity and sexual aggression are required in the male, if the race is to continue." (1953, p. 66) In fact, the whole theme of Deutsch's *Female Sexuality* is summed up in the first sentence of the book: "Nature does not always succeed in adapting organisms to function perfectly in their environment as we may clearly see from the far greater frequency of defective adaptation to the purely erotic function in women than in man." (p.1) Clearly, something very strange, indeed, happened to the view of female sexuality between the Middle Ages where women were supposedly so insatiable that they made out with the devil and this description of a sexual defective at the beginning of this century.

Let us recall here the standard psychoanalytic view of female sexuality and female masochism. For this purpose, a short summary of Freud's and Helene Deutsch's views will suffice. According to Freud the masochism of the female—as distinguished from female masochism in men—has two basic components: 1. The female's profound sense of inferiority vis-à-vis the male, and 2. generalized passivity. Both of these components are directly attributable to Freud's "Anatomical Distinction Between the Sexes" (1972b) that focuses on the problem of penis envy on the part of the female. Freud believed that once the little girl discovers the penis, she will immediately recognize it as the superior counterpart to her inconspicuous little organ, the clitoris. The resulting envy either can be absorbed in a reaction formation, namely the masculinity complex, or it will be displaced and manifest itself in the generalized character trait of jealousy. The corollary to her jealousy is her sense of inferiority. "After a woman has become aware of her wound to her narcissism, she develops like a scar, a sense of inferiority." (p. 188) Freud goes on: "she begins to share the contempt felt by men for a sex which is the lesser in so important a respect, and at least in holding that opinion, insists upon being like a man." (p. 188)

The recognition of her organ inferiority constitutes also the end of her masturbation since she is unwilling to settle for what seems to be second best. The penis envy on the part of the female, or rather her interpretation of the situation, has, according to Freud, a rather devastating bearing on the development of her superego. Given the fact that she recognizes herself as castrated, she has no compelling reason to work through her Oedipus complex.

> In girls the motive for the destruction of the Oedipus complex escapes the fate which it meets with in boys: it may either be slowly abandoned or got rid of by repression, or its effects may persist far into a woman's normal mental life. I cannot escape the notion, (though I hesitate to give it expression) that for women the level of what is ethically normal is different from what it is in men. Their superego is never so inexorable, so impersonal, so independent of its emotional origins as we require it to be in men. Character traits which critics of every epoch have brought up against women—that they are less ready to submit to the great necessities of life, that they are more often influenced in their judgments by feelings of affection or hostility—all these would be amply accounted for by the modification in the formation of their superego which we have already inferred." (192–193)

Another consequence of the young girl's recognition of her "castration" is a loosening of the tender bonds with her mother, whom she resents for having made her a girl. The mother then also becomes the object of jealousy once the girl turns to her father with the wish for a child. Her sexuality from that point on becomes passive in its orientation. Its long-range goals are twofold: 1. The shift from her masculine sexuality during her clitoral masturbation to her adult female sexuality which is passive, i.e. vaginal; 2. Her wish for having a penis changes to the wish to borrow the penis in the form of a baby, preferably a male one. The major theme that runs throughout Freud's psychology of women is that of "second best"; if you cannot have the prized penis, indirect means of attaining it become the expression of a woman's true nature. Reconciliation to loss and biological, intellectual, and moral inferiority represents femininity.

Deutsch's *Psychology of Women,* (it was published in 1944 and went into its 18th (!) printing in 1971) offers an interesting anthropological twist with respect to the origins of female masochism. She postulates that due to man's upright position and the location and structure of his genitals, he is the only animal who is fully capable of raping his female. On the basis of this presupposition, she argues that originally the sexual act was an act of violence, which the female, as the weaker of the two sexes was unable to resist and only gradually learned to experience as pleasurable. Deutsch's developmental theories are similar to those of Freud, but her interpretation of the genital trauma involves the entire character structure of the female. According to Freud, the young girl stops masturbating because she recognizes her clitoris as an inferior *sexual* organ. As a result of the genital trauma—Deutsch's version of the concept of penis envy—the little girl comes to the realization that the clitoris constitutes an insufficient outlet not only for her sexual drives but also for her active and aggressive ones. At this point in her development, she not only abandons masturbation, but her entire instinctual life takes a turn in the passive masochistic direction. In fact, the masochistic orientation of the female poses a potentially serious threat to her ego unless it is counteracted by considerable doses of narcissism. According to Deutsch, during the time between the end of the genital trauma and the advent of adult sexuality when the clitoris has been abandoned and the passive receptive organ, the vagina, is not yet available, the female is for the time period literally organless, a condition that tends to mobilize regressive tendencies focused on other passive organs, notably the mouth and the anus. The young girl's regressive passive stance and the repression of her aggressive drives are reinforced by her parents who offer her what Deutsch calls the "love bribe," which says that: "As long as you act like a sweet obedient little girl, mommy and daddy will love you."

The reawakening of the female's sexuality in adulthood is almost entirely contingent on the male's aggressive and persuasive powers—the 20th century version of "Sleeping Beauty."

(As a not unimportant aside, we might note the amazing extent to which Deutsch, who held an M.D. degree, insists that all sexual and reproductive functions are necessarily painful. Woman's life revolves around the triad of castration, violation, and childbirth. "In one of her functions, woman must have a certain amount of masochism if she is to be adjusted to reality. This is the reproductive function from beginning to end; even where it most serves the purpose of pleasure, it requires the toleration of considerable pain." (p. 277))

This view of woman's nature is as much prescription as it is description. In other words, on a descriptive level it contained quite a bit of truth, precisely because women, in the course of history, had, in fact, come to resemble these curious creatures described by the Freudians. The insatiable shrews of the *Malleus Maleficarum* had not only been largely tamed; they had learned to cooperate and they did so often beyond the call of duty. How and why did this happen?

To view the relationship between the sexes as one of oppression comparable to the oppression of social classes—or of ethnic and religious minorities—is from a sociological point of view, simply inaccurate. These oppressions do have a lot in common, but they are not identical. If nothing else, viewed in terms of sheer access to power and influence, the relationship between the sexes cannot be compared to that of social classes since men and women are about as intimate with each other as any two persons can be in their roles as husband and wife, parent and child. Every one of the oppressors—the male is literally the product of the oppressed—the female. The phenomenon of female masochism cannot be adequately explained in terms of the "identification with the oppressor" either, since this concept is based on the total powerlessness of the oppressed (Bettelheim's (1960) concentration camp victims). Women are *not* powerless, even though they may often feel that way. The relationship between the sexes, as reflected in the psychoanalytic literature that has just been examined, seems to constitute a sadomasochistic arrangement; one which contains all the elements that Fromm (1936) and others have identified as the prerequisite for a sadomasochistic bond: the partner who is weaker, smaller, more passive; biologically, intellectually and morally inferior, the female, subjugates herself to the stronger and superior partner—the male. His pleasure constitutes her pain that only gradually she learns to appreciate and to transform into pleasure. The weaker partner even shares the contempt which the stronger partner has for her sex and she compensates with obedience, "making nice," and by suffering. Freud, in his "The Taboo of Virginity" (1972a), spells out quite clearly the sadomasochistic elements in the process of defloration. By deflowering the bride, the male inflicts a narcissistic injury and, in so doing, truly takes possession of the woman. Although most normal women, according to Freud, react with sexual thralldom (Hörigkeit), many neurotic women react with a wish for revenge. For those women, only a second marriage may turn them into loving wives. I would argue that the term "loving" in this Freudian context can mean only the ability to repress the hostility and the fears that are invariably generated by a sadomasochistic arrangement. Although it is true that the Freudian psychology of women is a reflection of the sexual life of upper-middle class

Vienna at the turn of the century, a typical product of its time, it is even more important to note that as a *prescription* it is identical with God's punishment of Eve. If one compares the "psychoanalytic myth" with that of Adam and Eve, however, the big difference lies in the fact that the original threat, namely woman's natural sexuality, is no longer present. Ideology has won out over biology. Put differently, in the course of time, physiological impulses had yielded to social pressure; woman's crippled sexuality was perceived as the natural state of affairs, and in its distorted manifestation, biology was declared to be her destiny, a cruel dialectic indeed. Moreover—and Freud (1972a) himself was aware of this—it did not work. It was precisely in those instances where unbridled sexual impulses in women clashed with the sexual mores of the times, that the very "illnesses" in question emerged helping to give birth to psychoanalytic theory.

If we examine the history of women in other cultures and other ages, we have to conclude that in one form or another men have more or less successfully attempted to subjugate and curb female sexuality, and women have assented to it. It seems to be a constant in all known societies. The very staying power of this sadomasochistic interaction between the sexes is what needs explaining, particularly if one compares the role of women with that of other oppressed groups of people who, even though they were equally victimized, managed to liberate themselves and then, in turn, oppress others. The question that needs to be asked is: Why have men and women in all this time, or in any society, never switched roles or worked out an egalitarian relationship? In other words, what is the psycho-biological or cultural constant that explains the unique durability of this phenomenon?

In order even to begin to answer this question, one has to recall some of the basic psychodynamics of masochism. As stated in Chapter one, the masochistic stance, or rather the more masochistic end of the sadomasochistic continuum, develops most commonly during the oral stage, accounting for the masochist's need to be loved in a very passive, infantile way. The profound sense of being unwanted, so eloquently described by Berliner (1940; 1942; 1947; 1958) and others, or the experience of being less wanted than a sibling, (which, in my opinion, has the same effect) leaves the child with the difficult task of finding a mode of being insuring if not love itself, the illusion of it, the constituent core of the masochistic bond. Although both boys and girls can face the same dilemma in infancy, girls are more vulnerable in this respect than boys since there is reason to believe that the actual occur-rence of a non-loving or less loving maternal attitude toward the newborn is higher for girls than for boys. Furthermore, even if the sadomasochistic core is identical in both sexes, its transformation in the subsequent stages of infantile development, and the resulting adult behavior, is not.

First of all, the female stands a much better chance of being unwanted or the less wanted child. To this day, both males and females overwhelmingly prefer male children over female children. A total of twelve separate empirical studies have confirmed this (Sherman, 1971). In several samples, 90% of the males and between 70–80% of the females chose a *male* when asked what sex they would prefer if they could only have *one* child. Furthermore, as Westhoff, Potter, and Sagi (1963) have shown, when the first child is a girl, the interval before the second child is conceived averages three months shorter than if the first child is a boy. This difference is attributable not to the common-ly—and accurately—held belief that baby girls tend to be less trouble than boys, but to sex preference. It means that the parents, hoping for a boy, are simply in a greater hurry to try for another baby. Finally, the study of Gordon, Kapostins and Gordon (1967) has shown that post-partum depressions and other difficulties in postpartum adjustments are significantly correlated with the birth of girls rather than boys.

What this means is simply this: To the extent that a mother or father are inclined to feel negatively towards their children—and only the mythical perfect mother is free of such feelings—the girl is the more likely recipient of them. If the sense of being somewhat un-wanted is coupled with the recognition that the male sibling is the better loved one, a move toward the masochistic position—as opposed to the depressive position—is likely to result since the little girl can see that love on the parent's part is, indeed, available, whereupon the element of hope and its attendant unconscious fantasies are mobilized.

But even if the masochistic starting point, the experience of being unwanted or feeling less wanted than a sibling, is held constant, the average female is incomparably more likely than the male to develop a full-fledged masochistic stance—as opposed to the more sadistic one found in men—for a variety of reasons. It is known now that sex role stereotyping is not a feminist myth but an empirical reality. (Forisha, 1978; Lewis, 1976; Sherman, 1971; Frieze et al., 1978) The vast major-ity of traits identified with masochism are culturally encouraged in the female and culturally discouraged in the male. To list just a few: dependency, submissiveness, lack of competitiveness, altruism, "cute" manipulativeness, and self-depreciation. Conversely, the traits traditionally encouraged in the male by both his parents and his peers are independence, assertiveness, aggression, and competitiveness, all of which may not eliminate the tendency toward masochism but will certainly counteract a good bit of it. And according to the latest empirical evidence concerning sex-role perception among contemporary grade school children (Forisha, 1978), this difference will probably continue to exist for at least another generation. Furthermore, if one looks at the mother-daughter relationship and its relationship to masochism, one can see how even the loving and seemingly egalitarian mother is bound to relate to the baby girl differently than she does to the baby boy. Conversely, the way in which girls and boys relate to the maternal other during the early years is also different.

With respect to the "otherness" of the girl and its conformity with the mother's expectations, at least two possible patterns are easily discernible. 1. To the extent that the mother is uncomfortable with her own asocial, animalistic, delinquent, and willful impulses, the mirroring of these more or less unacknowledged traits on the part of the infant of the *same* sex will probably set off a greater degree of discomfort in the mother than that of the same behavior in a child of the *opposite* sex. After all, in the traditional nuclear family, the mothers learned that conformity with the basic sex role expectations got them to the point of marriage and motherhood, and many of them probably saw no reason not to want the same for their daughters. 2. Alternatively, the mother who secretly or overtly longed for a more assertive, independent and traditionally masculine stance in life for herself may project these wishes onto her daughter. Like most such projections, this agenda on the mother's part is not likely to succeed for two reasons: for one, encouragement for behavior patterns in small children without a same-sex role model is bound to produce conflict since the maternal message spells: "Do as I say, but don't do as I do." Second, if in the service of producing a more autonomous and independent girl, the mother makes an extra effort to insure that the girl stands on her own two feet as early as possible, she is likely to introduce the element of premature separation, loss of maternal assistance, and disillusionment in the goodness of the maternal other—experiences which tend to increase dependency, helplessness, a sense of failure, and worthlessness.

If one looks at the interaction from the young girl's point of view, the following conflicts are evident. The girl with the good enough "hatching" and symbiotic phase, (Mahler, 1968) will approach the individuation and separation phase with all the willfulness of children that age. All the power struggles typical for the toddler will come into play, just as they do in boys. There is one important difference, however: the differential response between boys and girls, respectively, to maternal, or rather, female power. As Dinnerstein (1976) has so aptly pointed out, the young girl, conscious of the fact that she too is a female, experiences the exercise of maternal power with very ambivalent feelings. Aside from the natural wish to assert her own will, to rebel, she is also aware that one day she will become the all-powerful other that she is now opposing. In other words, the girl's relationship to female power—which at that age is the only power she has known, the prototypical power so to speak, is highly ambivalent: On one hand she wants that power, but to become what one has learned to hate, is conflictual—so conflictual in fact that the suppression of her power-strivings seems preferable to its continued expressions. What remains is the unconscious fantasy "when I grow up I will be the perfect mother who poses no restrictions." Alternatively, if the frustrations were experienced as excessive, she may unconsciously plot revenge toward her mother through suffering, and at the same time comfort herself with the anticipation of enjoying equal powers over her own children.

Similar considerations pertain to the question of sexuality. If Friday's (1977) informal survey is representative—and I firmly believe it is—the subject of sex among mothers and daughters is still quite taboo. The delibidinization and depreciation of the girl's sexuality, one of the most important and central aspects of sex-role stereotyping, heavily contributes to the passive masochistic stance of the female. The examples and instances are too numerous and too well-known to recite here. If nothing else, the taboos surrounding menstruation, the conception of women as unclean and, therefore, dangerous are hardly designed to make the female feel good about her sexual self. The role of enforcing sexual restrictions, including the education towards asexuality, has been traditionally assigned to mothers or other older females. During the Oedipal period and during puberty, the age-appropriate exhibitionism and seductiveness on the part of the girl, if not prohibited or curbed by the mother, will result either in a severe rebuff by the father, a denial of his own sexual feelings, or alternatively in psychological or actual incest. In other words, the girl is taught to distrust her sexuality as a slightly dirty and potentially dangerous element of herself until such time as a male, through the ritual of marriage, suddenly legitimizes it, and when the law declares it as her marital duty.

If we look at the career opportunities for masochists in our society—and societies past—we find that social life is by no means an equal-opportunity employer. The professions or social roles that are based on the ability for self-sacrifice, which is often merely a disguised but socially acceptable form of masochism, are roles more likely to be occupied by females than by males. To wit: The thinking-only-of-her-family housewife, the secretary devoted to her male employer, as well as the entire range of the helping professions from Florence Nightingale on to the chronically helpful social worker.

All the elements that I have just listed as promoting the masochistic stance in the female today, have of course existed in abundance in the past. They have taken different forms and they have varied from one society to another, but the variations are rather minor. Thus, in view of what I have just said, it should no longer be surprising that women have so consistently occupied the masochistic end of the sadomasochistic arrangement between the sexes. But it does *not* explain why men have been equally consistent in defending what I have called the sadistic position. This question has to be raised, for no other reason than that all sadomasochistic arrangements are intrinsically unpleasant for both parties. If nothing else, they preclude any possibility for genuine love and intimacy.

It appears that in examining the origins of the male sadistic stance we will discover the painful truth that the "psychoanalytic myths of female masochism" and similar myths, are designed to conceal. This we will attempt to do in the next chapter.

Chapter 4

MALE SADISM:

Envy, Hostility, and Perversion*

As long ago as 1932, Horney in her paper, "The Dread of Women," suggested that to a large extent the boy's fear of the father is really a smokescreen for the fear of the vagina, the symbol of motherhood, life, and death. According to Horney, the fear of the vagina is two-fold, it is feared not only as the mysterious place where life and death originate, but also as a sexual goal that the young boy may want to pursue but for which he knows his penis is inadequate. Thus, the boy's sexuality is from the beginning tainted with fears of rejection, derision, or shame. Boehm, in 1930, pointed out that what he called the "femininity complex" in men is based on "parturition envy," the envy of the ability to bear and nourish babies and to create life. Womb-envy and breast-envy are both part of this syndrome. Even though this fundamental point about the relationship between the sexes, i.e. men's fear and envy of women, has been discussed and elaborated among others by Thompson (1959), Klein (1940), Mead (1949), Fromm (1951), Bettelheim (1954), Bak (1956), Reik (1960), Hays (1964), Lederer (1968),

*An earlier version of this chapter was presented at the 29th Annual Meeting of the New York Society of Clinical Psychologists; New York City, March 1977.

Stoller (1968), and Dinnerstein (1976), the subject has not really been incorporated into the mainstream of psychoanalytic thought. When Lederer published *The Fear of Women* in 1968, he found in the *Index of Psychoanalytic Writings* and *Psychoanalytic Abstracts* only two papers on the subject, one of them the Horney piece. And yet, mythology and literature are anything but subtle in revealing the connection between man's fear and his envy of woman's powers. In countless folklores and poems, the woman appears as the mysterious other who is both intensely desired, and at the same time, dreaded as the devourer and destroyer. Lorelei ensnares the boatmen by her beauty into certain death by drowning. Ulysses had to bind his sailors to the mast to protect them from the allurement by the Sirens. Those brave and clever men who solve the riddle of the Sphinx forfeit their lives. The Indian goddess Kali, a destroyer of men, adorns herself with the heads of her victims and drinks their blood from human skulls. All evil, all sickness and even death was contained in Pandora's box. These images are also alive and well today. When Mailer (1971) asked himself whether men and women could co-exist as equals, his answer was "No." He gave his reasons with characteristic candor. According to Mailer, equality between the sexes is impossible because men are afraid of women, afraid of the female's sexuality. In *The Prisoner of Sex*, he states in defense of Henry Miller:

> For he [Miller] captured something in the sexuality of men as it had never been seen before, precisely that it was man's sense of awe before woman, his dread of her position one step closer to eternity (for in that step were her powers) which made men detest women, revile them, defecate symbolically upon them, do everything to reduce them so one might dare enter them and to take pleasure of them. 'His shit dont smell like ice cream either', says a private to a general in a novel, and it is the cry of an enlisted man whose ego needs equality to breathe. So do men look to destroy every quality in a woman which will give her the powers of the male, for she is in their eyes already armed with the power that she brought them forth, and that is power beyond measure—the earliest etchings of memory go back to that woman between whose legs they were conceived, nurtured, and near strangled in the hours of birth. (p.66)

These images of women as the dreaded powerful other are countless and amazingly consistent. They hardly vary from one society to another.

It is hardly an exaggeration to state that the patriarchial system and patriarchial monotheism have consistently enforced male supremacy through the infantilization of women. Whether these social institutions arose as a result of, or revolt against, an earlier matriarchy is open to question and not really important in this context. What is important, however, is Goodman's (1979) astute observation that "unless women had been in a position of power, it would not have been necessary to strip them of their unique abilities, nor to belittle them in so many ways." (p. 41) Whether every male's experience during his first years of life in a matriarchial environment was once an anthropological reality will have to await empirical confirmation. Already, Freud however, was troubled by this question when he indicated that "I am at a loss to indicate the place of the great maternal deities who perhaps everywhere preceeded the paternal deities." (1955, p. 921)

If one examines that relationship between male and female in the Judeo-Christian tradition, the infantilization of women and their position as virginal child-brides is a hidden but powerful component. As Goodman has convincingly argued, if Eve was born from Adam's rib, then she is technically speaking Adam's daughter who then becomes his wife, one of the many creation—and marriage to the creator—myths encountered by anthropologists. "Her (Eve's) parthogenic birth from Adam's body makes Eve his daughter, so that the Judeo-Christian tradition rests on a primal father-daughter incest motif which is unrecognized and unspoken in male theology, scholarship and psychology, although it is basic to Western culture and thought." (p. 33) Thus, it is hardly surprising that in a patriarchial society such as ours the taboo against father-daughter incest is far less effective than that against mother-son incest, the latter being an affront to the father's male prerogatives.

Although no historical statistical data are available that would give an indicator as to the incidence of father-daughter incest in the past, it is known that among the 8,000 white middle-class women surveyed by Kinsey et al. in 1953, one out of 16 reported sexual contact with an adult male relative during childhood. Mother-son incest seems to occur only in severely disturbed families. (Justice and Justice, 1979; Butler, 1978) Sexual abuse of children seems to follow a similar pattern: 92% of the victims are female and 97% of the offenders are male. (Weinberg, 1955) To the extent that women and children are considered male property, these data do, indeed, make sense. Furthermore, as Herman and Hirshman (1977) have pointed out, in the case of father-daughter incest, there is no avenging father who could intervene and punish. Conversely, if we look at the Oedipus myth, there is no indication that Oedipus desired Jocasta, or that he fell in love with her. He simply married her because she came with the throne that Oedipus inherited after having solved the riddle of the Sphinx. Jocasta is the one who sets the whole chain of tragedies in motion when she abandons her son in order to save her husband, a seemingly excusable deed in a patriarchial society where even accidental patricide and mother-son incest are the ultimate crime, while infanticide is not. (Fromm, 1951)

Men's envy of woman's ability to produce life has been thoroughly demonstrated by Mead (1949), Fromm (1951), and Bettelheim (1954), in their examination of the practices of couvade (the masculine imitation of childbirth), male initiation rites (circumcision and subincision), and fertility rites. They concluded that the central mechanism operating in these rituals is the competition with, and awe of, the female's ability to menstruate and to give birth. After all, in all known societies and throughout history, it is the female who is experienced by the male as the first all-powerful other, the life giver, the life grower and also the first frustrator and, thereby, the object of his rage. The young boy can literally watch how mother, seemingly all by herself, grows a baby in her belly. He can watch as well as remember, how again, with no outside help, she can nourish a human creature. Since apparently she can grow her own food her powers must indeed appear limitless to him. To make matters worse, he knows that he, unlike his sisters, will never attain such powers. He can attempt to compete with her in the life and baby-producing business by becoming a gynecologist or obstetrician—which not accidentally are considered hotbeds of male chauvinism—but he can never be mother's equal. Men in preliterate societies were quite conscious of their awe before women's powers. Many of their rituals are clearly designed to give men the illusion that they, too, can give birth and menstruate. Zeus gave birth to Athena from his head and to Dionysus from his thigh. Among the tribal customs studied by Mead and Bettelheim, puberty rites for boys coincide with the onset of menstruation on the part of the girls, and the boy's rituals tend to be more elaborate than those of the girls. More-over, they are often conducted in secret. Since all of these societies did not understand the relationship between intercourse, impregnation and birth, the initiation rites focused on the female's ability to menstruate, since the menses indicated her ability to have children. In drawing blood in the process of circumcision, the boy becomes her equal, and together they now feel ready to accept their prescribed respective sexual roles. In the case of subincision, the attempt to imitate the female's sexual organs is even clearer. The long incision—resembling a vulva-like opening—is repeatedly and ritualistically reopened, thus drawing more blood in regular intervals, resembling menstruation. Since this operation also interferes with normal urination, the male now has to urinate in a squatting position, just like the females of the tribe. The subincision hole is variously called vagina, or penis-womb. It is important to note that the boys do not have to undergo those operations, and do not dread these mutilations that are usually voluntary; that, to the contrary, they are looked forward to for the adult status they confer.

The various customs of couvade—as *rebirth* by a male into the society of men—are equally common though varied. The principal dynamic is the following: the pretense that men, too, can give birth, and that a man is not a man until he is reborn by a man, which is the central theme of the Spartan cult of pederasty. (Vanggaard, 1972) For example, among the Liberian Poro society, the boys entering the ceremonial hut are assumed to be swallowed (or killed) by the Poro deity which is the crocodile spirit. In reality, the older men hide the boys in the forest. The older men then go out to resurrect them, and after several days they return with them, carrying the boys on their backs like infants, thus, creating the illusion of having brought them back to life. Moreover, the exhaustion exhibited by the older men, resembles the fatigue of a woman after childbirth, and their wives have to nurse them back to health. Symbolically, the boys have reentered the womb through the *vagina dentata*—the mouth of the crocodile (or a dragon in other societies)—and, thus, reversed the process of their birth in order to be reborn by a man. It is important to note, however, that the male rites of couvade are almost invariably carried out in secret, in order to disguise the fact that the desired goal was not reached. At a later stage of social development, when the true biological process of gestation can no longer be denied, the contribution of the semen is overstressed and the female contribution is considered neg-ligible. The concept that the male sperm contained the entire human being—the homunculus—and that the mother's womb is merely a breeding ground also has been a rather popular theory in many societies.

In the Christian tradition, baptism, confirmation in the faith, and communion also contain an element of couvade. Although the child has been born by a woman, the infant only acquires a chance of immortality through baptism by a male priest. The souls of infants who are not thus baptized—or born—and who through no fault of their own die in infancy, are not permitted to enter heaven but are con-signed to either limbo, purgatory, or hell.

What all these rites, cults, and myth have in common in their intent is the understandable desire to render harmless the all-powerful, dangerous, female love object. Put differently, what I am suggesting is that patriarchial social institutions and ideologies, including the "psychoanalytic myth of female masochism," are basically a monumental culturally-valued reaction formation to man's dread and envy of women. Moreover, as will be shown below, the fact that this essentially sadomasochistic arrangement has alleviated the fears of both sexes is what accounts for its unique durability.

Since this book addresses itself to the problems of sadomasochism in contemporary society, however, the question as to how that sadistic component in the sadomasochistic substratum in the psyche of the average male manifests itself *today*, has to be examined. What empirical proof or evidence—if any—does one have for this contention? In order to answer this question, one has to clarify first for what one is looking. Male sexuality, the male's relationship to the female body and the memory traces it evokes, is characterized by a considerable amount of ambivalence. The same is not true for the female and her relationship toward the male body, since the body of her first love object—the mother—differs from that of her later attachment—the father. The father, who during the oedipal period becomes the symbol of her sexual desires, is not the parent of earliest infancy and, thus, uncon-taminated by either the longing or the grievances of that time. His slate is clean, so to speak. As Dinnerstein (1976) has pointed out, her relationship to him is much more neutral and much less charged. The ambivalence toward her mother may be transferred to the father and later in life to the man she loves, but the experience is once removed, it does not have the same *physical* authenticity as the relationship between the boy or the grown man and the female body. The male has to make the difficult transition of relating sexually to a body that is the repository of all the grief as well as the bliss of the nursery, a fact which heavily contributes to what Dinnerstein has called the "sexual malaise." Moreover, because the female is usually the first primary caretaker, the "core gender identity" of the male is also much less stable than that of the female. (Stoller 1968 and 1975)

The male ambivalence toward the female body is composed of the following components: bliss, security, and warmth on one hand, and fear, envy, hostility, and rage on the other. In early infancy, the moment there is even a glimmer of the experience of the otherness of the mother, rather than the feeling of oneness with her, the sense of bliss and security becomes mingled with fear then envy, and later, rebellion. After all, the experience of the separateness on the part of the mother spells impotence in the infant. The baby's survival depends first of all on the supply of milk. But even the most conscientious mother cannot ever guarantee a steady flow of milk, the compatability of the milk with the infant's digestive system, the timing between her feeding and the infant's hunger. Consequently, every baby develops an ambivalent attitude toward the female breast. The baby sees it on one hand as the most valuable object in his limited universe, but on the other, because it does not function like a mechanical water fountain, it also becomes the object of his rage. To the extent that the breast is experienced as a frustrating object, the infant has to cope with two sets of terrors: oral sadism, the temptation to bite the breast, and the wish to swallow the breast, i.e. the mother. As the saying goes: You cannot have your cake—breast—and eat it, too. Often, the wish to incorporate is defended against by the fear of being swallowed up.

The experience of the mother as the first frustrating and, thus, rage-provoking object, however, extends to all aspects of the young boy's existence. She is teaching him a very hard lesson, namely: "You do it my way, or else . . . " During the second year of life, she is in charge of toilet training, a process which no matter how benignly it is conducted, spells renunciation of very gratifying experiences, and at each attempt the mother is the witness to both his successes and his failures. Now, she is not only totally in charge of everything that goes *into* the body but also of everything that comes *out* of his body, an experience which in adult life is only approximated by a line-by-line audit by the

Internal Revenue Service. A certain amount of maternal invasiveness is inevitable, and so is the experience of humiliation. In fact, the fear of humiliation goes far beyond the process of toilet training. The toddler, with his insatiable need to explore the entire environment, meets with a string of prohibitions and warnings. Even though he is told time and again not to touch the stove, the electric outlet, or to pull the dog's tail, chances are he will do one or all of these things, get burned, shocked, or bitten, and on top of the shock of the pain, he is likely to encounter a perfectly understandable "I told you so" reaction on the part of his exasperated mother. Mother knows best and her omniscience is both reassuring and infuriating.

In the process of establishing both his separateness and his dignity, he will have to oppose her time and again, but the price of opposing her, is quite often to fall flat on his face and to expose himself to ridicule and corresponding shame. Superman, after all, does not trip over his own high-chair. If the young boy finds the task of separating through opposition too overwhelming, he is faced with another danger: regressson, i.e. the wish to be a baby again. But that wish spells the loss of his precious autonomy, the fear of becoming unborn, and on top of that censure and ridicule from both mother and father. Thus, it is vital, that in the process of establishing his male autonomy in opposition to the preoedipal mother, he can connect with his father and draw strength from his strength. If the father is either unavailable or rejecting, the young boy is then thrown back into the only too unequal power struggle with his omnipotent mother.

We have no reason to believe that the envy and the dread of the lifegiving powers of the mother, her vagina, womb, and breasts is any less pronounced in the young boy than it was for the men of the preliterate tribes discussed earlier, and he knows just as they did, that unlike his sisters, he will never attain such powers. While the young boy is pondering these matters, his father may well singlehandedly arrange the merger of two major corporations, invent the polio vaccine or fly to the moon, but these enterprises are first of all incomprehensible to the little boy, and to the extent that they were, they are in his view hardly matters of consequence compared to mother's powers. By the time they do acquire significance, he is already so much more of a little person, rather than a symbiotically connected extension of his mother, that his father's powers may impress him, but they will not overwhelm him. Put differently, the father may be *humanly* powerful, but mother's powers are *divine*. Even the genius of Dr. Frankenstein could only produce a caricature of a human being, and even that creation turned into a nightmare.

Before going on to distill from these considerations a list of unconscious fears, fantasies, and perverse impulses that one expects to find in varying degrees in the psyche of the average male, and before setting out to look for empirical indicators for them, it seems necessary to discuss the concepts of "core sexual identity" and "perversion" as postulated by Stoller's work first, since his research has added a powerful dimension to our knowledge about the origins of male sadism.

Due to parental reinforcement of masculine and feminine behavior, and given normal development, the core gender identity of both sexes is set by the end of the first year and more or less irreversibly consolidated by the age of three. Establishing a gender identity, however, is much harder for the male than it is for the female, since for both sexes the earliest identification is with the female body. Thus, the male establishes his gender identity in opposition to—or away from—his primary identification. The nonpathological mother, who takes delight in the maleness of her infant will subtly encourage maleness by the way she holds, handles, and caresses the boy, which slightly differs from the way she handles the girl. In this manner, the boy "disidentifies" with the mother, a process which for the girl is not necessary, and his maleness becomes an integral part of his self.

> . . . these earliest experiences 'imprinted' permanently into the psyche (and brain?), act as inexorably and unalterably as do 'instincts,' and while not primarily originating in biological drives, they create permanent intrapsychic demands that will be felt by the individual as if they were 'instinctual'. (Stoller, 1968, p. 36–37)

In order to truly desire the mother as a sexual object—as opposed to the feeling or wish to be like her—individuation and separation would have to be complete and conflict-free—a contradiction in terms. First of all, the ever-present pull back to the symbiotic way of relating is a continuous danger that may be present in the mother as well as the boy, since it weakens the necessary barrier, i.e. symbiosis anxiety, between mother and son which allows him to consolidate his male identity. Moreover, even if the mother does not interfere with the boy's attempt to separate and individuate as a male child, his envy of her powers, the parturition complex, makes the route toward untroubled masculinity a hazardous one. If one adds to this all that has been said before about the power struggle between the toddler and his mother, it is easy to see that the interference with the boy's willfulness and aggressiveness is also experienced as an assault on his maleness, since to him the opposition is—at that moment—experienced as global. The girl, in contrast, who does not have to disidentify with her mother's gender, opposition is just that, and, therefore, usually not a threat to her gender identity. This does not mean that a mother may not also assault her daughter's femininity, but here we are talking about *normal* development, not pathological behavior. For the male, a more or less firm gender identity, and, therefore, heterosexuality are not a biological preordained given, but a painfully acquired accomplishment, which under extreme conditions, may not succeed at all. The relationship between the mother of a transsexual and her son is a case in point and perhaps the best example for how things can go entirely wrong. According to Stoller, these mothers, who usually harbor a profound hatred toward men, choose one of their sons to be a completely feminine narcissistic extension of themselves. They allow the boy to separate and to individuate in all areas except that of gender identity. Consequently, a male identity never develops in the first place, and, thus, the transsexual's feelings of being a male trapped in a female body reflects an accurate inner reality and experience. In all other male sexual deviations—including "normal" heterosexuality—a male identity *was* developed and then threatened, leaving in its wake if not concrete perversions, traces of perverse impulses and fantasies.

What I want to propose, is this: it seems that what Dinnerstein (1976) has called the "sexual malaise" and what Stoller (1975) has identified as the perverse component which is necessary and present in all human sexuality, are both almost identical with what I have called the sadomasochistic substratum in the relationship between the sexes. Stoller defines perversion as follows: "Perversion, the erotic form of hatred, is a fantasy, usually acted out but occasionally restricted to daydream (either self-produced or packaged by others, that is, pornography)." (1975, p. 4) Whether the choice of the term, namely perversion, for something so utterly universal is a courageous or a foolish one—I tend to think of it as courageous—depends on our willingness to accept the fact that remnants of real hostility toward the primary caretaker, which in our society is usually the mother, are present in all of us, and that these grievances must be redressed over and over again. Although Stoller acknowledges the necessity for these needs for redress, nowhere does he express happiness about it. In order to understand the meaning of the term perversion as Stoller uses it, and its relationship to male sadism, the psychodynamics of fetishism (or fetishistic crossdressing), a seemingly victimless act, is perhaps the best illustration. Moreover, fetishism is considered by Stoller and Bak (1956) as the prototype of all perversions. "One who cannot bear another's totality will fragment—split and dehumanize—that object in keeping with past traumas and escapes; he may then isolate a neutral fragment—aspect—of that person and displace his potential sexual response from the whole person to the part that more safely represents that person (fetishization)" (p. 132) Thus, at the core of all perversions is hostility and a fantasy of revenge designed to convert a once real childhood trauma into an adult triumph. The element of risk-taking, provided it is not too great, lends excitement to the perverse act. The original trauma is an assault on, or threat to, the child's gender identity as for example in the case of the fetishistic crossdresser, the habitual dressing of the young boy in girl's clothing as a humiliating punishment. To see the resulting anxiety and humiliated fury as merely responses to castration anxiety is too narrow a view. It is a threat to one of the most vital parts of the boy's identity—the core of the male self—which is a far more encompassing threat than that of the loss of the penis which is *a* symbol of maleness. Thus, the fetishistic crossdresser, for whom the employment of the fetish is a prerequisite for orgasm, relives the original trauma by wearing female garments. Now he is not only *like* a woman, but he is also the most superior woman, since unlike *them* he also has a penis. Thus, the element of triumph lies in the fact that he is fully potent in the presence of the original trauma. He takes his revenge in the fantasy that by proving over and over again that she—mother—failed in her attempt to de-masculanize him. Frustrating her (the mother) in that way satisfies his hostility. As was indicated in chapter two, the same mechanism operates in the sado-masochistic perversions: The original trauma—usually a humiliation—is relived, controlled, and, thus, rendered harmless through redress. If one accepts the fact—and I believe one must—that childhood is never without trauma, that men raised in the nuclear family never completely lose their awe, fear and envy of women, then it would follow that a certain and minute element of perversion—as well as perversity—and sadomasochism are present in the relationship between all men and women. Where Stoller's work, in my opinion, has often been misunderstood is in the fact that he concludes—*not advocates*—that in light of the above the inclusion of a certain amount of perversion adds excitement to the sexual act. Thus, I am proposing that, in varying degrees, traces of the following elements are likely to be present in the conscious or unconscious of the average male psyche: fear and envy, and consequently, hostility, denial, fantasies of role-reversals and revenge, and finally, outright sadism. These feelings can apply to the female breast, vagina, womb, the female's power to impose her will on his, her ability to give or withhold life-giving supplies, oedipal rage, and, depending on the individual case, probably a host of others.

Unfortunately, there is not a reliable and representative in-depth survey of male sexual fantasies that could empirically verify this hypothesis. Instead, I have looked for an empirical indicator that does not prove the hypothesis but, in my opinion, clearly supports it. It appears that the most likely place for the manifestation of these fears and fantasies would be pornography.

The choice of pornography or sex magazines as a social indicator for this hypothesis has several advantages:

1. It is read almost exclusively by men; women are bored by it.
2. It has the aura of the semi-forbidden.
3. The men who read these magazines hardly constitute a deviant minority. To the contrary, in February, 1977 when this study was conducted, the circulation figures for *Playboy* were 5.4 million, followed by *Penthouse* with 5.3 million and *Hustler* with 2.8 million, to name just the most widely circulated magazines with a combined circulation of 13.5 million.* Moreover, circulation figures constitute only a fraction of the actual readership.
4. Unlike literature, pornography the self-expression of a particular author and his particular quirks, in not at issue. To the contrary, what is being dealt with is a literary product that has

*These figures were obtained from the circulation desk of these magazines. However all figures pertaining to readership are estimates since one reader may buy more than one magazine and each magazine may have many readers.

been written to order to satisfy the largest number of male customers. They are truly single purpose magazines—to provide sexual stimulation—and unlike novels, nobody can claim to read them for their literary merits. In fact, one of the magazines in my sample contained an intelligent piece which offered sound advice on how to write pornography in terms of plot, location, vocabulary, themes, dialogue, fantasy material, titles, audience appeal and the reminder that "a porn book should be no shorter than 183 pages and no longer than 187 pages. In other words, long enough for pleasure but not so thick that the reader has to use both hands in order to hold it." (Swank, p. 54)

The material I examined represents a cross section of pornographic magazines published in February, 1977. It consisted of 20 magazines sold in local candy stores, 10 magazines sold in the pornography stores at Times Square and 2 novels. All told, this adds up to 2500 pages of print with an approximate circulation of 15 million. These magazines obviously constitute only a sample of what is sold nation- or even city-wide since two thirds of this material was bought in various stores in one respectable residential neighborhood in Manhattan. Since the material bought at Times Square did not differ in any significant way from that bought locally, all the examples quoted below have been taken from the more "respectable" material.

Considering the widespread consumption of pornographic literature by heterosexual American men, an estimated 18 million copies are sold monthly, one must conclude that among other things, it satisfies a continuous need on the part of its consumers that cannot be explained in terms of simple sexual curiosity, since one issue would satisfy that need. Thus, the question had to be raised whether pornography appeals to the sadomasochistic—or perverse—substratum in the male psyche, a response to the sexual malaise. In my opinion, the answer is an unqualified "yes," since in my sample of just *one* month, I found *at least one example* for each and every preoedipal fear and fantasy discussed earlier in this chapter. The more "touchy" subjects though, such as outright sadism were often dealt with not by portrayal but by denial and through humor. This is what I have found:

The Breast—Although the female with oversized breasts (up to

48D) no longer predominates the centerfolds, she has by no means disappeared. She is still quite common, and the caption underneath a series of photos of a woman with a 42-inch bust reads as follows: " 'People like me' she says, 'and they like to confide in me. Maybe I look like the mother they wish they'd had' "(Cheri, Feb. 1977) In four instances, big-busted women were sucking their own breasts, confirming the young boy's notion that women can, indeed, feed themselves as well as others. The flip-side of oral greed, namely, oral sadism, is present in the following cartoon: An enraged man—naked except for his shirt which is covered with blood,—with a huge butcher knife in his hand snarls at a horrified woman whose breast he has just cut off: "Now do you believe I'm a leg man not a tit man?" (Swank, March 77) The reversal of the feeding situation is portrayed by a cartoon in which a naked man and a woman put on bibs. In the next frame the man is sitting on a table with a bottle of wine, food, and one place setting. In the third frame, he proceeds to eat while the woman crawls under the table and "eats" him. One of the curious fantasies that I have encountered in all pieces dealing with oral sex is the notion that the woman can never get enough of the male sperm, she always hates to waste a single drop. The insistence that the penis feeds as well as the breast is a curious distortion since during breast feeding, the infant's gratification, depends not just on the quantity of the milk but also on the even flow of it. This equation of the two types of feeding experience also often contains a sadistic or retaliatory element: although the female is invariably described as gagging on the sperm, she is also alleged to adore her encounter with the experience of almost choking to death.

The Vagina—Horney's (1939) belief that the young boy fears that his penis is inadequate to satisfy his mother, is sadly acknowledged by a cartoonist who portrays a giant of a woman who looks disappointedly at a little man who brings home a vibrator the size of his torso and states with an apologetic expression on his face: "It's the biggest one they had!" (Swank, March 77) This cartoon conveys apology and mockery at the same time. The fear of the vagina as a smelly and dirty place appeared quite often. Two examples will suffice. One, a cartoon of a wedding. The bride is considerably taller than the groom. An angry minister holding his nose addresses the bride as follows: "And do you, Karen, promise to love, honor, cherish and douche once and a while?" (Hustler, March 77) In another cartoon, a naked and monstrously fat and ugly woman sits on a bed with her legs spread. She pulls out of her vagina not only a tampon but also a host of insects and bugs. While doing this she says into the phone: "I'll be ready when you get home, Carl. I am cleaning it out now." (*Hustler*, March 77)

The fear of the vagina dentata was found in three separate instances. One, a naked woman sitting on the head of a tiger, and the caption supplies the reader with the information that "the vagina dentata, said to afflict flamenco dancers. It seems that vag.d. was nature's answer to the problem of what do you do when you're out in public and your castanets are at home."(*Oui*, March 77) A more frightening possibility is expressed in the other example. The first frame shows a voluptuous female, seemingly treading water in the ocean and waving her arms for help. In the next frame the man, in eager anticipation swims toward her. In the third frame, we see that it is really a hungry crocodile (!) with a toothy smile who holds in one of his claws the puppet figure of a female as a decoy. (*Cheri*, March 77) Finally, a preview of "Deep Fang" that is considered "The newest kink in horror Porn is babes like Draculina, here, with an oversexed overbite and blood lust to boot. The twist is that vampire love could either get you very hot—or leave you cold." (*Cheri*, April 77)

The Penis—The fear of the vagina finds its corollary in the fear of the inadequacy of the penis. In my sample of magazines, I have found almost as many ads for penis enlargers as for all other products combined. A full-page ad by Leisure Time Products, for example, combines fear of inadequacy, outright phallic sadism, phallic exhibitionism, and threats to male identity. It states on one hand: "Sure the medical authorities say size doesn't count; but as long as women have a need to be filled, they'll demand a full measure of devotion. And no amount of psychological reassurance will fill the gap between expectation and reality." (*Hustler*, March 77) Alongside this statement, however, is a cartoon portraying the same brutally sadistic male who was mentioned earlier as having cut off a woman's breast. This time he is holding her in his lap while standing up, and penetrating her so deeply that his penis comes out of her mouth, causing her unspeakable agony, pain, and horror.

Diagonally across from this cartoon we see a photo of a proud male with an enormous penis. The rest of the body is not seen, just his hips and his sexual organ. Between these two images, the advertiser displays a huge "Peter Meter" in the form of a tape measure that has the following divisions: "Should have been a girl"; "Mostly Imagination"; "Small Change"; "Tickler"; "Getting There"; "A Nymph's Delight"; "For Use with Small Cattle"; "All Bets Are Off": and "Gulp!" In another full-page ad, the same manufacturer, promoting "Dueling Dildoes" that can be used as dildoes or can be worn over a man's penis, tells the reader the following: "Leisure Time knows that when you go into battle you need to be well armed. That's why we've called good old 'Doc' Johnson to help you choose the right weapon." (*Hustler*, March 77) The war-like element in this ad has two components: the male competitive element, which shows a traditional dueling scene,—only the men are holding penises instead of pistols; and the hostile sadistic component. A demure but happy young woman is shown with a huge jewelry tray holding all the various "weapons." Proportionally, however, the size of the dildoes, if applied, would probaby cause internal hemorrhages rather than pleasure.

Womb Envy—I found this topic dealt with through what appears as a double denial. The cartoon shows a delivery room with the two doctors holding an object resembling a small egg-shaped balloon with a string. The two doctors announce to the surprised woman on the table: "Congratulations, Mrs. Stanley. It's a six-pound seven ounce sperm." (*Hustler*, March 77)

Female Domination—This turned out to be one of the most commonly encountered topics both in the "stories" as well as in the jokes and cartoons. One frequent solution is to turn the humiliation into enjoyment. *Swank* (March, 1977) has this to say on the subject of "Dominating Bitches:"

> Why do men like dominant women? Psychologist Helmut von Atta wrote, in his *Geschichte von dem Uberfräulein:* 'The figure of the Dominatrix. . . . is a slightly refracted image of man's primal overlord, His Mother. At her breast he was fed—or denied. At her hands he was caressed—or disciplined. In his image of the Huge Mother is the male infant's first perception of awesome power. Growing into adulthood, men will often find themselves still cowed by an almost instinctual worship of the Mother and, by extension (to spare the inevitable Oedipal grief), of Womankind. This adoration is sublimated by most males into so-called normal rela-

tionships. . . . other men, more imaginative perhaps, are determined to precisely realize their feelings of homage to Supreme Femininity. Those who act out these feelings are submissives and spend their lives in the pursuit of an approximately accommodating Mistress or Dominatrix.' " (p. 56)

Role reversal, as a theme is equally common. *Club* (March 77) shows an elaborate spread of photos showing an urbane business man and his secretary—he wearing a large sign that says "I can dictate"—she wearing a button that reads "I can type." In this series, her genitals are inspected by the "dictator" and are shown off for appreciation by the reader. She then goes on to service him sexually and she winds up in a position of almost statuesque obedience lying on his desk, while he stands over her in a King Kong pose. Secretaries who become the sexual servants of their bosses is a fairly common topic. In this case, however, the male starts out objectively in a superior position. Even more common, is the scenario wherein the male turns the superior female into his sexual slave. Examples are: male students and their female teachers; upper-class housewives and their delivery boys, electricians, plumbers, mailmen, and T.V. repairmen. Outright revenge as the central theme was found in a piece titled "Getting even with cheating Chicks" (*Swingle,* 1977) which proposes elaborate torture scenes. Women bound and gagged and trussed up like chickens were also found in four of the magazines. Usually at least one rope cuts sharply into her vagina and across her breasts. Direct retaliation for harsh toilet training appeared in a cartoon which shows an elderly couple eating in a restaurant. A young, blind man stands in front of them and he urinates into the woman's soup. The couple looks horrified. The waiter, however, politely explains to the blind man: "Excuse me, sir, but the rest rooms are to your right." (*Hustler,* March 77)

Fear of Women—For the male for whom the fear of the female seems too insurmountable, mechanical models are available that are widely advertised. Life-sized solid foam dolls, with clothing to match, long silky hair and a teenage body and electronic four-way action with remote control are here. And the advertiser, Frankfort Sales, explains that: "Even her sensuous lips, and deep throat mouth, powered by air suction, can open and close gently," and her vagina responds in a similar fashion. These mechanical wonders sell for $50–$90. For the man who wants his sexual pleasures more circumscribed, Emerson

Industries suggests the "Suck-U-Lator." "It duplicates the exotic feeling of a real expert *you-know-what* job—but it feels even better! For one thing, the Suck-U-Lator has built in humming, vibrating action that will drive you up the wall with toying, teasing, tumultuous blasts of frenzied delight. (*Gent,* April 1977)

Sex and Death—The awareness that through the female body one first learns about not only life but also death, is directly acknowledged by a cartoon that shows two elderly ladies knitting. One explains to the other: "Poor Sam. Whoever thought that 'once more for old times sake' was gonna blow out his pacemaker?" (*Gent,* April 1977) A reversal of that relationship, however, was found in two instances. In both stories, the women are so insatiable that they pursue sexual stimulation, mechanically administered by a man, until the woman suffers "Death by Orgasm." (*Light and Day,* March 77)

Oedipal Material—Finally, the following "letter to an advice columnist" (*He and She,* March, 1977, p. 60) combines oedipal and oral material, with the woman cast in the role of the seducer:

Dear Miss Sharpe:

You're not going to believe this one. I used to have a problem getting sexually aroused. Sex was a dreary, boring affair until last month, when my husband and I had a baby son. He was a complete joy to both of us, but we never expected him to be *this* much of a joy. I am an earthy sensuous woman, which is why I chose to breastfeed my son. My husband gets very turned on watching his infant son (who looks just like him) suck hungrily on my full, overflowing breasts. But what turns me on is having my baby sucking and pulling on my tits. I become like a bitch in heat. I get so turned on that I can't wait for my husband to fuck me, which he often does with the baby still sucking. It's wonderful! We've been balling at least twice a day, and our marriage has never been better. My question is this. Our pediatrician has said to wean Junior by the time he is one year old, otherwise he will become spoiled. By now, Junior has become an integral part of our sex life. . . . I don't want to lose my new found sensuality. What should we do?

Jocasta R.
Cedarhurst, N.Y.

To the extent that this sample of pornographic material can be considered to be representative, and I believe this to be so, one can conclude that sexual fantasies that involve preoedipal sadomasochistic components, based on envy, fear, and hostility toward women are common enough in the psyche of the average American male to support a major industry. The similarities between the psychic mechanisms operating in initiation rites, couvade, mythology and those found in contemporary pornography are too striking to be accidental. It could be argued however, that the examples given above only constitute a small fraction of the overall material examined. This is true. In evaluating pornography as a whole, however, I am in full agreement with Stoller, (1975) who argues that there is no such thing as non-perverse—or non-sadomasochistic—pornography, even when it only portrays heterosexual intercourse, genitals and other seemingly erotic scenes or objects. For one, the pleasure is strictly voyeuristic, an expression of hostility, fear, and triumph over the unwilling object. The people on the page do what the reader wants them to do. The consumer, as the invisible third, can direct, fragment "fetishize," and lord over the mysterious other. A full-page photo of a vagina outside of a medical textbook, has no other function than to demystify and to dehumanize the female and her genital. Paper, after all, cannot talk back. The simple nudes, according to Stoller,

> reduce the actual woman to a two-dimensional, frozen creature helplessly impaled on the page, so that she cannot defend herself or strike back, as she might in the real world. Even if she has a dangerous look about her, that implied risk is negated by her imprisonment on the paper. She can be insulted, dirtied, forced to act according to the viewer's will, and remain uncomplaining, smiling, or even phallic—whatever is necessary—but immobile. (1975, p. 133)

Before concluding this chapter we have to return to the original question, namely what fears motivate both sexes to have cooperated throughout history in what clearly constitutes a sadomasochistic arrangement? The answer seems to lie in the fundamental sense of human dependency implanted in infancy. After all, the most archaic human fear, from which all others derive, is the fear of abandonment. Although the masochistic stance and its sadistic counterpart develop in response to a non-loving love object, the fear of abandonment constitutes its base, regardless of whether the love object is good or bad. It represents the threat of not having any love object at all, which spells death. It is simply part of the human condition. Although in the child with the good enough mother this dread will be reduced to quite manageable proportions, traces remain in all of us, a fact which the love literature through the ages amply demonstrates. Romeo and Juliet prefer self-inflicted death to separation; so did Goethe's young Werther; and Johann Sebastian Bach wrote for his wife Anna Magdalena a song that in translation goes as follows: "If you are with me then I will meet death and eternal rest with joy. Oh how happy were my end if your loving hands were to close my faithful eyes." (David & Mendel, 1945). *(trans. mine)*

Viewed in this way, the plight of both sexes, namely their need for sadomasochistic arrangements, should now be intelligible. When Indian widows let themselves be burned after the death of their husbands, they did not only deny their separateness but were in fact expressing a sentiment not dissimilar from that of Johann Sebastian and Anna Magdalena, namely, that they will accompany their spouses into their ultimate sleep which is death. The Chinese women who bound their feet were giving their men the following message: "If I cripple myself to the point where I lose my self-sufficiency as well as my powers to abandon you—my feet—will you love me in return?" The women who submitted to clitorectomies surrendered their sexuality which might have tempted them to leave their husbands for someone else. They did this in the knowledge that as sexual property they would not be abandoned.

It bears repeating at this point, that the universal sadomasochistic substratum discussed here, differs qualitatively from the sadomasochistic character formation. The manifestations and treatment of the latter will be discussed in the next five chapters.

Chapter 5

CASE HISTORIES

PRESENTING PROBLEMS AND DIAGNOSIS

In order to illustrate the etiology of sadomasochism as the predominant pathology, and the proposed treatment process, four patients have been chosen: Karl, Bob, Larry, and Anna. Their life histor-
ies and their progress in treatment will be presented in detail in the
following chapters. Although all four of them exhibited a preponderance of a sadomasochistic personality formation or life style, substan-
tial differences in terms of the extent of their ego impairment, self-
pathology, sexual orientation, and motivation for treatment were evident at the beginning of treatment. Although all of them have made an
enormous amount of progress—in fact Karl, Larry, and Anna will most
likely have terminated therapy by the time this book goes to press—
Bob is only now, after seven years, beginning to enter therapy in
earnest. His case history has been included to exemplify the contention
that the self-pathology—in contrast to the degree of ego impairment—
is the more important variable in determining the sadomasochistic
patient's ability to benefit from treatment *quickly*. In many ways, Bob
resembles the case of Mr. M. described by Kohut (1977), with one
important difference: termination has never been really an issue in

either of our minds. Fortunately, since all parents of these patients are still alive, I have been able to verify most of the hypotheses concerning the early history of these patients including most pertinent aspects of the parent's pathology.

Presenting Problems

Originally, Karl, a 30-year-old male homosexual did *not* present himself as a patient at all. It was his lover Tom, a paranoid schizophrenic, who called for an appointment because he had had a fight with Karl, in the course of which he (Tom) almost succeeded in killing him. In the days following this fight, Tom had experienced several episodes of almost unmanageable homicidal impulses towards his co-workers as well as strangers in the street. When he came for his first session, Karl walked him to my office for moral support, and had intended to wait for him in my waiting room until the end of the session. It had not occurred to Karl that he, too, might need some help. Neither had the thought crossed his mind that living with his lover might be a peril to his life. I suggested during this initial consultation that I ought to speak to Karl also, in order to assess (for myself) the degree of destructiveness in their interaction. For a variety of reasons—the imminent danger to Karl's life and the fact that Karl would only deal with a German-speaking therapist, being two of them—it was decided that I would see both of them individually twice per week and the two of them as a couple once a week in order to diffuse the malignant aspects of their symbiosis. Although this treatment setting seemed hardly ideal—in fact it had all the makings of a therapist's nightmare—there was also that indefinable something that spells a commitment to health. Although I would never recommend such an arrangement, given other alternatives, patients do not always accept alternatives, and, therefore, we have to decide between not accepting them at all, or, for the time being, to go along with the limited options with which they provide us.

If one defines the term "presenting problem" as the difficulty that patients bring into the first session as "the problem" or "problems" that they want help with, then—strictly speaking—Karl had no presenting problem. His current situation did not seem unusual to him, since it was no different from life as he knew it. He had been born during the war as the second child of a lower class family and had grown up in a climate of violence. His father had beaten him unmercifully and had occasionally threatened him with a butcher knife. These threats had been reinforced by the fact that his father regularly gave Karl pets which sooner or later disappeared mysteriously. The parents always claimed that those pets had run away, but he invariably found them in the garbage can with their throats slit. His mother confronted the advancing Red Army by holding her two children in front of her and stating: "You will have to shoot my children first, before you can rape me."Although this memory only emerged later in treatment, the memories of the war and of his father's treatment of him were readily available and constituted almost the main focus during the first year of therapy. Karl had barely managed to graduate from the Gymnasium, the branch of the German school-system entitling the student to enter the university. He attended several universities, never completing any systematic course of studies, and never holding down any job for any length of time. In his early twenties, he married a woman who had given birth to his two children. Karl claimed that he had no idea how this had come about, and he doubted that he had had any part in those events. The couple had lived together on and off but the memories of that marriage were vague. Eventually, when Karl's homosexual impulses broke through, he withdrew even more from life and in a fit of drunken depression, attempted suicide. He was hospitalized briefly with a diagnosis of "disturbance of the vegetative nervous system," given some tranquillizers and the admonishment to stay away from men. After this episode, he took a trip to the United States to visit a relative and it was during this trip that he met Tom and decided to leave Germany and live with him. Tom had promised to take care of him. Karl worked occasionally but his recurrent fits of depression prevented him from either going to school or working on any regular basis. When he started therapy, his presentation of self was that of an extremely passive, depressed, and compliant young man whose life never seemed quite real to him. He experienced it essentially as a bad movie that he could only escape from by tuning it out.

Bob, a 25-year-old male homosexual, a former school-teacher, entered therapy because he had never been able to combine love and sex. He had a few close women friends, never yet a lover, and a few male acquaintances. All his sexual activities took place near the piers on the West Side of Manhattan where most of the leather bars are located and where a great deal of anonymous sex takes place in the abandoned warehouses and the trucks. Bob was compulsively drawn to the trucks and he was deeply ashamed. He was also quite troubled by recurring impulses to push people into the street into oncoming traffic. Sometimes, he felt this way toward strangers and sometimes towards friends and acquaintances as well. He was afraid, that sooner or later, he would act on this impulse.

Bob is the oldest son of an Irish Catholic working-class family with nine children. He had managed to graduate from college, even though he had consistently provoked male authority figures into "victimizing" him by giving him grades that did not correlate with his intelligence. After graduation, he taught high school for a few years. He was quite popular with his students but his relationships with his superiors rapidly deteriorated until he was fired from his job for insubordination. His rage over this persecution was as profound as his rage toward his father who had beaten him regularly and severely until he was old enough to fight back. Although he considered his sexual proclivities and homicidal impulses to be problems for which he needed psychotherapy, he did not feel this way about his relationship with authority figures. *They* were the ones with the problem; he was merely the victim. Bob did not reveal his recurrent and rather extensive drug abuse during the initial sessions; this information only emerged after several months of treatment.

Larry is the second child and only son of a middle-class professional family with five children. He came into therapy at the age of 24 with the following symptoms: Massive anxiety, a numbing pain in his penis, severe and disorienting ringing in his ears, and a host of other hysterical symptoms. Larry had started on an unusually promising career as an actor; in fact, he had just received a rave review for his stage debut, but he found himself totally incapable of continuing because (a) he was terrified of even getting near a theater or reading a play; (b) he felt entirely incapable of facing an audience, no matter how small, and (c) he had to be able to keep his hand on his penis most of the time in order to know that it was still there. Before coming to me, he had consulted a male psychiatrist who had put him on Thorazine which had aggravated his symptoms. When hospitalization was suggested, Larry became frightened because he felt that while he was definitely "crazy," he was *not* "crazy-crazy." He believed he needed someone to talk to rather than drugs. When he arrived for his first session, he came half an hour early. He bypassed the waiting room and headed straight for my office, totally oblivious to the fact that I was busy with another patient. He simply collapsed in one of the armchairs, looked at the two of us not knowing who was who and simply said: "Help!" The patient whose session he had interrupted, a therapist herself, yielded to that big, long-haired and unmovable presence in the armchair, good-naturedly wished me luck, and quietly departed. Interestingly enough, Larry later remembered that hour quite differently. He was convinced that the earlier patient had walked into *his* session, rather than the other way around. In fact it had annoyed him greatly. After relating his various symptoms, Larry stated that his mother was a warm and wonderful person, that he had three sisters whom he had always liked, particularly the younger ones, and that his father was a cold and cruel man who never loved him. In fact, Larry felt that he had never been able to figure out what his mother saw in his father.

Larry had married right after finishing college. His wife seems to have been extremely frightened, submissive, and masochistic. He had chosen her because he felt unbearably lonely once he left home and attended graduate school, and he had been afraid that no other woman would want him. As soon as he married, he became quite cruel and sadistic toward his wife; after two years of marriage, he became obsessed with another woman who was much more attractive than his wife and who seemed much freer sexually. As soon as he was through making love to this woman—even though according to Larry it was pure lust not love—he practically ran home to his wife in order to 'confess'—an act that was as much designed to punish her as to relieve his overwhelming sense of guilt. After this episode, the marriage fell apart and the incapacitating symptoms appeared which brought him into therapy.

Anna was a 27-year-old overworked and underpaid social worker, the middle child of a lower middle class Polish Catholic family with five daughters. She sought therapy because of an unbearably painful involvement with a married psychiatrist. Sex with this man consisted of his inviting her to come to his office when he had a cancellation or some other break between patients. Anna complied each and every time. He never came to her apartment or took her out for a date, in order to keep the affair from his wife. Only once did he invite her for a weekend skiing trip together with his wife, claiming she was just a coworker he was friendly with, who was new in New York and terribly lonely. Anna, however, was well aware of the fact that in this instance, she was the instrument in some marital squabble, a suspicion that was later confirmed. What made this relationship even more unbearable was the fact that having come face-to-face with her lover's wife, Anna experienced an overwhelming sense of guilt and, at the same time, realized that she was hopelessly addicted to this man.

Anna married the day she had graduated from college—with a major in nursing—in order to be able to leave her parents' home. Although sex with her fiancé was reasonably good before her marriage, she developed dyspareunia during her honeymoon. Thus, sexual intercourse was either extremely painful or impossible. The marriage deteriorated soon and they were divorced within a year. Her mother was so ashamed of Anna that she kept the divorce a secret and forbade Anna to come to their house if relatives were present. From the beginning of treatment, Anna focused on the unloving and often hateful treatment she had received from her mother, and she idealized her father. She felt unwanted by her mother, a feeling that was strongly supported in her mind by the fact that prior to Anna's birth, her mother had undergone two D&Cs, which in the case of a strict Catholic might, indeed, have been a disguised attempt at an abortion. This appeared to be a valid interpretation in view of the fact that Anna's mother had informed her about this event when Anna was still quite young and she later made repeated references to it.

Diagnosis

In keeping with a modified descriptive approach, we intend to examine the material just presented in the following order: (a) reality testing; (b) quality of object relations; (c) reality functioning; (d) super-ego development; (e) self-pathology or pathological narcissism; (f) ego ideal; and (g) additional features of relevance for the treatment of the sadomasochistic patient. The quality of object relationships and ego functioning, taken together, represent the degree of ego impairment, which combined with the severity of the self-pathology, lends itself to a tentative—and admittedly fluid—distinction between schizophrenic or borderline-schizophrenic, borderline and character disorder as diagnostic entities. Although perhaps in the case of a structural neurosis the therapist will probably be able to arrive at a reasonably accurate diagnosis and treatment plan after the first session, with the more disturbed patients this is usually neither feasible nor desirable. First of all, the very act of entering therapy can be interpreted as an active, self-affirming exercise of will which, in and by itself, represents a small but important change in the diagnosis, since the capacity to exercise positive willing is particularly poorly developed in the sadomasochistic patient. Moreover, patients with more severe pathology must be allowed to present themselves in whatever fashion they see fit and are comfortable. Since therapy commences with the very first phone call to the therapist (Blanck and Blanck, 1974), the therapist's desire to arrive at an accurate diagnosis has to be subjugated to the patients' need to state their problems safely, i.e. in accordance with their expectations. Thus, they may overemphasize some problems, and conceal others. Typically, the more masochistic patients feel that help is not readily offered unless they can "sell" themselves. Depending on what they think makes for an "interesting patient" they may either omit or overemphasize their more bizarre symptoms. For example, Bob's reluctance (or rather dishonesty) to talk about his drug abuse was due to two factors: shame; and fear of punitive actions on the part of the mental health clinic under whose auspices he had come into treatment with me.

Since the experience of shame plays such a vital role in the sadomasochistic patient, the importance of respecting the shame barrier cannot *ever* be overstated. Sexual material, especially if sadomasochistic practices are suspected, should not be elicited until a modicum of trust has been established, and patients are able to talk about it on their own initiative.

Typically—if all goes well—after five or six sessions, we will be able to arrive at a reasonably accurate diagnosis. This, however, does not mean that there will not be some surprises later in treatment but that hopefully they are minor. The material presented in the previous section of this chapter summarizes the salient facts that were obtained during the first six sessions of treatment.

Reality Testing   Obviously, the question whether a given patient is a schizophrenic has to be answered first, since some therapists in private practice believe that they cannot be treated on an outpatient basis. I believe that many of them can, even though this can mean that some of them may need short-term hospitalizations if for whatever reasons their psyches become overtaxed. As challenging and as rewarding as I have found working with schizophrenics, however, I personally have never been able to treat more than two or three at the same time and still retain my own inner equilibrium.

The clearest, though by no means only indications for the presence of ambulatory schizophrenia are: impaired reality testing, the existence of thought disorder and primary process thinking. Of the four patients under discussion only Karl exhibited all three of those symptoms. His reality testing with respect to the physical danger he was in, just by living with Tom, was clearly impaired. He simply experienced no fear, even though after his fight with Tom, the apartment was in shambles, most dishes and glasses had been smashed, and Karl only started to defend himself against Tom's attempt to strangle him when he began to turn blue in the face. Karl's judgment of the situation was simply that Tom had become very angry and probably for legitimate reasons. His account of the events during his adult life, notably his marriage, consisted mostly of "I don't know's," contradictory statements, and an occasional confusion between the subject and the object of an interaction. For example: "She (the wife) only told me I was pregnant until it was too late for an abortion." Or: "She was so angry, I felt like slapping her in the face." His affect was either totally flat or depressed. Also, even though he had insisted on a German-speaking therapist, he found himself incapable of speaking German except for a few words or expressions. After almost 50 sessions, when speaking about particular war memories, he temporarily lost complete contact with reality. He had to be physically restrained; however, the strength required to do so was only the strength one has to apply to restrain a very angry four or five year old boy.

Quality of Object Relations   In order to differentiate between a borderline structure and a character disorder on one hand and a neurotic on the other, the quality of object relations and the patient's reality functioning are perhaps the most important indicators for the degree of ego-impairment. Following Kernberg (1976), I take rapid shifts of affective states or alternating ego states and contradictory values pertaining to identical moral and ethical questions as prima facie evidence for a borderline structure.

Bob's splitting of me into an all-good and all-bad component was, at times, almost comical. Since we both lived and worked within a few blocks from each other, encounters on the street or the supermarket were not infrequent. No matter how angry he was with me during a session—and after the first two months he was often very angry, indeed—he would positively beam when he met me in the street. In the course of 12 hours, he could call me the most brutal, selfish, cold and authoritarian therapist in town and then refer his friends to me as patients, praising my skills and personality.

The few times Bob had sought sexual encounters outside of the trucks and the S&M bars and had picked up a one night stand in a regular gay bar, he would become impotent if his lover for the night showed signs of civility; if the lover's behavior resembled affection, Bob's panic became so unmanageable that he would be unable to sleep until the lover had left. His interaction with his friends was equally indicative of his habit of ego and object splitting. The woman with whom he had developed the longest lasting and deepest friendship was Bob's characteriological carbon copy of both his good and his bad qualities. He alternately identified with her or berated for her inability to accept any rational authority and for her poor choice of love objects. She did the same thing with him and they fought constantly. Projection and projective identification of his own paranoid ideation were constantly operating and defied any attempts at interpretation. On the contrary, no matter how tentative a suggestion was offered that possibly he had some input into the situations he complained about so bitterly, it would produce unneutralized rage and disappointment in the therapist. Although Bob was forever complaining about the exploitation and "ripoffs" that the world subjected him to, he saw nothing morally or ethically wrong with his own often sadistic and callous exploitation of others, particularly if the objects of his exploitations were institutions.

Karl's defensive maneuvers were much more archaic. Although by-and-large his transference appeared to be positive, under stress he would either depersonalize the therapist or other threatening objects, or, if the stress became overwhelming, transform them into figures from his past. Due to his outstanding artistic talents, he was able to draw his inner visions of people around him, and they often looked like the monsters found in paintings by Hieronyinus Bosch. At the same time, he experienced himself as a filthy, slimy, and often unbearably smelly toad-like creature. At times, he felt that his own stench was so intolerable that he took shower after shower, but nothing helped in removing the smell of mud and feces. He complained time and again that he felt like a pig that had rolled around in the gutter.

Larry and Anna on the other hand, had a much more stable sense of self and other, and consequently, ego and object splitting only occurred in times of unusual stress. Although neither of them were capable of true object love—as typical for the neurotic—their object relationships and object representations were rather stable. Anna had no illusions about her lover's commitment to her, but she experienced the excitement of the "bad love object" as too irresistible. She stated over and over: "In my rational mind I know he is a bastard and that he will never change, but the times when we are together, I feel too good to give him up." Larry, who at the beginning of therapy was obsessed with a rather simple-minded, confused and rejecting 17 year old, was also quite clear about the fact that he was pursuing a bad love object, but her physical beauty—"big boobs" and her unpredictability— proved too alluring to resist.

The quality of Anna's and Larry's transference also had a much more stable and continuous quality than that of either Bob or Karl. Obviously, it had its ups and downs that will be discussed later, but both of them experienced me as one and the same person toward whom they had both positive and negative feelings. The number of times when object constancy was lost and I became in their minds an out-and-out monster that had fooled them all along (the Jim Jones of the profession as Anna recently put it) were far fewer, and the problem was usually resolved in the course of two or three sessions. Larry, in his disarmingly unselfconscious way, expressed his ambivalence and his tolerance of it quite clearly in the fifth month of therapy when he said: "I love you because you take such good care of me, and I feel you understand me like nobody ever did before, but I hate you for not being available 24 hours a day. Well, that's life, I suppose, and I have to try to live with it." Also, unlike Bob and Karl, Anna and Larry had a stable set of friends, whom they neither idealized nor excessively devalued. Anna, who more often than not related to her friends submissively and sometimes masochistically, usually projected her rage onto them and spent a good deal of time worrying whether one of her friends was angry with her. Eventually, however, she would always be able to recognize that the problems that came up were due to her inability to take a firmer stand and that the anger she feared was really her own rage rather than theirs. Larry's friendships were firm but lacked intimacy. His friends were essentially playmates. But he explained to me quite realistically that, "since they are all actors they are as crazy as I am, only they are not in therapy." Thus, his arrangements with his playmates were in effect quite functional; they kept each other from being lonely—talking shop at 3 a.m. was quite common—and they respected each other's eccentricities.

Reality Functioning   The ability to cope effectively with the realistic demands of adult life is not only an indicator of a patient's separateness from the internalized parental other, but also of the degree of ego-strength. Prognostically, it is an invaluable indicator for the patient's capacity to withstand the stresses generated by therapy and the readiness to conscientiously apply themselves to the task of working in their own behalf in good faith. Karl, except for graduating from the Gymnasium had never functioned effectively on any level of adult life. He was unable to perform as a student, wage-earner, husband, or father. He did some part-time work but he was essentially supported by Tom. Once he had started therapy, however, he was extremely punctual, conscientious about his bills, and about cancellations. As it turned out later, the fact that I never cancelled a session or ran late was of decisive importance in our weathering some major crises in treatment. Karl had never known any dependable other in his life and he had not expected to ever find one. The surprise value of finding it time and again in therapy did not wear off for several years.

Bob's coping capacities *seemed* to be adequately developed. He had graduated from college and obtained a teaching position. He had, in fact, completed the transition from the working class into the middle class. When he started therapy, however, he was unemployed and, therefore, expected to be treated for a minimal fee. Even though he stated that he wanted to look for another job when his unemployment ran out, his statement carried no conviction. His commitment to himself and to his life appeared to have been used up; there was a quality of being burned-out about him that did not augur well for serious analytic work. His frustration tolerance was very low, and he was seething with resentment against the middle class of which he had made himself a member. When he realized, after several months of treatment, that the job market in his field had begun to shrink, he quickly gave up looking for a job and settled back with the not so hidden agenda of being supported by "the system" which he despised.

Larry, who had also started therapy after he had stopped working, nevertheless, presented quite a different picture. He had functioned well in high school, college and graduate school and his record in some subjects had been truly excellent; so much so in fact, that even though for several years he took a leave from his chosen career, his former teachers never lost faith in him and they stood by with support and encouragement. Larry worked several part-time jobs that were related to his field, mainly coaching, and he was, therefore, able to support himself. During his first year in therapy, he asked his parents to pay for his treatment, something they could well afford. But this decision was a willful choice on Larry's part; it was intended as punishment for all the wrongs they had committed, rather than a necessity. In retrospect, I am quite certain that if they had not been able to pay, Larry would have done so himself. After all, at the beginning of his second year, Larry informed his parents that he was going to pay for half of his therapy, and six months later, he told them that their financial help was no longer needed even though his parents were quite willing to continue helping him financially. His coaching jobs had no direct bearing on his job and they bored him. In spite of this, his work must have been so outstanding that his employers did everything in their power to make the job pleasant for him and tried to entice him to work more hours than he wanted to.

In terms of ego strength and coping capacity, Anna presented the most promising picture, since she had always functioned extremely well even under the most adverse of circumstances. Her parents had labelled her as "the strong one" and expected her—unlike her sisters—to earn part of her tuition in her parochial high school by working as a student-custodian. In a similar vein, she had to earn the money for expenses ordinarily assumed by parents with a middle class income such as dental work, clothes, college tuition, and her wedding. In spite of all these difficulties—15 hours of baby-sitting paid for the filling of one cavity—she was an honor student all the way through. Right after her marriage fell apart, she applied to a very good university for admission for a masters degree and also graduated with honors even though she had to work part-time. No matter how badly she felt, and when she started therapy she was in a great deal of emotional pain most of the time, it never affected her work. If anything, it spurned her on to greater efforts, a trait that can be considered as a mixed blessing since it may indicate that suffering is an integral part of the ego-ideal.

Super-Ego Development   The super-ego of the sadomasochist almost by definition is archaic, punitive and sadistic. This does not mean, however, that it is consistent with respect to ethical conduct. On the contrary, large lacunae are often present which allow the sadism to emerge in a more-or-less disguised or sophisticated form. Anna, for example, whose super-ego was the most consistently harsh and sadistic one to begin with, and which had been fortified by massive dosages of Catholicism, expressed her sadism primarily in the form of a rather priggish display of moral superiority. Thus, it escaped the censorship of her super-ego. In all other areas of life, however, her tyrannical super-ego made her existence quite torturous. At the beginning of treatment, insomnia was one of her major complaints. To her, a couple of glasses of wine at bedtime spelled incipient alcoholism; taking a Valium when she awoke at 2 a.m. meant she was on her way to turning into a "junkie." Rest equaled sloth, dressing well meant pride. The same was true for the pursuit of intellectual activities that were not job-related such as classical music or any other enterprise that would make her "better than other people." Her mother had given her the message that the pursuit of any knowledge not contained in the Bible or the curriculum of the parochial school system was somewhat sinful since it implied pride which after all, according to Catholic dogma, constitutes the first of the seven deadly sins. Since covetousness is the second of the deadly sins, Anna's affair with a married man produced an almost unbearable conflict even though Anna had allegedly long before, ceased to be overtly religious. Fortunately, Anna's innate and rather pronounced sense of humor helped her in poking fun at some of her moral obsessions and, thus, get at least some temporary relief from her self-inflicted torments.

Bob, on the other hand, who had also been brought up Catholic, had not been able to develop any consistent super-ego at all, since the moral and religious teachings he was exposed to from a very early age on were so oppressive and so unattuned to the emotional abilities of the small child, that he realized very early in life that there was no way in which he could ever live up to the moral imperatives that were presented to him. Moreover, the constant portrayals of the various punishments awaiting him in purgatory and in hell kept him in a constant state of panic throughout childhood. What finally put him on the troubled road of an almost holy crusade against religion in general, and Catholicism in particular, was the recognition of his homosexuality in early puberty. Given the prevalence of latent or overt homosexuality among the clergy, Bob could not possibly escape the dim awareness that some of the verbal and physical abuse that he suffered at the hands of the priests were not only sexual in nature but that he was, in fact, at times punished for *their* sins. Although this awareness was not a conscious one, it, nevertheless, deepened his generalized suspiciousness and paranoia. Also, given the fact that his father had singled him out as one of the children who received constant beatings that had no relation to their actual misdeeds, his experiences in the Catholic school-system were, in effect, an extension of his home life which required the *suspension* of a super-ego which otherwise would have made mere living impossible. Thus, in contrast to Anna, Bob was hardly ever plagued by moral scruples. On the contrary, he obsessively concerned himself with the moral shortcomings of others.

When Larry began therapy, he seemed to have a rather benign superego; after all, he had allowed himself to collapse and had assumed a rather childlike persona. His presentation of self was so much that of a little boy that when he mentioned in some other context that he had driven a car, I found myself virtually unable to picture him performing such an adult activity. Having adopted this childlike stance, he made a neat division between *acting* the part of the obedient little boy but nevertheless sharing with me his delight in his destructive sadistic fantasies. For example, although he took great pleasure in thinking about the idea of urinating on my carpet, couch, and the pillows, he always took his shoes off in the waiting room in order not to track in any dirt on the very carpet that he longed to urinate on. His truly sadistic masturbatory fantasies, which will be discussed in Chapters 6 and 7, produced shame rather than guilt. Thus, except for the perfectionistic standards that he applied to his acting, his superego development was essentially immature, rather than sadistic.

Karl's psyche was in such a state of fragmentation, that it is almost impossible to separate ego impairment from superego pathology. His moral failures as a small child with respect to honesty, obedience, school performance, etc. were experienced as so gigantic, that he never felt that his existence was at all justified. By his own standards, he had forfeited his right to live before he even entered the first grade. Once he entered school, his compulsion to make-up stories that might impress his teachers and fellow students compounded his sense of shame and moral turpitude. The final touch to his sense of doom and condemnation, however, was the discovery of his homosexuality that had precipitated his first suicide attempt. It brought together all the elements of his earlier failures: Karl's mother had been unable to toilet train him. He defecated into his pants until age five when his father returned from the war. When his father learned that the child was still not toilet trained, he announced that he would "fix that little pig" and did so with a beating worse than any Karl had experienced before. It must have been so severe, even by German standards, the Karl never had another lapse and he also never forgot it. When Karl reached puberty, his mother, who was extraordinarily seductive, and who had dressed him as a girl until age 12, started to talk to him about homosexuality continuously. She informed him that several cultural figures of renown had been homosexuals. Furthermore, she told him that homosexual men engaged in anal intercourse. As a result, she said to him, they soon lost control over their rectal muscles and consequently, their bowel movements. Karl took this information to be the truth. Thus, when his homosexuality emerged, he rather condemned himself to death than suffer another paternal beating. In order to avoid the encounter with his archaic and sadistic superego, he became more and more passive as he grew older, playing the role of the eternal victim. The fact that he had two children, however, whom he had indeed abandoned, was something he could not block out for any length of time, even though he tried hard to do so. Every time he heard about them either from his parents or his former wife, his guilt feelings became so overwhelming that he became suicidal.

Self-Pathology of Pathological Narcissism   All four patients under discussion exhibited in varying degrees pathology of the self in addition to, and separate from, their degree of ego impairment and superego pathology. None of them had had parents who were empathic enough to allow the child to develop a stable and cohesive self. In fact, both Bob's and Karl's parents had quite actively attacked their children's sense of self, integrity, and sexual identity.

Anna's presentation of self and her reality self were that of a meek, fearful, unassuming, and chronically helpful young woman. Her appearance was mousey, harrassed, worried, and apologetic. Nothing seemed to go right in her life and she made no claims that it should. In a highly obsessional manner, she would present her various calamities, forever searching for causal chains or interpersonal connections that would make sense out of her miserable existence. Her obsessional style was clearly a defensive structure since any real or imagined lapse in empathy and sympathy on my part would result either in angry and self-depreciating tears or rather severe depressive reactions. The hypothesis that her mother had experienced her primarily as a burden and had been unable to respond to the child's needs and to serve as a stimulus barrier to the very young infant was supported by the fact that insomnia was one of Anna's most severe presenting problems. Her incessant preoccupation with the use of tranquillizers and alcohol was both real and hypochondriacal. The unreal part has been discussed in the section on superego pathology. What complicated matters even further was the fact that Anna's mother had forever berated her father for his alcoholism, when in fact he seems not to have been an alcoholic at all. He was a problem drinker who occasionally got drunk and silly and on a few occasions acted very irresponsibly toward the children. In one instance, he took them to another city for a sports event, disappeared into a bar and returned home without his children. Anna found it extremely difficult to square this memory and her mother's accusations with the idealized image of him and her wish for a positive identification.

On the other hand, in my own mind, I took Anna's preoccupation with the subject of addiction quite seriously since they seemed to represent an uneasy attraction to substances that temporarily supplied her with the missing structures of the self, i.e. with what Kohut (1971) has termed "transmuting internalizations." This does not mean that there was ever any real danger of addiction, but that the incessant hypochondriacal preoccupation with the subject was the symptom of a rather severe narcissistic disturbance. The repression barrier between her reality self and her unconscious "archaic, narcissistic and exhibitionistic strivings" (Kohut, 1977) was quite firm, so firm, in fact, that these conflicts did not come to her attention until all other structural defects had been all but fully rehabilitated. To the extent, that Anna's infantile exhibitionistic strivings were in evidence at the beginning of treatment they had a negative valence. It took the form of an almost provocative display of her "craziness," helplessness, pain, and her inability to properly tie her metaphorical shoelaces. On the other hand, her compensatory structures were solid—though in need of modification—to make them more rewarding and less of a daily grind. In order to do so, her sadistic superego had to be toned down first, before more constructive solutions could be found that were not in conflict with her ego ideal.

Larry, on the surface also presented a meek reality self. The term pseudo-meek, however, is perhaps more appropriate, since he had only hit upon the innocent, incompetent little boy persona after his professional collapse. On the other hand, this choice was not an arbitrary one. As it is so often the case with young people who make it through life on the basis of one outstanding talent, he had never felt the need to develop any adult social graces. Being a *wunderkind* seemed to be sufficient and excused many of his eccentricities. His hypochondria was pronounced, he obsessed about each and every one of his hysterical symptoms endlessly and he worried incessantly over his use of Valium, to combat his insomnia.

His need for sadistic omnipotent control over women, so indicative for a narcissistic disturbance in heterosexual men, encompassed a wide variety of actions and fantasies. Some of them were immediately evident, others emerged only later. By that I do not mean that they were not in existence, but that the shame barrier and his need to present himself as a victim prevented him from talking about them in therapy. Larry had come to me on the recommendation of one of his friends who was a patient of mine. It seemed that he had developed an instant idealizing transference even before he saw me and that the wish for omnipotent control was part and parcel of that idealization. His first session (see section on presenting problem) illustrates this quite clearly. With the single-minded determintion of a St. Bernard puppy with a toothache, he took up residence in my office and expected to be taken care of immediately. Also, the transformation of the patient whose session he had disrupted into the intruder that had to be removed seemed to indicate that contrary to his stated feelings, the birth of his younger sisters must have constituted quite a severe narcissistic injury. His extreme state of agitation at the beginning of this session and his fury at his father prompted me to suggest that he visualize his father as sitting in the chair opposite him and to simply say, "Please!" This suggestion produced an immediate outburst of tears; it was as if a dam had broken. After about 20 minutes of uninterrupted crying, Larry was calm and I had become a magician in his eyes.

This definition of reality also determined the terms of our interaction: (1) Given *his* helplessness and *my* magical powers my availability became an overriding concern, a power struggle. The fact that I saw other patients besides him was something he could not yet handle, and had to be blocked out. That I would only see him for 45 minutes at a time and that this time had to be paid for, he experienced as another outrage and misuse of my powers. What he wanted was unlimited access to my space and time with no financial obligations in return. Even though for the first six months of therapy his disarming gratitude outweighed his resentment, the resentment was, nevertheless, quite discernible. But a patient who experiences his therapist essentially as an intensive care unit, is not much in a position to argue with the details. (2) Thus, the only way in which Larry could exercise his wish for control was by asking me at the beginning of each session for some cue that would release his tears, usually some imaginary encounter with his father. He would then proceed to hug or beat pillows, in a state of total self absorption. Although he ignored me completely during these exercises, my attention was never allowed to wander. Later on in treatment, he escalated his battle for control by testing my patience. He made a deliberate attempt to bore me to death with his obsessions and later with an even more direct campaign of provoking me into losing my temper. The details of these two campaigns, together with Larry's masturbatory fantasies, will be discussed later. Unlike Bob and Karl, however, his regressive stance was quite deliberate and to a large extent in the service of the ego. Despite his infantile longings and his seeming inability to tolerate the parameters of the treatment contract, he tolerated them quite well. No matter how helpless he felt when he left a session, he always managed to go straight to work and to perform well. Furthermore, regardless of how badly he felt at night, he never opted for emergency phone calls. For a long time, however, he insisted that there was a real possibility of his truly going crazy and that if that happened I would have to make a house call.

In his relationship with his ex-wife and the women he dated, his covert sadism and wish for control was even more clear cut and for a long time did not yield to any insight. He habitually pursued very young, dumb, meek, but rejecting women, who had to resemble *Playboy* centerfolds. His idea of an ideal sexual encounter was the following scenario: at first, the woman should spend about an hour passionately sucking his penis and stroking his entire body. After that, they would engage in an ecstatic intercourse until exhaustion would allow him to fall asleep peacefully. Needless to say, given the women he chose, he had little success, but that did not deter him from pursuing his goal anyway. It seemed that his fear of his own sadistic impulses prevented him from ever realizing his dream. This assumption was further substantiated by the fact that Larry could not tolerate to have a woman in his house while he was sleeping. For reasons that he could not identify, the thought scared him. It was not until two years later that he came to realize that the fear of killing the woman prevented him from spending the night with her.

Larry's compensatory structures—his acting ability—had provided him with an outlet for many of his grandiose and exhibitionistic strivings in a way that was not only socially acceptable but highly-rewarding and had provided him with a continuous source of narcissistic gratification. His inability to act, however, after his first major success, clearly shows that the public acclaim did not sufficiently satisfy the exhibitionistic and grandiose strivings of the pre-oedipal unresponded to infant. Originally, he attributed his deprivation on that level to his father who seems to have considered physical contact and expressions of affection such as kissing as "both unnecessary and unsanitary." Thus, we have to conclude that Larry's initial success threatened him because it appeared to cut him off forever from the attainment of his real ambition, namely to get from his parents the affection, care, and recognition that he had missed in earliest infancy. On the other hand, the very fact that his debut had shown him that he had what it takes to really excel and achieve fame, allowed him to take time off, and to attend to his emotional problems.

Bob, like Larry, also developed a spontaneous idealizing transference. As indicated earlier, though, the idealization was contingent on the therapist sharing his paranoid ideation and mirroring his chronic narcissistic rage. He had entered therapy at the point where his fragile compensatory structures had collapsed. Neither his father nor his superiors were particularly impressed by his intellectual and professional accomplishments. Whatever repression barrier there might have been that could have prevented the breakthrough of his archaic grandiose and exhibitionistic strivings, it was clearly absent when he came for treatment. My sense is that it was never strongly developed in the first place and that the loss of his job consolidated the vertical split in his psyche. His exhibitionism took the form of displaying the extent and the depth of his victimizations, intricate perversity of his adversaries, and depth of his sexual pathology. His grandiosity manifested itself in his contempt for the Church, the middle class establishment and for all "the poor suckers" who tried to function rationally in an irrational social system. He believed that he had tried to do right by his students who had appreciated his efforts, but since "the establishment" seemed to value appearances such as proper clothes and a haircut more than his revolutionary pedagogical talents, he was clearly wasting his intellect on narrow minds. His outbursts of often quite unneutralized rage against a world that refused to value him, were a desperate but ineffectual attempt to ward off a serious depression. Yet his addictive, self-destructive sexuality, combined with his drug and alcohol abuse, created a vicious cycle. In order to feel less depressed, he would resort to amphetamines, which he bought off the street, usually from highly unreliable connections. The same was true for the other drugs he bought. Once he was high, he would go out to have sex, either in the trucks, warehouses or leather bars. In the course of the evening, he often took more drugs, mixed with alcohol and this mixture could get him so disoriented that he would be out most of the night with little recollection as to where he had been and what he had done. Thus, he exposed himself to the following sources of danger: (1) Harrassment by the police; (2) V.D.; (3) Assault and battery (queer-rolling); and (4) Overdosing on drugs and alcohol. Although these real dangers did not bother him, the damage to his self-esteem and the constant fear of exposure and concomitant humiliation, were more than he could handle. The only way he knew how to deal with his shame was to "drown it out," so to speak, with another escapade in the same way in which an alcoholic takes a drink to combat his hangover. Viewed in the light of his earliest experiences, this behavior pattern is quite intelligible; it represented a neat package that was composed of the combined toxic influences of his mother, father, and grandmother: His mother, a typical borderline structure herself, had married at 17. Apparently, she experienced marriage and pregnancy as an unwelcome trap that put an end to her youthful pleasures. She must have felt so unprepared for motherhood—and I would hazard to guess—so resentful toward her first child, that she wore a surgical mask whenever she handled the infant, lest he catch her germs. Moreover, she did not allow anybody else to handle the infant for the same reasons. All the relatives had to wear surgical masks, too, when looking at the infant. Since eight younger siblings were born in rapid succession, it seems that both the quality as well as the quantity of the mothering was toxic and insufficient, leaving the child with an intense "object hunger" that later on, he relieved with the combination of alcohol, drugs, and impersonal sex. In order to understand why Bob's father had singled out some of the children for his arbitrary beatings and spared others, I asked Bob to bring in whatever childhood photos he could find. When he pointed out which children had been the objects of his father's wrath, it turned out that the father had chosen those children who in their looks took after the mother, and had spared the ones that looked more like himself. It seems that Bob, unresponded to by his mother, had turned to his father who *did* give him attention, though in the form of beatings and expressions of contempt. The one person who gave Bob some genuine affection was his grandmother. She was also the one who bombarded him with her visions of purgatory and hell, however, places Bob was sure were awaiting him, since her religious teachings made the perpetration of sins inevitable: sins of commission, omission, or thought. It seems that hell was exactly what Bob was looking for in his nightly escapades. He seemed to be saying, "Since I am bound to go to hell, I might as well get it done and over with."

Though not overtly delinquent, Bob was less than conscientious in financial matters, and when it came to dealing with institutions, he was, on occasion, outright dishonest. This can be interpreted as both an expression of grandiosity—the assumption that he was exempt from the rules and regulations applicable to ordinary folks—as well as the flip side of that attitude, namely that he felt so unworthy of things that without cutting corners he would not be able to get anything at all. Both interpretations are accurate in this case.

Karl's self pathology was qualitatively different from that of the other three patients, since in addition to the insufficiency of the mothering, his identity had been openly attacked. Since Karl's older sister had been born slightly crippled, his mother had hoped that her second child would be a "perfect baby girl," who would soon grow up to be her helpmate in caring for the older child. Thus, when she gave birth to a son, she simply disregarded his sex and dressed him like a girl. Karl remembered how he masturbated compulsively in her presence, and how she consistently ignored his efforts to let her know that he was a male. Since Karl had to wear his dresses in public, he was too ashamed to make any friends either in kindergarten or grade school and, therefore, he did not even have other boys with which to identify. The malignant bond with his mother was further strengthened by the fact that she made him her confidante about her marital troubles and by burdening him with tasks and demands that he was far too young for, such as taking care of his sister, and riding the subways to pick up the ration cards. Furthermore, she often asked him to play the role of a personal maid. He was asked to brush her hair for hours, and in return, was allowed to play with her make-up.

All through his childhood, Karl was terrified of his father, who on one hand never objected to his wife's crossdressing of their son, and who on the other, attacked Karl for not being more of a man. After work, his father spent most of the time dozing on the couch, but every so often when the oppressive atmosphere in their one-bedroom apartment got to be too much for him, he would suddenly jump up from the couch, hitting everybody who got in his way and screaming that he, too, was a human being. Since these outbursts were entirely unpredictable—at least for the children—they made any closeness between father and son impossible. Deprived of any non-schizophrenic mirroring from either parent, Karl grew up with an almost bottomless sense of shame for his very existence. The shame for the self was compounded by, and confused with his shame *for* his parents. While they espoused all the moral and ethical values of the *petite bourgeosie,* his father, like so many Germans during the years after the war, regularly stole food for the dinner table. His mother with her narrow sexual mores, after a couple of drinks, would play the part of a "femme fatale" at their weekend parties. Although preaching pride and dignity, both parents slouched and drivelled in the face of any middle class authority. Attending the gymnasium, in and by itself a difficult task for a working class youth, (approximately 5% of the German gymnasium population came from a working-class background) was made even more difficult by his parents who, on one hand, expected him to do well so that *they* did not have to feel ashamed, and on the other, accused him of trying to be better than they. Thus, he felt double bound between the push to succeed and the constant reminder of the futility of his efforts since, according to his parents, "people like us never get anyplace anyway, and are only looking for trouble if they stick their necks out."

When Karl entered therapy and looked at his chaotic life, it more than confirmed all of his parents' dire predictions and the only direction that his grandiose and exhibitionistic strivings could take was through his display of worthlessness, pseudostupidity, and pathology. For a long time, Karl's shaky self-esteem rested on the unwarranted assumption that he was my craziest patient, a position he did not easily relinquish even in the face of a great deal of evidence to the contrary. Only in the secret world of his drawings and his writing, could Karl build a grandiose role for himself. Pen and pencil allowed him to play the part of the great indictor, the ultimate judge who exposed the world with all its follies. The nature of the transference can only be described as a life-jacket transference. He clung to me—and later group—for dear life even though he insisted over and over again that his case was truly hopeless.

Ego-Ideal Since the ego-ideal is composed of the internalized postoedipal representations of parents or idealized parent figures as well as parental expectations, the ego-ideal of the predominantly sado-masochistic patient has to be examined primarily—though not exclusively—for two facets: (1) the distance between the actual ego functioning and its ideal; and (2) the degree to which suffering or the infliction of pain is part of the ego-ideal. Although I am entirely in agreement with Kernberg (1977) who claims that the extent to which suffering is part of the ego-ideal is inversely correlated with the hopefulness of the prognosis (1976), I believe that this statement needs a small modification. The poorest prognosis is for those patients where the ego-ideal isnonrealistic or outright impossible *and* has suffering as one of its major conponents. Fantasies of being Jesus Christ would be the ultimate example for this toxic combination. On one hand, death and suffering are rewarded by the son's return to heaven and his father's love; on the other, while on earth he was the adored, though misunderstood, infant that kings feared and paid their respects to.

At the beginning of treatment, I always ask every patient what ideally he or she would like to be, reality nonwithstanding. In a similar vein, questions about childhood daydreams, what the child in its fantasy would have liked to have been once it grew up, are equally important. Taken together they indicate 1. the child's archaic wishes for greatness and admiration; 2. the patient's sublimatory potential; and 3. the ego's ability to transform these archaic strivings into more-or-less realistic pursuits, i.e. pursuits that are realistic both in terms of the patient's abilities and talents as well as the restraints and opportunities in real life.

Neither Karl nor Bob could answer questions about their childhood dreams or their aspirations for their adult life. Shame and confusion prevented them from revealing their grandiose childhood dreams. The recognition of the vast abyss between their actual accomplishments and their ideal self was too shame provoking to allow them to reveal their dreams. During adolescence, they had both shifted from pursuing a positive rewarding goal that would gain admiration and respect from their parents and the community where they grew up, to the wish to be the ultimate judge and indictor of the agents of their primary and secondary socialization.

Karl had developed the fantasy of becoming a great cultural critic who could use his artistic talents to expose bourgeois society in the tradition of men like Wedekind, Tucholsky and Brecht. Having had no real live role models to shape himself after, and having met only impossible parental expectations, his ego-ideal was a mixture of the earlier wish to transcend, or at least escape, from the chaos of war, starvation, and the demoralizing milieu of the Berlin tenements, as well as a genuine desire to emulate the critical minds whose works he had studied in school. Having met with nothing but failure in his adult life, however, the pursuit of a career as a mental patient seemed to be the only alternative. For Karl it had three attractive features: 1. freedom from the task of taking care of himself; 2. revenge against a pathological and confusing environment that had indeed incapacitated him and 3. the dubious distinction of being a mad genius.

Bob's transition from the childhood wish of being a "good Catholic boy who would go to heaven" was transformed into the desire to conquer the Catholic Church—to become the 12-year-old Jesus who unmasked and dismissed the High Priests. His stance vis-à-vis the Church—and male authority in general—however, never lost its strong undercurrent of competitiveness. The wish to destroy the pope was as strong as the desire to *become* the next pope. Having been frustrated on both scores, he was left with little else but the choice of being a monumental failure who would wrest from the social system all the reparations he could get. What he was saying, in effect, was "If I am not appreciated, then at least you have to support me." Underneath this adult stance, however, was the profound conviction that suffering and failure in this world would eventually redeem him in his father's eyes and transform the sadistic rejecting parent into a good and loving one. This particular constellation of his ego-ideal and his ego functioning did, indeed, result in a very poor prognosis since it combined an impossible goal and the need for suffering as the vehicle of the achievement of his ideal self. Even his aspiration to become the embodiment of depravity was too much in conflict with his superego to allow him a distinguished career as a serious sexual sadomasochist. This very poverty of options heavily contributed to his suicidal ideation. Not being able to be very accomplished as either saint or sinner, death seemed an attractive alternative.

Larry's ego ideal was quite straightforward: he was determined to become one of America's leading actors, a goal that had been supported by his environment ever since his pre-school days when his unusual talent caught the attention of his parents. It was continuously reinforced by his teachers and coaches. He received the special treatment often given to child prodigies by his peers and teachers, though not by his parents who treated him no differently than they treated the other children. Larry quite consciously banked on the fact that if he were to become famous and acclaimed that then his father would adore him and love him. On a deeper conscious level, he aimed for his mother's unqualified and undivided love, a love that required no accomplishments on his part and which excluded his father and siblings.

Though his competitive streak was strong, and the need to excel could not find an outlet on the stage for many years, Larry was able to channel it rather easily into competitive play. For example, he became one of the meanest anagram players imaginable. But again, natural talent was supplemented by his conscientiousness in collecting every legitimate palindronic word grouping in the English language. Without his flexibility in his pursuit of excellence, his "time out" from his career would have been much more of a hardship, and the demands of therapy would have been more difficult to deal with.

The major conflict between his ego ideal and his actual behavior revolved around his sadism toward women. Although his ultimate goal was to become the indulged and adored little boy of earliest infancy, he could only see his adult sexual interactions as a victimization by womanhood. He had to deny any consciousness of his sadistic impulses as well as his provocative behavior that was clearly designed to elicit sadistic responses from his girl friends, therapist, and female group members.

Anna's ego-ideal provides an illuminating contrast to that of Bob's since in her case, too, suffering was an integral part of her ego-ideal and had been heavily shaped by Catholicism both at home and in school. Being much less grandiose to begin with, however, she channeled it from an early age on into much more realistic aspirations. Unlike Bob's ego ideal, which required suffering to the point of self

destruction, Anna's ego ideal consisted essentially in seeking deprivation rather than self-annihilation or suffering per se. Moreover, her
goals consisted basically in subordinating her needs to those of another
person rather than a god. Consequently, whatever rewards are associated with suffering, they were essentially obtained during life rather
than in a life hereafter. Anna's earliest aspiration was to become
mother's little helper in order to make up for her feelings of having
been unwanted and a burden. The shift from the helpful child to
nursing and later to social work is a logical progression that is both
realistic and socially acceptable and rewarded. Thus, there was no need
to abolish her ego ideal; it needed toning down, or rather a shifting of
emphasis on her needs rather than the needs of others, and to understand that the two are not incompatible. In Bob's case, most of the
content of his ego-ideal had to be abandoned to fit the real world.
Therapeutically, this is a major difference, because even though the
elimination of the masochistic elements of Anna's ego-ideal turned out
to be hard and protracted work, it could be accomplished within the
context of her professional career. Therefore, she never lost a basic
sense of continuity and identity since she could continue doing what
she had set out to do, but slowly do it differently. Bob's ego ideal was
doomed to failure right from the beginning, not only because short of
entering a monastery he could not have lived up to the moral imperatives that were presented to him and which he had introjected, but also
because his homosexuality, ambivalence toward religion, and inordinate need for social power were incompatible with monastic life.

Additional Features of Relevance in the Sadomasochistic Patient

In the process of forming a treatment plan and for prognostic
purposes, the therapist who deals with the predominantly sadomasochistic patient is well advised to look for some symptoms or symptom
clusters that may interfere with the therapeutic work. This is particularly true for the more disturbed patients and it may require some
modifications of the therapeutic contract.

Impulse Control   If a patient gives evidence of poor impulse control, the therapist may want to state at the beginning of treatment that
major decisions such as changing the frequency of appointments,
interruptions of therapy, divorce, marriage, pregnancy, moves to

another city or another job should be given several months in order to examine jointly the sensibility of such a decision before it is acted upon. Although such an agreement is no cure for poor impulse control, it may well prevent the patient from making mistakes that are irreversible or seriously interfere with the patient's ability to continue therapy. In one instance, for example, I feel that if such a cooling off period had been agreed upon, I might not have lost a particularly masochistic patient who insisted on marrying a man she knew for only two weeks. She became pregnant within a month. She has since left this man, but child care, her job and the shame barrier of having to admit a major mistake, have prevented her from re-entering therapy with me or another therapist.

Care of the Body   Sadomasochistic patients very often include their bodies as targets for their conscious or unconscious sadism. This may take the form of outright neglect or somatization. Neglect includes poor eating habits, including fad diets, unwillingness to get dental work done, or one's vision tested, repeated exposure to V.D., or other forms of reckless disregard for physical safety. Although my patient population is hardly a representative sample, I find it, nevertheless, noteworthy that I have *never* encountered a sadomasochistic patient whose teeth were cared for properly. Poor eating habits and insufficient dental care are two obvious arenas for the expression of oral conflicts. Consequently, one may hope that, as these conflicts get worked through, healthier habits will emerge. In the case of dental care and alcohol and drug abuse, however, waiting for a natural resolution of the underlying psychodynamics can be a dangerous gamble, since we may lose the patient long before we get a chance to work on these particular problem areas. They may have become addicted or they may find themselves in a position where they require such extensive medical attention that they have to choose between the expense of their medical care and psychotherapy. Talking about this possibility early in treatment, preferably during Phase I when the parameters of the treatment in general are discussed, may prevent it from happening. For example, one of my patients reported later, that he went to the dentist only because I referred to poor dental care as "such a common maneuver" and he only wanted to have "original" symptoms.

Patients who somatize in my experience will do so more-or-less through most of their therapy, though hopefully to a lesser extent. In this case too, gentle pressure to obtain qualified medical help, and to take out health insurance constitutes not only an expression of genuine concern, but it can also prevent serious and incapacitating illness from hitting the patient seemingly "out of nowhere."

There is essentially very little we can do for the accident-prone patient except to make certain safety precautions part of the therapeutic contract. One of my patients with whom I had made such a contract, insisted on riding her 10-speed bicycle through midtown traffic *after* having smoked pot. Although she refused for a long time to give up this dangerous habit she did at least agree to wear a crash helmet.

Sexualization of Sadomasochism   For the reasons given in Chapter 2 patients whose sadomasochism extends into their sexual life should be weaned gently but firmly, particularly those patients whose sexual practices are hazardous not only to their sense of inner integrity but to their very life and health. The therapist may have to ascertain *exactly* what specific dangers patients expose themselves to. This may require some extra reading and some field work on the part of the therapist. Under *no* circumstances should actual experimentation with sexual sadomasochism be encouraged in patients who are merely fantasizing about the subject.

Karl, fortunately was quite conscientious about his health, though not always of his safety. After his involvement with Tom was over, and he had time to reflect upon it, he took very few risks that might have endangered his life or physical well-being. Bob, on the other hand neglected his health and particularly his teeth to such an extent, and with such relish, that his dental bills eventually played a considerable part in his decision to cut down on his therapy. I have always regretted the fact that I did not take a firmer stand at the beginning of treatment. On the other hand when excruciating pain finally sent him to the dentist, he refused to follow his orders with the predictable result that temporary work was destroyed and the work had to be done all over again together with additional repair work. His disregard for even the most elementary safety precautions with respect to the purchase of drugs and his sexual escapades has been discussed earlier. In his case, the combination of poor impulse control and the strong need to defy authority resulted in a host of particularly difficult extra-therapeutic problems.

Larry, a typical product of upper-middle class upbringing, exhibited only one of the symptoms described above. He took regular medical and ophthalmological check-ups for granted. He avoided the dentist for five years, however, in spite of recurrent toothaches.

Anna, though reasonably cautious with her health, took serious risks in terms of her physical safety in the subways and in the streets of New York. Her concept of "helpfulness" and dedication to the poor, resulted in her working in a clinic in a part of New York where even the police are afraid to leave their patrol cars. She traveled to work on a subway that has earned itself the reputation as New York's "mugging express" and the neighborhood she lived in was highly unsafe. Although with patients like Anna little can—or should—be done to change their dedication to their work, it is often quite helpful to point out that they will be able to do their duties *better*, if they don't arrive at work in a state of panic, injured or robbed. In other words, an appeal to their sense of *duty* is usually quite effective in enrolling their superego to the task of protecting the patients' life. Now, no longer doing it for herself, she will do it in the service of her calling.

CONCLUSIONS

Developmentally, what all four patients had in common are the following elements: 1. A more-or-less profound sense of having been unwanted, insufficient mothering during the first three years of life, maternal persecution; and 2. hostile and repressive mirroring of their infantile grandiose and exhibitionistic strivings. Attempts at connecting with an idealized father image had failed in Bob's and Karl's cases and had succeeded in Anna's and Larry's, even though the breakdown of Larry's idealization had precipitated his breakdown and Anna's idealization of her father seriously interfered with her self-concept as a woman and with her realistic evaluations of men.

In terms of ego impairment and self pathology, Karl can be diagnosed as schizophrenic, or a borderline schizophrenic. Bob presented a typical picture of a borderline structure and Anna and Larry were lower-level character disorders.

Chapter 6

THE TREATMENT PROCESS; PHASE I:*

Hatching or Establishing a Working Alliance

Psychoanalysis and Psychotherapy

Psychotherapy as distinguished from psychoanalysis is the treatment of choice for the patients discussed in this book. In fact, I would argue that psychotherapy is a perfectly appropriate tool for almost every form of psychopathology encountered in the work of the average therapist with the possible exception of the structural neuroses. Moreover, I feel very strongly that psychotherapy is the functional equal of psychoanalysis, not its stepchild, and should be regarded as such by patients and therapists alike. Even though this point of view is now widely accepted, I feel it still needs unambiguous reiteration. For example, even Blanck and Blanck (1974), eminent advocates of psychotherapy as a technique, state that "while we ourselves prefer to have our psychotherapy patients sit, especially if object representations are blurred, some of them prefer to lie down and there is usually no reason to deprive them of *this status symbol.*" (p. 129, emphasis mine) What does such a seemingly innocuous and humane response imply? It

*An earlier version of this chapter was presented at the Meeting of the Eastern Association for Sex Therapy; New York City, March 1978.

seems to me, that statements of this sort reflect and reify the position advocated by many leading theorists in the field, notably Waelder (1960), Gill (1954), Eissler (1953), Kernberg (1975), Kohut (1971), namely that only psychoanalysis enables patients to work through their oedipal problems. In other words, psychotherapy would be the pre-soak so to speak, as opposed to the actual wash, which is psychoanalysis. This, in my opinion, is simply not true. Moreover, particularly the masochistically inclined patients who enter psychotherapy can experience this to mean that they are too disturbed to benefit from "the real thing," that they are receiving merely scotch-tape therapy. Instead, I am in full agreement with Chassell (1953) who defines psychoanalysis as a "procedure of limited but significant usefulness in certain cases" (p. 552), one which presupposes the existence of an intact ego that is capable of entering into a transference neurosis. In my professional experience, the vast majority of today's patients in private practice have neither the ego strength nor motivation and financial resources that would make them suitable candidates for psychoanalysis. Fortunately, however, in the last two decades our knowledge about the development and structure of the ego, the preoedipal development of normal children and the advances in object relations theory have increased to such an extent that a tentative "mapping out" of techniques of ego modification, rehabilitation and structure building, is now possible. It appears that we have come reasonably close in meeting Eissler's requirements for a successful psychotherapy: "If our knowledge of the structure of the ego were complete, then a variety of techniques—ideally adapted to the requirements of the individual disturbance—could be perfected, thus we could assure definite mastery of the ego over those areas in which it had suffered defeat, that is to say, assure complete recovery." (1953, p. 104)

I believe that in the absence of an intact ego, a radical departure from the "classical mirror model" (Loewald, 1960, p. 25) is indicated. Moreover, it has to be replaced with a model that has been derived from the early parent-child relationship, and translates them into therapeutic techniques taking into account that the patient is definitely an *adult*, but one whose ego functions resemble those of a small child. Consequently, the therapeutic model proposed here is definitely not psychoanalytic in that it is not based on either dual instinct theory or traditional psychoanalytic techniques. Rather, it is interpersonal and developmental. Depending on the degree of pathology at the begin-

ning of treatment, or in response to severe regresssions later in treatment, its parameters range from a purely supportive approach—"pacification," (Gedo and Goldberg, 1973) to a strictly interpretive mode
and include "unification" and "optimal disillusionment" as intermedi-
ary techniques. It will be argued that the process of psychotherapy that
is based on developmental psychology, is essentially one of corrective
parenting. That means that it is the responsibility of the therapist to
lead the patient through the different phases of infantile growth and to
adapt his or her techniques to the changing emotional needs of the
patient—infant. Also to be shown is that the shift from one phase to
another is marked by distinct transition points or crises.

Before going any further, it seems necessary to spell out what is
meant by the terms phases, or stages, of development and corrective
parenting. Based on the findings of developmental psychology the
observation of the development of normal children, one knows that
infantile development can be roughly mapped out in terms of the
major sources of anxiety (Gedo and Goldberg, 1973), the principal
tasks (Mahler, 1975) and cognitive development (Piaget, 1966). These
findings have given us some very valuable tools with which to sharpen
our therapeutic techniques. Since one has a reasonably accurate idea as
to what specific tasks the child has to master at the various stages of
growth, one can now trace approximately how and when the maternal
environment interfered with the natural growth processes of the child.
What is more, this information suggests what kinds of structural defects one can expect in a patient, given certain traumatic climates in
early childhood. In order to devise therapeutic tools that respond to
preoedipal, even preverbal traumas, one has to ask the following: How
does the sadism of the object become the masochism of the subject? In
chronological developmental terms, what do the concepts "libidinization of suffering" "illusion of maternal love" etc., actually mean?
Adaptation to a non-loving environment obviously means something
different at age six than it does at the age of five months. Although in
the first chapter of this book I have examined what types of parental
behavior are instrumental in the formation of the sadomasochistic
stance, we will now look at the interaction from the child's point of
view. In this chapter, we will begin with the preverbal stage.

We now do have a variety of developmental models to choose
from. The major points at which they differ pertain to (a) the precise
timetable of events; and (b) the conceptualization of how and when

structures are built and defenses are erected. Some of the disagreements are major, others are minor, and they have been discussed elsewhere. (Chessick 1977) Since the empirical research on cognitive development suggests that extreme caution has to be applied in attributing any thought processes to the infant prior to age two, in what follows I have tried to err on the conservative side in conceptualizing the ways in which the sadomasochistic personality formed. By that, I mean in discussing the probable events in the various developmental stages, I shall adhere to psychoanalytic theories and concepts that are congruent with, or at least possible, in light of Piaget's findings about cognitive development.

Perhaps the most widely accepted model of infantile development is that of Margret Mahler's (1975). I have adopted it for the purposes of, first, generally mapping out the emergence of the sadomasochistic stance; and, based on this, a strategy of treatment. Briefly stated, the four stages are:

1. The hatching stage (0-3 month) the normal autistic phase during which the mother serves as an external executive ego whose function it is to protect the child from traumatic overstimulation.

2. The symbiotic phase, (2 or 3 months to 6 or 8 months) during which the child becomes slowly and intermittently aware of the fact that the satisfactions of needs are contingent on an "other," i.e. something outside of its own body. Thus, the loss of that object becomes the major source of anxiety.

3. Separation and Individuation with four sub-phases: (a) Differentiation (6 to 10 months): The child discovers locomotion and derives pleasure from its own body and actively approaches the environment for pleasure and stimulation. (b) The practicing period (10-18 months) during which upright locomotion, exploration, and the development of representational intelligence all contribute to the child's inflated grandiosity. (c) Rapproachment (16-24 months) the child's attempts to balance independence and separation anxiety, resulting in a gradual deflation of its grandiosity. (d) The fourth sub-phase (roughly the third year) characterized by the unfolding of the more complex cognitive functions, verbal communications, etc. At the end of the third year,

"psychological birth" is complete; the toddler has become a little person in its own right. Psychological birth and the establishment of a cohesive self essentially coincide.

The fact that the sadomasochistic character formation develops in a climate of parental rejection that was present *at birth* poses a particularly difficult problem for two reasons. We have to speculate about processes that take place at a preverbal level; and the time period under discussion is that of sensorimotor intelligence rather than representational intelligence. What this means is this: Even though the baby has no speech, thoughts, signals, symbols, or self- and object-representations, it has, nevertheless, the capacity for archaic forms of problem solving. Consequently, much of what will be said about the hatching stage and the symbiotic phase will have to be imprecise simply because we do not know enough about the psychological aspects of early infancy to state as an empirical fact what exactly goes on in the baby's mind when it is faced with continuous frustrations and impingements. What we do know is the fact that we can observe the results in terms of behavior or symptoms such as marasmus, coma, anaclitic depressions, three-month colic, infantile eczema, hypermotility or fecal play, but we know nothing about the *inner experience* of the baby. We have countless theories about the subject, but all of them are derived from the analysis of adults, and many of them do not conform to the empirical information we do have about the cognitive development of normal infants. For example, we know from Piaget's studies (1976) that the baby during the first year of life has no ideas, only experiences which have a cumulative effect and will leave memory traces, probably in the form of body memories. When I used the term "illusion of maternal love" in early infancy earlier, this cannot possibly mean a conceptual distortion of the maternal object. All it can refer to is the intrinsic and biologically given object seeking quality of the infantile psyche, the imperative need for attachment or bonding. The infant instinctively turns to the maternal other for the purpose of finding something good and gratifying there, and it does so even in the face of repeated disappointments. Only after the child has acquired the capacity for stable object representations between the ages of 18 and 24 months can the term "illusion" mean a distorted image of the maternal other. Also, Bemporad (1980) has convincingly argued that without stable object representations, objects cannot be introjected or incorporated as whole objects which then operate as "inner objects." At best, what can be introjected are the experiences of the relationship between the infant and the object such as positive or negative mutual cuing, mirroring, experiences of comfort or impingement, gratification or deprivation, soothing, or assault. Exactly how these early experiences shape the emergent psyche, however, is for the time being, an unknown. The only thing we do know as a fact is that it has an effect, and we must presume that it acquires the impact and the quality of what Khan (1974) has described as "cumulative trauma" and what Shengold (1979) has termed "soul murder." Thus, in treading the thin line between what is suggested on the basis of retrospection and what is possible in terms of cognitive development, we have to conclude that the cumulative trauma, experienced by the future sadomasochist during the early developmental phases, i.e. everything preceding individuation and separation are essentially characterized by what might be called a "bad universe" experience, which, in time, tilts toward a "bad me" distortion. What I mean is simply this: during the phase of the undifferentiated matrix, where the child and the world constitute a whole, bad experiences cannot be attributed to anything or anybody. The baby, being co-existent with the universe, feels badly. Only in the course of self-object differentiation does it become imperative for the child to attribute the bad experiences to the self in order to depend on the goodness of the maternal other.

We are assuming that in what Winnicott (1965) has labeled the good enough holding environment during the hatching phase (also the phase of primary narcissism), the mother's function as an auxiliary ego builds the rudiments of a protective shield (Khan, 1974) that protects the baby from traumatic overstimulations. The soothing and pacifying functions of the mother are later internalized and their cumulative acquisition constitute what Kohut refers to as transmuting internalizations. Without any self-object differentiation, we can, at this stage, only think of cumulative good universe experiences that can serve as the first building blocks for what later becomes an ego. Winnicott's and Guntrip's conception of the libidinal ego during the hatching phase then, must be thought of as the product of a mostly rewarding interaction between mother and child, the ability on the part of the mother to intuit what the baby needs. In other words, the natural development of the emerging ego, that is by definition, pleasure-seeking or libidinal is not interfered with. Conversely, it seems that the anti-libidinal ego is built up as a result of incorporating repeated states of unrelieved terror and rage by a baby whose mother could not soothe the child. If we examine an anaclitic depression that results from emotional abandonment, the child walls itself off from the mother, and it becomes unresponsive. Gedo and Goldberg have called the defensive modes of this stage "primal repression" and "hallucinatory omnipotence." Primal repression seems to be exemplified by that walling off process, the shrinking away not from an object, but probably from the experience of unmanageable inner turmoil. In other words, primal repression seems to be the obverse of the protective shield. In adult patients with a history of neglect during early childhood, I have often found a marked insensitivity to physical pain, fear, hunger and thirst, and external stimuli such as disturbing noises, which, in the course of treatment, slowly revealed a considerable and troublesome hypersensitivity to those stimuli and an apparent inability to cope with them. This leads me to conclude, that the adult behavior in question represents a continuation of a defensive mode that probably originated during the hatching phase.

What all of this means for the psychotherapy of the sadomasochistic patient is that we will have to devise techniques that allow the patient to relive and reexperience these preverbal traumas and to find effective ways of dealing with inner discomfort through pacification. In chapters 7, 8, and 9, we shall examine the developmental task of the subsequent phases and corresponding modes of treatment. More generally, what I am suggesting is that a successful psychotherapy of the sadomasochistic patient will have to encompass techniques that resemble the optimal mothering required in all stages of infantile development.

Furthermore, we are postulating the existence of transition points between the different stages of development in therapy, a signalling on the part of the patient, who can let the therapist know that a developmental task has begun to be ego-syntonic. By borrowing from the terminology of Gedo and Goldberg and that of Mahlers, we shall call the four phases of treatment: 1. Hatching or establishing a working alliance; 2. Symbiosis or "Make it All Good Again"; 3. Separation and Individuation; and 4. Maturation or the Pursuit of Internal Integrity. The transition points will be called: a. getting in touch with one's sadism; b. confronting self-responsibility; and c. superego integration. Although the progression through these phases can often only become evident in retrospect, it is, nevertheless, discernible in spite of all the regressive moves on the part of the patient. It is the responsibility of the therapist to determine throughout the treatment, and in each session—sometimes even from one minute to the next—on what particular developmental level a patient is operating and to choose a response that matches the patient's needs. A regression on the part of the patient may either be just that, or it may indicate the presence of a toxic element in the patient-therapist interaction, or it may be a response to a traumatic event in the patient's life. Often a patient will move through a phase or phases with deceptive speed and emerge in a state of pseudomaturity only to start all over again, but this time more earnestly. What these patients are saying is: "I don't have to be a dependent child, I can grow myself up without needing you very much." Having made this point, they can then settle down and grow at their own pace. Other patients, after the same quick once-over, can get stuck in one phase until they have made some major changes in their external lives that provide them with the emotional scaffold that can allow them to confront their more archaic impulses. During such times, the therapist's work will have to consist of supportive therapy only, and it is important that the therapist does not misunderstand the situation and become frustrated and impatient. Even though the linear development through the four phases of treatment is disrupted by many detours and regressions, the concept of transition points is a very important one because they are moments of insight, shared by patient and therapist that can never be really undone. Patients will try to forget them, but they cannot do so with the same firm conviction as before. In the case of the sadomasochistic patients for example, who started therapy with the self concept of a total victim, who thought that they could not hurt a fly, and who have reached the point where they expressed for the first time their own sadistic impulses, will not be able to return to their victimized position with the same degree of innocence. This is particularly true if the therapist has alerted the patient to the fact that the treatment has entered a new phase and has been able to honestly welcome this new development. The same holds true for the other transition points. The argument could be made that all psychopathology originates in a specific developmental phase and that therefore the treatment process should focus primarily on the vicissitudes of that particular developmental phase. Masterson's work with borderline patients is perhaps the most brilliant example of this approach, and it works extremely well with the patients he described. His patients, however, are quite different from the one's discussed in this book. For example, although a sadomasochistic character disorder may have received enough mothering to "get by," i.e. to avoid more serious form of pathology, the general emotional climate of being unwanted, usually began at birth. Conversely, overindulgence during the symbiotic phase,—or for that matter, during any of the other stages—is precisely what was absent in the childhood of the future sadomasochist. Emotional and physical deprivation tend to be the rule. Therefore, the therapist dealing with predominantly sadomasochistic patients should assume that "repair work" will probably be needed on *all* developmental levels.

The term "corrective parenting," unfortunately, has created many confusions. In some circles, it has been understood to mean that the responsibility of the therapist is merely one of being a nice, comforting, indulgent mother—in other words a travesty of the "good enough mother." The parenting advocated *here* is characterized by two major components: respect and a vision of what the patient is striving to become; and empathy for the patient's temporary limitations.

Respect implies the simultaneous acceptance that the patient is in treatment with the goal to terminate; to become what his life experiences have prevented him from becoming. The good parent-therapist conveys a message of expectation for change and growth. As Loewald put it: "This 'more' that the parent sees and knows, he mediates to the child, so that the child in identification with it can grow." (1960, p. 20) The other side of the same coin is the empathy with the needs and limitations of the patient who is still in the process of becoming. Tension reduction through self-soothing activities, for example, is learned behavior; it is the product of a great deal of soothing and pacifying on the part of the mother of earliest infancy. In the absence of this input, the adult patient may be utterly helpless in dealing with threats to his inner equilibrium, and the therapist may have to actively provide soothing and comfort until the patient has reached the point where he is able to provide these things for himself. By expecting him to do otherwise, we would merely duplicate the patient's earlier experiences, which, after all, brought him into treatment in the first place. As Fleming pointed out: "I have been increasingly impressed with the fact that we expect our adult patients to possess a degree of maturity on their psychosocial developmental line that would almost preclude any need for analysis." (1975 p. 756) Respect and empathy thus are the essence of good corrective parenting because they simultaneously deal with what the patient is and what he is capable of becoming. For example, the patient who soaks up the comforts of companionable silence should be seen as a person who practices scales in order to learn to eventually play a symphony. Alternatively he can be seen as an advanced musician who feels he has to temporarily go back to practicing scales. In other words in treating preoedipal conditions we have to be prepared to utilize a very wide range of techniques that are geared to the problems originating in earliest infancy as well as those of the toddler stage.

One of the tools that I personally have found to be extremely effective is the presence of a suitable pet in the office, such as a dog or a cat. Needless to say, this only works if the therapist happens to be a dog or cat lover, and if the pet in question is small, affectionate, non-threatening and reasonably unobtrusive. Aside from the obvious function of representing a cuddly nonhuman transitional object to the patient—a self object—that may be easier to relate to than the therapist, it is also a representation *of* the therapist. Since to some extent, pets always take on their owner's characteristics, including those that the owner disavows, a set of subtle communications is established that adds valuable dimensions to the therapeutic exchange. The presence of my own dog, Giulietta, in my office has figured prominently in the dreamworld and the fantasy life of the patients discussed in this book. Being a quintessential mutt, small, skinny to the point of scrawniness, guileless and demanding, with a regal disregard for such elementary canine duties as guarding the house, she has endeared herself to all my patients in two ways: one, by identifying with her playful childhood persona that is valued just for being, rather than doing, an experience these patients have never had. My obvious love for her is therefore experienced as comforting. Two, on a more subtle, unconscious level, there is the recognition that this pet must also represent an aspect of their therapist, one which in small ways counteracts some of the most negative transferential projections. Anna for example, who for a long time saw me as a slave driver, was given a photo of Giulietta to keep on her nighttable to look at whenever her obsessions over work yet to be done kept her from sleeping.

PHASE I: HATCHING OR ESTABLISHING A WORKING ALLIANCE

Hatching or Phase I of the treatment denotes the process by which two total strangers, patient and therapist, establish a unique and special relationship with each other. This does not mean that once this relationship exists that the patient will not go through many moments of feeling estranged from his therapist, himself, and his surroundings. During those times, when alienation and loneliness are the predominant feeling states, a temporary regression to the hatching phase will occur, and the treatment objectives and techniques appropriate for this phase will have to be employed. Such regressions can last anywhere from 10 minutes to 10 weeks depending on the severity of the trauma that produced the regression.

The specific treatment goals or objectives are the following: 1. to induce the patient to "come in from the cold," to settle in; 2. to build a tentative sense of trust, safety, and welcome that allows patients to air their grievances without fear of censure or retaliation; and 3. to get to the point where they can shift from the self-absorbed preoccupation with their troubles to a dialogue with the therapist, so that therapy becomes a joint effort rather than one person complaining to another. In order to achieve these objectives the stance of the therapist should resemble that of the optimal parent of earliest infancy who only becomes an object *for* the infant on the basis of a continuous expression of empathy and genuine acceptance. When sadomasochistic patients have reached the point where they are ready for a real dialogue, they will invariably signal this development with an expression of sadism, directed either at the therapist or their environment. The shared acknowledgment of the patient's own sadism marks the transition point from Phase I of the treatment to Phase II.

The First Hour

Obviously, we cannot be equally good—or even adequate—for every patient who applies for therapy. The reverse is equally true. Also, the wish to balance one's patient population in terms of age, pathology, sex, and sexual orientation is a legitimate consideration in the selection of patients. Patients who bore one therapist can be of great interest to a colleague. To accept a patient whose values, ethics and/or politics are offensive to us would be extremely unfair to the patient as well as to ourselves. Whether a pronounced negative reaction to a patient, who for example works as a pimp, constitutes countertransference, is really immaterial. The only thing that matters is the recognition that our tolerance has limits and that these limits will have to be respected.

Consequently, before starting therapy with any patient, the two most important questions that have to be answered are: 1. Do I want this particular patient?; and 2. Will I be able to do justice to this person? Patients like Karl and Bob are not everybody's cup of tea since they make extraordinary demands on their therapists, particularly during the first two or three years. Since they also tend to be poor, (see chapter 5 discussion of ego functioning) they will also be unable to pay more than a minimal fee for a long time. Masochists, even if their ego functions are more intact, are often quite reluctant to improve their incomes and living conditions; this is part of what Freud termed the "negative therapeutic reaction." A therapist, who for whatever reasons is financially strapped, should think twice before committing him or herself to years of treating somebody for a negligible fee. Otherwise, resentment is bound to develop, and the treatment suffers. For all of those reasons, it is best *never* to accept any patient sight unseen, but to call the first session or sessions a consultation for the purpose of determining how well they can work together, or whether a referral to a colleague is indicated. This point should be made clearly and un-ambiguously at the first encounter over the phone or by mail. This statement, however, has to be made in such a way that patients do not, in any way, feel that they have to sell themselves, or that they may wind up getting no help at all. On the contrary, it should be stated very clearly that a. *A* competent therapist will see them; b. that the decision between being accepted or referred is contingent primarily on the compatability between the patient's and the therapist's schedule, and c. that the patients, too, have every right to look over the therapist before committing themselves to treatment.

Once the decision has been made by both parties to begin therapy, the treatment contract has to be spelled out as clearly as possible. It has to spell out the therapist's obligations, frequency of appointments, vacation times, and the availability of standbys, fees, policy concerning cancellations, the therapist's availability between sessions, and special restrictions for the impulsive patient. Patients have to understand that they are freely entering a contractual agreement that is not subject to subsequent negotiations by either party. This does not mean that, in the course of treatment, hours cannot be rearranged and fees be adjusted by mutual agreement; what it does mean, however, is that patients know that as long as they fulfill their part of the bargain, the therapist will do likewise. It introduces the element of security and predictability, something that the patient may have never known before. The best way to introduce the subject is to say something to the effect: "This is the way I work . . . " and to follow it up with "If this is agreeable to you, we are in business." Usually, I explain to patients: 1. that as their therapist, I commit myself to the best of my ability to their emotional growth for as long as they need me; that as long as they adhere to the rules agreed upon, only *they* can choose to terminate the treatment. 2. That the therapy hours are theirs and theirs alone to be utilized in whatever fashion they see fit. In return, they are expected to: 1. report as honestly as possible their troubles; 2. bring in their dreams; and 3. pay their bills on time even if, for whatever reason, they choose to cancel a session.

The more disturbed patients have to know that in an emergency the therapist is available between hours, provided it is, indeed, an emergency. The therapist's vacation times should be spelled out clearly, including the place and precise dates, so that patients can make their own plans accordingly. Although the therapist's vacations always spell hardship for the patient, this hardship can be minimized if 1. standby's are available; and 2. if the therapist can be reached during this time, either by mail or by phone; and 3. if the vacation time is announced without defensiveness on the part of the therapist. Even though I take off two months in the summer and two weeks in the winter, this has never been an insurmountable problem for any of my patients. With a vacation schedule like mine, however, one should not accept any new patients after April first. A colleague of mine, who travels and lectures extensivly during the summer months, gives each and every one of her patients a detailed itinerary, complete with mailing addresses and telephone numbers. This is a highly commendable procedure because her patients know that she has not disappeared from the face of the earth and that she can always be reached. The difference between abandonment and temporary physical absence can be crucial. I might also add that it is a thorough misunderstanding of the rule of abstinence not to tell our patients where we are during our vacation and what we plan to do. A patient who can find our vacation spot on the map will feel more assured that we still exist. Patients who have been told that the therapist is taking time off to rest, catch up with the professional literature, and write, may still feel deprived but not quite so rejected. Moreover, they may eventually come to feel that at least some of the therapist's time off will ultimately benefit them. These considerations are particularly crucial with sadomasochistic patients who have experienced the sense of being unwanted throughout their childhoods and who are, therefore, likely to experience the therapist's absence as yet another narcissistic injury. Very impulsive sadomasochistic patients will have to be told that unless they can agree to postpone major decisions, and to eliminate clearly dangerous habits, therapy will have to be discontinued until such time when they can abstain from them. Examples are the use of LSD or other heavy hallucinative and/or addictive drugs, drag-racing, barroom brawls, prostitution, possession of firearms and explosives and other forms of disregard for the most elementary precautions for physical safety. The rationale for these restrictions should be expressed in very simple terms, namely that therapy cannot extend to a hospital, mental institution, or the city morgue.

Treatment Goals and Objectives

Without a single exception, patients come to us because of a deep-rooted, but sometimes unconscious belief, that in some way life has handed them a dirty deal. I, for one, take this belief to be a fact. Consequently, in the initial phase of treatment, the establishment of trust, through the validation of the patient's subjective reality—not the therapist's—is the main treatment goal. The patient, who has never been able to trust either his own or other people's reality cannot even begin to look at his own contributions to his problems until he can believe that unlike the original parent, he has found someone at long last who can see the world through his eyes. This is someone who can fully empathize with his pain, his terrors and his pleasures, twisted as they may be, and who can accept him the way he is. Since the experience of being unwanted, rejected or outright hated is so central in the psychodynamics of sadomasochism, the necessity of first "taming" the patient cannot be overstressed. The term "taming" has been borrowed from Saint Exupéry's moving fable, *The Little Prince*. In his travels through the different planets, the little prince finally lands on earth. In his endeavor to find a friend he encounters a fox, and the ensuing dialogue is worth quoting in full since it poetically captures the essence of what this initial interaction should be all about:

> "No," said the little prince. "I am looking for friends. What does that mean 'tame'?"
>
> "It is an act too often neglected," said the fox. "It means to establish ties."
>
> " 'To establish ties'?"
>
> "Just that," said the fox. "To me you are still nothing more than a little boy who is just like a hundred thousand other little boys. And I have no need of you. And you, on your part, have no need of me. To you I am nothing more than a fox like a hundred thousand other foxes. But if you tame me, then we shall need each other. To me, you will be unique in all the world. To you, I shall be unique in all the world . . ."
>
> "I am beginning to understand," said the little prince. "There is a flower . . . I think that she has tamed me . . ."
>
> "It is possible" said the fox . . .
>
> "My life is very monotonous," he said. "I hunt chickens; men hunt me. All the chickens are just alike, and all the men are just alike. And, in consequence, I am a little bored. But if you tame me, it will be as if the sun came to shine on my life I shall know the sound of a step that will be different from all others. Other steps send me hurrying back underneath the ground. Yours will call me, like music, out of my burrow. And then look: you see the grain fields down yonder? I do not eat bread. Wheat is of no use to me. And that is sad. But you have hair that is the color of gold. Think how wonderful that will be when you have tamed me! The grain, which is also golden, will bring me back to the thought of you. And I shall love to listen to the wind in the wheat. . . ."
>
> The fox gazed at the little prince, for a long time.
>
> "Please—tame me!" he said.
>
> "I want to, very much," the little prince replied. "But I have not much time. I have friends to discover, and a great many things to understand."
>
> "One only understands the things that one tames," said the fox. Men have no more time to understand anything. They buy things already made at the shops. But there is no shop anywhere where

one can buy friendship, and so men have no friends anymore. If you want a friend, tame me. . . ."

"What must I do, to tame you?" asked the little prince.

"You must be very patient," replied the fox. "First you will sit down at a little distance from me—like that—in the grass. I shall look at you out of the corner of my eye, and you will say nothing. Words are the source of misunderstandings. But you will sit a little closer to me, every day. . . ."

The next day the little prince came back.

"It would have been better to come back at the same hour," said the fox.

"If, for example, you come at four o'clock in the afternoon, then at three o'clock I shall begin to be happy. I shall feel happier and happier as the hour advances. At four o'clock, I shall already be worrying and jumping about. I shall show you how happy I am! But if you come at just any time, I shall never know at what hour my heart is to be ready to greet you . . . One must observe the proper rites. . . ." (p. 66/68)

Saint Exupéry's concept of taming contains the two key ingredients of the initial patient-therapist encounter: 1. A predictably good, reliable, and accepting other who slowly becomes unique and special in the patient's eyes; that can be counted on to always be there at the appointed hour, and 2. the fact that this dependable other makes no demands, offers no criticisms and has no expectations with respect to the patient's performance. During Phase I, we do, indeed, have to offer ourselves as the all-good—though not yet differentiated—self-object of earliest infancy. The objection could be raised that this initial procedure constitutes unnecessary "coddling" or that it gives the patient false hopes and the wrong idea of what hard therapeutic work is all about. It is even conceivable to view this process as a form of seduction. To some extent, this is accurate and not at all wrong. After all, the course of a complete and successful treatment of a severely sadomasochistic patient can be an extremely painful and often upsetting experience. Patients who embark on this enterprise will find themselves tempted, time and again, to simply live with their misery, rather than endure the pain of having to cope with shame, guilt, and the corrosion of their old identity. Most of our patients, at the beginning of treatment, mercifully do not know what they have let themselves in for. The reason they seek help is because the cumulative effect of their suffering has propelled them into the risky proposition of delivering their bruised psyches into the hands of a total stranger. This decision takes courage, and this courage requires some bolstering particularly since they have so little experience with human kindness. Moreover, by the time sadomasochistic patients enter therapy, they often come with such a backlog of unexpressed pain, resentment, rage and loneliness, that they have no free attention for anything other than their inner turmoil. In other words, even if we wanted to, we could not start "serious work" in the second or even the tenth session because even though the patient may *look* like he is paying attention, he is really not. I have often tested patients' recall of the early month of therapy, and they have come up with no memories of what was said. They remember colors, textures, blurry recollections of parts of my body, Giulietta's playful presence, knick-knacks in my office, etc., but very little else. What all of them do remember though—without a single exception—was the gnawing questions in their minds: "When will she attack me?" and "Where do I run when she does?" Needless to say, this is hardly the time for interpretative comments on the part of the therapist since if an attack is what is foremost on the patient's mind, any comment might be interpreted as being critical, if not assaultive. The fact that the predominantly masochistic patient will ask for precisely that, does not mean that it should be given; to the contrary, it should be deliberately withheld. The high drop-out rate by severely sadomasochistic patients may well be partially explained by the therapist's insufficient attention to the real needs of the patient at the beginning of treatment as opposed to the stated needs. The patient who in the second session asks; "Doc, tell me what's wrong with me?" may well be setting the stage for his or her disappearance if the question is answered truthfully and comprehensively.

Since Kadushin's (1969) research has shown that the average time lapse between the onset of symptoms and the beginning of psychotherapy is approximately one-and-a-half years, and often involves trips to the family physician, minister and other members of the helping profession, who slowly convince the future patient that the problems are not medical, spiritual, or environmental, but emotional, these one-and-a-half years of unrelieved pain and confusion may well require three to six months of ventilation and validation. When I use the term validation, I do not mean that we should agree with the patient's often distorted view of the world, but validation of their *feelings* of hurt, confusion, rejection, and despair. To merely agree that their unhappiness is real, that their confusion is legitimate, and that they have probably good reasons for resenting some of their parents' actions, is all that is called for. The purpose of this consistent expression of compassion is, among other things, to get patients to the point where they have enough free attention to utilize interpretations and to fortify them for the hard work ahead.

The initial phase of treatment, however, does not have merely a preparatory function; to the contrary, it is already a form of active intervention, and it has the following components: 1. The experience of a soothing or pacifying other is a new experience in the patient's life. The empathic responses from the therapist can be internalized and, thus, clearly aid in the building, consolidating, or modifying of more or less archaic structures. 2. The unconscious, and sometimes conscious fantasy, that every sadomasochistic patient brings into therapy, (and to life, for that matter) is: if they could find only *one* human being who could give them the unilateral acceptance of the good mother of earliest infancy, who does not intrude with her subjectivity into the self-contained world of the baby, all would be well. By playing this role for as long as our patients ask us to, we can, indeed, supply some of the corrective parenting that was absent during this period of our patients' lives. But more important, by going along with the patients' demands, they, themselves, become the discoverers of the fact that their "If only . . ." is an illusion. They will come to recognize that paradise is, indeed, lost, not because they cannot have what they want, but because they, themselves, have lost the necessary innocence that would make this "If only . . ." blissful. Thus, by putting the patients fully in charge of their sessions, by accepting their definition of reality, two objectives are accomplished simultaneously: the autonomy of the patients is preserved, since nothing is forced on them. They are the one's who question at least the unilateral validity of their "If only's. . . ."; given the fact that they, themselves, do the leaving of a position that they expected to spell bliss, it is not "spoiled" for them by parental prohibition or disapproval, and, therefore, they can feel free to return to it when the going gets rough without a sense of shame.

One last objection has to be discussed. The question could be raised: How do we know that with this approach, patients do move? Won't they simply regress and stay put? First of all, I have never seen this happen with any patient who has brought into treatment a modicum of good faith. Second, the ventilation of pain, anger and, loneliness after all results in relief and, therefore, enables patients to start asking the question as to what would make things better. It is this very question that compels the sadomasochistic patient to look at his therapist for help, and at that moment the initial self-absorption turns into a dialogue.

In other words, during phase I of the treatment, compassion, pacification, empathy, understanding, and patience are the only therapeutic tools that benefit the patient. The *only* thing these patients do *not* need during phase I is an interpretation that contradicts their victimized view of themselves. Sooner or later, they will make this discovery all by themselves, while a premature interpretation would not only delay this insight, but might even induce them to leave therapy—which is something that the sadomasochistic patient is only too ready to do anyway.

TRANSFERENCE

One of the most important things that the therapist of the sadomasochistic patient has to keep in mind, is the fact that no matter how accepting and kind we are, nothing will ever be good enough for the patient. Although some of them will not express this openly, they may feel it strongly nevertheless. A patient, who all his life has experienced hatred or rejection as if they were love, will not be able to easily deal with an object that is consistently kind and dependable. The need to provoke the good object into acting sadistically, is everpresent, and the therapist will have to be extremely alert, not to fall into that trap. We do have to remember, that with respect to the art of provocation, we, as therapists, are probably mere amateurs, dealing with pros.

Given the fact that our presentation of self during Phase I is uniformly that of unwavering attention, the precise nature of the transference varies from patient to patient depending on the degree of ego impairment and the balance between sadomasochism and narcissism. In the case of the schizophrenic, to the extent that their relationship to the therapist can be called a transference at all, we are more of an institution than an object. Inanimate objects in our office may be of greater importance than our person. If all goes well, however, the schizophrenic will develop a tenuous "life-line" transference at the beginning of treatment, which applies to therapy itself more than to the therapist. In my personal experience, I have found it helpful to begin treatment with schizophrenics like Karl, on a two to three times a week basis, because of the rapid fluctuations of moods and perceptions of those patients, and because of the danger of emotional flooding. No matter how carefully we may try to keep a schizophrenic patient from drowning in their material, however, flooding is likely to occur at times and with it, the depersonalization of the therapist. They will transform us into threatening figures of the past and the experience will be *real.* In Karl's case, there were several instances where I actually became the father threatening him with a butcher knife and his terror during those psychotic episodes was truly bonechilling. With essentially no good introjects to call upon and to mobilize (no memories of pleasant and rewarding interactions with people were available to him), only good and safe *places,* (the village where he had spent his summer vacations), the connection had to be made between the good place in the past and the safe place in the present to contain the hallucinations. Thus, the reliance on the objects in the office, which are particularly meaningful to such a patient, can be very helpful. During those episodes Karl experienced himself as four or five years-old. In his attempt to flee from the office, he had to be restrained; this was possible since he did not use most of the strength in his six foot body. And by alternating between English and German, the connection between the past and the present was facilitated. Harrowing as many of these episodes were, they did help Karl in recognizing that in addition to the good place and the therapeutic process, there was also a strong *being* that could be relied upon to contain his madness without fear, and who understood and accepted what, until this point, had been his own secret world.

In the case of a borderline patient, the transference is characterized by ego and object splitting. Depending on the nature and degree of the narcissistic disturbance, the transference will also have either an idealizing or mirror component. In the case of a borderline patient whose archaic narcissistic and exhibitionistic impulses are repressed (Kohut's horizontal split, 1971) the transference situation, difficult as it may be, is still infinitely less complicated than that of a borderline patient with openly-displayed narcissistic strivings, (Kohut's vertical split). The latter will develop primarily a mirror transference. In the first case, if the therapist is sufficiently unintrusive, and supportive, defensive splitting will be employed primarily toward people on the outside and only secondarily toward the therapist, who most of the time, is idealized. The inevitable lapses of empathy on the part of the therapist, however, will result in a disturbance of the transference. These lapses are experienced as bereavement, object loss, and a sense of profound emptiness resulting in depression. Without an omnipotent self-object, the patient feels depleted and withdraws. These situations are best resolved if the therapist offers a suggestion such as: "It seems I have misunderstood you, and I know how hurtful that can be. Please forgive me and let's go over the entire story again." Such an explanation usually allows the patient to freely express his disappointment and hurt and then restore the idealized self-object to its proper place. Since during Phase I hardly any interpretations are given, the splitting of the therapist into an all-good and all-bad part is essentially restricted to real or imagined lapses in empathy and results in depression rather than rage. Rapid alterations between love and hate only emerge during Phase II.

The borderline structure with a vertical split, however, is a very different story, and perhaps one of *the* most difficult patients to treat. The complex nature of his transference, almost from the beginning, puts patient and therapist alike in a no-win situation. The following vicious cycle is established: the transference that develops is primarily a mirror transference, wherein the therapist is expected to respond to the patient's overt display of his exhibitionism and grandiosity. This however presents problems. The patient's illusions of hidden greatness are often patently exaggerated, even absurd if not pathetic and they tend to be accompanied by a bottomless contempt for the rest of the world. Alternatively, the patient's claim to specialness may rest on little more than the depth of his pathology or the perfidy of those who refuse to acknowledge his genius. Consequently, positive mirroring is an almost impossible task and what can be given will usually not satisfy the patient. Obviously the therapist cannot, in good conscience, respond enthusiastically to the grandiosity; since it would be clearly disrespectful of the patient's potential. Thus, he can only offer compassion for the patient's enormous need for appreciation. This response is usually ignored, while the guarded response to the patient's grandiosity is experienced as a narcissistic injury that produces rage. In the patient's eyes, the therapist becomes all-bad. The often quite vicious attacks on the therapist by such a patient lead to fear of loss of love, guilt, and shame. The experience of shame mobilizes the grandiosity anew and the cycle starts all over again. Since the main defense of the borderline patient consists of ego- and object-splitting, no insight into the nature of this vicious cycle during Phase I is possible. In fact, to attempt to interpret this behavior would only make matters worse. Thus, the most hopeful area of work is to focus primarily on the patient's childhood, a subject where the expression of understanding and compassion can be most genuine. We do have to keep in mind, however, that only a fraction of our positive responses will register, most of them will be devalued or ignored. Needless to say, progress is made by millimeters rather than inches.

The transference of the sadomasochistic character disorder during Phase I typically has two components: overt idealization; and a covert need to devalue. Wall-to-wall support and acceptance are the response that such patients feel they have always striven for, even though it is apparent that unconsciously they have avoided it meticulously as evidenced by their choice of bad love objects. For the masochist, the absence of negative attention—or even persecution—leaves them at a loss. Their habitual ways of obtaining love, namely suffering and self abasement goes unrewarded, while their "badness" i.e. their selfishness is encouraged. The inner dynamic that operates is that the self has to be kept bad in order to keep the love object all-good. The tension between the positive and negative self-representations is relieved by self punishment, or by punishment meted out by an exciting bad love object. A good love object, such as an empathic therapist, disrupts the delicate balance between guilt and reparation and, therefore, must be devalued. Patients who employ their suffering primarily in the service of revenge, i.e. sadistically, tend to become enraged at the therapist if their masochistic behavior elicits concern, but no remorse on the part of the therapist. In this case, the self is kept good by keeping the love object all bad. By indicting it over and over again with one's suffering, the hope is maintained that eventually the bad object will repent and change. Although in both cases the transference is an ambivalent one, the more sadistic patient will do the devaluing overtly and provocatively, while the more masochistic patient will do it secretly.

There is also another reason for some sadomasochists' need to devalue the therapist, namely their own conception of values, of what constitutes good and bad behavior. The predominantly masochistic patient, views healthy self-respect and assertiveness as morally bad since the component of martyrdom is missing. Thus, the masochistic component of their ego-ideal receives no positive mirroring and support. Conversely, the sadistic aspects of their personality, the element of ruthlessness, though not responded to by the therapist during Phase I by its very absence or lack of encouragement, leads the more sadistically-inclined patient to conclude that the therapist must be a *shlep,* a patsy or a goody-two-shoes. This problem can become quite acute when such patients attempt to involve the therapist in fraudulent schemes against unemployment, welfare organizations, insurance agencies, the I.R.S., prospective employers, or schools. In Bob's case, the moral dilemma was particularly acute since his regular use of amphetamines left only two options: either to let him continue to buy it off the street from highly unreliable sources and, thus, with no guarantees about either the purity or the dosage of the drug, or to find a physician who could give him a prescription and deal with the possible physical and emotional side effects.

TECHNIQUES

Many of the techniques described in this book are clearly "unorthodox" by traditional analytic standards, and I do not expect analytically-oriented therapists to agree with them. On the other hand, I do hope that no one confuses the techniques discussed here with those advocated by the vast army of "wild therapists" who believe that anything goes and whose techniques are not rooted in anything deserving of the term "theory." It is this writer's belief that the reliance on the verbal and cognitive-intellectual facilities of our patients—though the goal of therapy—are often insufficient for the more disturbed patients and should, therefore, be complemented by body memories and bodily expressions. I expect that the greatest source of disagreement, however, will revolve not around the "rule of abstinence" per se, but its interpretation. Obviously, therapeutic techniques have to be tailored to the patient's needs and not to those of therapists and their shifting interests in therapeutic fads. For example, therapists who literally provide food, are clearly feeding themselves and infantilizing their patients. A chicken-soup mother is not a therapist. On the other hand, to make it an absolute rule that no real nourishment should ever under any circumstances cross our office doors is an example of rigid thinking. For example, a strategically placed cup of tea with a patient who has little or no inner resources for self soothing, can be enormously effective if it is timed properly and interpreted afterwards. Similar considerations apply where patients are in the middle of serious traumatic events, illnesses, accidents or merely got drenched in the rain. If the rule of abstinence is interpreted to mean that we should tacitly encourage unnecessary suffering by inaction and rigidity, it ceases to be therapeutic.

Another source of confusion and disagreement is the following: Much has been written about the contamination of the transference by a variety of factors:

1. The therapist being a real object; by maintaining the blank screen theory that implies that every statement made by the patient about the therapist is essentially a transferential projection, we are essentially deluding nobody but ourselves. Worse yet, it can become a form of active mystification, hardly a commendable therapeutic mode of operating. If patients are determined to learn something about our private lives, they will do so, and some of them with an ingenuity that would put the F.B.I. to shame. Conversely, patients who need to see the therapist in a certain way will continue to believe in whatever fantasy they have regardless of how much evidence to the contrary may be sitting right under their noses. Moreover, the ethnomethodologists among the sociologists have shown quite clearly just how much "our presentation of self in everyday life" is a communication to the other, geared toward eliciting specific responses by giving out clues about our expectations. Our way of dressing, grooming, talking, even our office decor, all contain clear messages about who we are and how we expect others to respond to us. In other words, try as we may, we cannot help being real objects. The important point is not to obfuscate this obvious fact but to be conscious of what we convey nonverbally and to utilize it *if and when* it truly benefits the patient.

2. The fear of contaminating the transference has also been applied to the giving and receiving of gifts. Obviously, patients who give their therapists expensive presents need to be questioned about their real motives, and the therapist may conclude that it is wiser not to accept the gift. But here again, no hard and fast rules apply. For example, in the case of the

highly narcissistic patient it can be a sign of real emotional growth, if for the first time he can give something of himself, particularly if the gift is something he himself created such as a drawing, photo or a particularly pretty seashell he collected on the beach. Even more noteworthy is a gift that is both handmade *and* geared to the therapist's particular tastes and interests. Not to acknowledge the real shift of orientation symbolized by the gift would not only be unnecessarily cruel but clearly untherapeutic. The argument that it would be better if such patients could simply verbalize these inner changes—valid as it may be—should not mean that until patients learn to do things "just right" that their efforts should not be welcomed. Conversely, a well chosen symbolic gift given *to* a patient can also be extremely valuable if object constancy is still shaky. Rather than constituting a bribe, it can be a very growth-promoting exchange. The same holds true for the loan of inexpensive objects from the therapist's office during the therapist's vacation, or other traumatic separations such as a prolonged illness or a stay in a hospital. A patient who cannot yet function without a transitional object, should not be deprived of one. After all, the best climate for emotional growth is one of optimal frustration, not one of unmanageable deprivation.

3. Physical contact between patient and therapist has been declared a cardinal sin by some writers and a cure-all by others. It is neither. If it is used properly and sparingly, well-timed and truly geared to the patient's needs, it can be very useful indeed, and it can even, at times, prevent or shortcircuit a psychotic episode. Patients who panic because of their fear that the self is disintegrating may need a restraining arm or a hand to hold onto, until the crisis has passed. In other words, in treating the more disturbed patients, many of the traditional rules of therapy will have to be modified, provided these modifications are truly in the best interest of the patient.

The techniques employed during Phase I of the treatment are determined by two factors: treatment goals and the ego strength of the patient. For example, when it comes to encouraging patients to ventilate feelings of hurt and rage, techniques that are highly effective with a character disorder, might be disastrous if applied to a borderline or a schizophrenic. Obviously the ultimate goal with patients is to get them to the point where they can verbalize *all* thoughts and feelings effectively and integrate the interpretations offered to them. Most of our more disturbed patients, however, are unable to do so. The therapeutic tasks for Phase I are essentially these: 1. to establish the therapeutic situation as one of safety; 2. to give patients the sense that they are being understood even if words fail them; 3. to allow them to soak up as much compassion as they are capable of; and 4. to ventilate some of the backlog of unexpressed feelings. First of all, and this point is rarely mentioned in the literature except by Searles (1965), an office that is bright, sunny and cheerful and that offers enough space for the patient to determine the optimal degree of distance or closeness from the therapist is an invaluable asset. A patient who feels closed in, physically uncomfortable and unable to clearly see his surroundings, will not be able to concentrate on what is going on. Thus, at the very beginning of treatment it is usually helpful to suggest to patients to make themselves comfortable by choosing the chair that establishes a safe distance between them and the therapist, and to invite them to walk around the office in order to get to know the place where, after all, they will be spending hundreds of hours. The initial walk around the office accomplishes three goals; 1. it alleviates the fear of hidden dangers that might be lurking in the corners—fantasies of trap doors and instruments of torture are not uncommon among sadomasochistic patients; 2. it gives patients a sense of autonomy, that they need not be glued to their seats but can move around the room freely if they are so inclined; and 3. by studying the decor, including the clutter, they get a chance to know us also, even if at the beginning much of what they see is mysterious to them.

Typically, a patient at the beginning of therapy, has at least *one* immediate focus of unhappiness, a particular person or situation either in the past or in the present. If the predominant feelings are either anger or hurt, one has to evaluate very carefully how much a patient will need to express in order to get some relief, and how much the ego can tolerate without getting flooded. The patient who seems out of touch with his or her feelings needs encouragement and help in expressing them. This can be done verbally by inviting the patient to visualize the object of his hurt or rage as sitting opposite him and to tell this person how hurt or angry he really is. The therapist should *not* offer his or her own person for this purpose in order to avoid transferential conflict and confusion. To invite the patient, however, to choose a symbolic object, such as a pillow, stuffed animal, or doll may well facilitate the process for the inhibited patient. Alternatively, patients who are too frightened by their own anger, may feel reassured if during this exercise they, themselves, can hang on to any of the objects mentioned above. Larry for example, almost always clutched a red pillow for comfort and often elected a stuffed toy unicorn (!) to represent his father. When he was finished with it, he soon developed the habit of putting it back on its place on the mantelpiece, but facing the wall; a neat role reversal of a child standing the parent in the corner for punishment.

Once a patient has settled in and has developed a good working alliance but still feels incapable of expressing any anger verbally, he may be able to do so with his hands, by hitting a pillow, or better yet, a stack of pillows. Although the major problem is usually to get the patient to do more than just give the pillows a few gentle pats, this is not always the case. A surprising amount of anger may sometimes come to the fore. The sadomasochistic patient may, without proper instruction, do the pillow exercise in such a way that they, themselves, get hurt. This possibility has to be avoided at all cost. In order to do so, several precautions have to be taken: 1. the patient must remove glasses, jewelry, tight jackets, and shoes. The pillows have to be wide and soft enough so that there is no chance of hitting the floor; 2. for that reason it is best if the therapist sits next to the pillows to make sure that they remain in front of the patient; 3. should the patient "accidentally" slip and hit the floor the exercise must be discontinued with the explanation that nobody is allowed to inflict pain on themselves while expressing anger. The patient should also be encouraged to make sounds while hitting the pillows. It can hardly be overstressed that such techniques must be used not only very selectively and sparingly but also *only* in the presence of the therapist and *only* at the beginning of a session and never at the end of it. Otherwise, there is no opportunity for closure and interpretation and, thus, the patient might do harm to himself or others after he leaves. It should be remembered that hitting pillows should be reserved for patients who cannot verbalize their anger at all but who are visibly choking on it. It is never a suitable method for a schizophrenic and only very occasionally for a borderline.

Usually, the expression of rage, if it is to be therapeutically useful, is a waystation for the expression of the underlying hurt and the injury to the patient's self esteem. Almost invariably, the expression of anger will lead to tears. After the anger and the hurt have been expressed, patients should talk about their experiences and whatever insight the exercise produced, which quite often means the uncovering of a repressed childhood memory. Sufficient time will have to be set aside, for patients to fully collect themselves so that when they leave they are again firmly rooted in the present tense. While most of the time the major problem is the reluctance on the part of the patient to let go, sometimes there is also the danger that they may get carried away. In that event, they will have to be interrupted kindly but firmly. As a rule of thumb, 15 out of 45 minutes should be set aside for talking about the experience and 15 minutes for reorienting patients firmly in the here and now. For predominantly masochistic patients, like Anna, who cried herself through the first eight months of therapy, the experience of beating the pillows—instead of berating herself—constituted a real turning point in her therapy and it prepared the way for her separation from her callous lover.

Patients who talk about their childhoods with a great deal of detachment can be helped with a technique that I will call guided regression. Instead of letting the patient talk *about* what happened in their childhoods, I invite them to *be* that child in that particular situation and to replay the specific event under discussion. An extremely useful variation of this technique is to actually recreate a traumatic event in group therapy where the patient can direct the scene by choosing group members to play the parts of the other members of the family—or the classroom. First, patients can direct the scene in the way they remember it. The second time around, the patient will ask the other actors to play the scene as he would have *wanted it* to have happened, i.e. by providing a happy ending. What often becomes painfully obvious in exercises of this sort is, how poorly equipped many of these patients are in even having a good fantasy and in being able to direct others firmly to re-enact the rewarding rewrite of the original scene. Conversely, the patient who becomes silent and is visibly slipping away should be given a couple of minutes to do so, and then be asked "How old are you right now?" Usually we will get an answer of an approximate age. We should then proceed to ask the patient unintrusive but concrete questions such as "Is it winter or summer?" "What are you wearing?" "What do you see, hear, smell and who besides you is present?" Chances are that slowly a repressed memory will emerge, and with it, feelings of anger, hurt, or shame. Once the scene has been re-lived, it should be followed by the question: "Is there anything you could think of *now* that might have made things better?" For example, I have encountered several patients whose mothers punished them by locking them out of the house, often during the winter time when the children were not dressed for the cold. Patients who are reliving such a scene, including their desperate attempts of banging on the door in order to be let back in, may eventually realize that *today*—symbolically speaking—they would have the option of going to a neighbor's house. To picture themselves in front of a warm fire-place at a neighbor's house can be the beginning of two important psychic tasks: it counteracts the patient's sense of impotence; and it gives them a self-soothing fantasy that they can conjure up if they feel anxious and depleted. Lastly, patients who, under stress, cannot verbalize their experiences in any meaningful way, as for example many ambulatory schizophrenics, pose a particularly difficult problem because other means of communication will have to be found. Examples are drawings, paintings, music, sculpture, mime, even dance. When anxiety and emotional flooding are an everpresent danger and the patient has not yet learned to say "I'd rather not talk about this," or "please stop, I am drowning," we have to learn from such patients the meaning of their non-verbal signals of impending panic attacks. Alternatively we can instruct them to simply raise both hands, or to reach for a particular object or any other signal that has been mutually agreed upon. Such arrangements greatly add to the feeling of safety that, after all, is the prerequisite for any meaningful therapeutic work. Often, participating in a patient's silence—accepting the need to carve out private space—is more valuable than trying to figure out the meaning of the silence. Usually, the body language of the patient will tell us whether the silence represents a contented "being with" or a wish to be rescued from depression or regression.

By and large, during Phase I, however, the therapist's main job is to carefully and patiently listen to whatever material the patient chooses to bring into the session. Interpretations are avoided. Questions pertaining to actual events should be raised whenever the actual sequence of events are unclear. Confusion on the patient's part that are due to parents' mystifications—or outright lies—should be probed very gently. If they encounter resistance, they will have to be put aside until some later time. During the hatching phase, it could be quite devastating if we were to deprive patients of parental objects before they are ready to do so on their own. A premature critique of important love objects may leave a patient bereft—objectless—and can induce an unnecessary depression, resulting in the patient's wanting to give up. Only after we have become important and reliable objects in the patient's mind, can we risk to examine the family dynamics and family mystiques. All the major family skeletons, such as real or attempted matricide or patricide, rape, incest, child abuse and the like, are best left alone during Phase I unless the patient clearly wishes to examine them. Questions like, "How come you had an abortion at 14 when you don't even remember having had a boyfriend?" are an invitation for disaster. Phase I reaches its natural termination point when patients start to express their own sadism and overtly or covertly call the therapist's attention to it. How this signalling evolves will be shown in the case material below.

CASE MATERIAL

Karl

Karl spent the first eight months of therapy (close to 100 hours) primarily dealing with three subjects: his father's treatment of him; war memories; and his relationship with Tom. During this time he never missed a session, and he was never late. His demeanor—except for the duration of his psychotic episodes—was that of a passive, obedient, and fearful young man who most of the time found himself unable to understand what was happening around him and why. The common theme that linked the three subjects, war, father, and Tom, was Karl's inability to determine cause and effect and his seeming inability to distinguish between reality and fantasy. The bombings toward the end of the war were as unpredictable as his father's rages and he felt the same way about Tom's outbursts, which he quite subtly provoked with his passive-aggressive stance. For the longest time, he denied Tom's homicidal potential. At the same time, he was haunted by a childhood memory of having seen hundreds of slaughtered farm animals lying in pools of blood. Given the scarcity of food in 1945, he believed that this memory must have been a bad dream that, for some reasons, he could not shake. Yet it was so powerful, that every time he felt compelled to talk about it he ended up losing contact with reality. What Karl had seen was quite clear, namely the product of one of Hitler's last edicts that nothing but "scorched earth" was to be left to the enemy. This order included the butchering of all livestock before fleeing from the various advancing armies. The fact that Karl was assured that his memory was real, that it was planned rather than arbitrary, produced very ambivalent feelings in him. On one hand, he was quite relieved to know that his memory was not a hallucination, but on the other, he was terrified at the thought that perhaps many of his other nightmares had also a basis in reality. Living in a world where nothing makes sense, terrifying as this may be, also has its advantages, namely it relieves the actor of any responsibility for his own actions. It allowed Karl not to think about his two children as well as his input into the explosive relationship with Tom and his own inability to hold down a job. As it turned out, for many years to come, the "reality" of this particular memory became the high-water mark of Karl's ability to accept the continuity of his life and his own contributions to his fate.

During Phase I of the treatment of a schizophrenic patient, an extraordinarily delicate balance has to be maintained between too much insight (or rather reality testing) and enough contact with the realities of life to keep the patient out of trouble. Aside from the general objectives of treatment, patients like Karl often live under reality pressures that have to be dealt with first in order to make the pursuit of these objectives possible. Karl clearly had to be separated from Tom without further violence. After four months of treatment, however, the symbiotic tie between the two of them was as tight as ever. Although the intensity of their fights diminished, they also became more frequent. Since neither of them had any close friends or family to turn to, they clung primarily to each other, with the therapist in the role of the arbiter. Although this situation was a clear improvement over that of the past, it also limited any further progress. Since group therapy is contraindicated during Phase I, the therapist in such a situation has two choices: to wait it out, in the hope that both parties stay alive, and wait for the time when the symbiosis has run its course and dies on its own accord, (a risky proposition); or to take the calcu-lated risk of putting both parties into their own therapy groups. A tight-knit, well functioning group can always accommodate *one* schizophrenic member and in fact be quite protective of him or her. Moreover, if the patient can extend his fragile sense of trust to the group, it may help him or her separate from a malignant symbiosis. On the other hand, the fact that too much pressure is put on too fragile a psyche before the hatching process is completed, means that only under extraordinary circumstance should group be considered. In Karl's and Tom's case, I reluctantly took this gamble. The results were mixed. Karl "took to" group even though he spent many a session in stony silence and claimed that he disliked the group immensely. Tom made himself quickly the center of attention with his sharp wit and intelligence, and clearly aimed for the position of co-therapist. When Karl sensed Tom's interest in people other than himself, he exaggerated his passive aggressive stance. Tom, with the support of his group, slowly gave up on his "crazy lover." He became increasingly disgusted with Karl and three months later left him. Unfortunately, shortly after this separation he also left therapy and moved to another city, ostensibly to return to graduate school. (As of this date, he is in school and doing quite well.) Karl on the other hand, after the first shock had worn off, became quite depressed and despondent. He quit his part-time job and went on welfare and psychiatric disability. Since he was in the same group as Bob, he shifted his symbiotic needs onto him, and for a very short while, the two became secret lovers. This soon changed into an intense, but ambivalent, friendship.

Toward the end of the first year, Karl had come to trust me enough to also show some occasional signs of irritation with me and my work. He also became conscious of the importance that the other group members had for me and he expressed traces of jealousy. His passivity gave way to outbursts of anger which he, himself, found quite puzzling. His self concept as a perpetual victim, and the transition from Phase I to Phase II, however, came to an end in the following way: when his birthday approached, he very timidly informed me that he would like a little frog for a birthday present. I gave him a very large Steiff-type stuffed frog that surprised and delighted him. At first, he cherished this toy; he hugged it and slept with it. Shortly thereafter, however, the frog began first to annoy him and then to infuriate him. He alternated between throwing it from wall to wall, and embracing it. Eventually, he began to stomp on it, then pick it up again with an enormous sense of remorse only to repeat the sequence. In the course of two months, he admitted that the frog had been entirely torn to shreds. Needless to say, he was extremely distressed when he talked about this. Even though, his seeming "ingratitude" and inexplicable rages troubled him a lot, there was also a challenging tone to his voice when he related the story to me. He was cleary angry with me as well as with himself for having destroyed a valued birthday present and an upgraded symbolic self-representation (a funny frog instead of an ugly toad). There was no denying of cause and effect, no escaping from the realization that *he* had been the person responsible. What differentiates the transition crisis during which the patient moves from Phase I to Phase II is not the expression of sadism per se, but the combination of the patient's awareness of it and his need to call the therapist's attention to it. Although there had been plenty of evidence of Karl's sadism before this incident, particularly in his "humorous" cartoons portraying group and me which were so potentially explosive that I felt it necessary to carefully hide them, lest they fall into the wrong hands, I had deliberately refrained from commenting on their sadistic sexual content. Also, his involvement with Bob could be seen as defiance and as an attempt to destroy "the family." Although this may be objectively true, and certainly applies to Bob's motivation, I am convinced that for Karl this was not the main purpose. On the other hand, the attack on the frog was qualitatively different, since he, himself, identified the problem. When this happens with any sadomasochistic patient, it is vitally important that the therapist does not mystify the message by a noncommittal response, but gives a straightforward, unambiguous interpretation. In Karl's case, all that needed to be said was: "Given all the things that happened to you when you grew up, don't you think it is only natural that you became very angry as a child? And since you could not express this anger for fear of punishment, this anger is still with you. I am also very glad that you trust me enough to tell me how angry you are, so that we can now work on it."

Bob

After a very short honeymoon period of unmitigated idealization, Bob spent the first year of therapy by focusing on little else but his life-long victimizations by his father, sexual partners, school, former boss, roommate, friends and acquaintances. Unlike the other three patients, however, he seemed unable to accept anything but wholehearted approval. When I stated earlier that during phase I validation is what the patient needs, and therefore what the patient should get, that does *not* imply that the therapist should ever be dishonest—a toxic element under any circumstances—and thereby strengthen the victimized position. It is one thing to agree that having lost a job is hurtful, it is quite another to reiterate to the patient that he is totally innocent in having brought this situation about, particularly if the patient's provocations are patently obvious. Although Karl, Larry, and Anna never pressed the point about their own contributions to their calamities, Bob almost incessantly insisted on hearing my opinion, even though he sensed quite clearly how I felt about his deliberate self-destructiveness and his vendetta against the world. Patients like Bob, thereby, put the therapist in one of the most difficult situations imaginable. Like all help-rejecting complainers, they press for an honest response in order to either devalue it or to use as an excuse to leave therapy. A dishonest response will satisfy them for a while and then get them to the point where they end up dismissing the therapist for his or her dishonesty. To get around this double-bind, the therapist will have to try to focus as much as possible on the patient's childhood history where the victimization was indeed real. Although I generally feel very strongly that patients should be entirely in charge of their sessions, this is not always possible with patients like Bob. The therapist has to be quite directive in avoiding these head-on collisions that the patient is seeking, either by leading the patient back to similar events in childhood, or by encouraging them to express many of their feelings nonverbally. By that, I do not mean the ventilation of feelings, for that they need no prompting and it would be far too taxing for their fragile egos. What I mean is for example to suggest that the patient seek peace and comfort by lying down, holding on to a pillow or a blanket and gently rocking him- or herself. One can also suggest that the patient visualize one particularly happy place or event in his life and to recapture it in fantasy until he feels a little calmer. These maneuvers allow us to slip in some warmth and compassion—almost through the back door as it were—with the hope that the cumulative effect of this process will counteract the patient's bad faith and his paranoia. In Bob's case, this approach worked. By that, I mean that the positive elements of the transference outweighed the negative one's and that he stayed in therapy. On the other hand, his investment in indicting his father through his suffering was so strong that every productive session was followed by one of his nightly escapades to the S&M bars. He fought his depression with amphetamines and he soon gave up his attempts at finding a job. When his unemployment benefits ran out, he went on welfare and psychiatric disability. The very process of applying for these social services in New York City, however, is quite humiliating and depressing under any circumstances, and Bob responded with unneutralized rage, alternating with severe depressive states. Since his shame over his external circumstances also resulted in isolation from the few friends that he had, the rule about the contraindication of group therapy during Phase I also had to be broken. His feelings about group were as ambivalent as his feelings about the therapist, but his bond with Karl who also went through the process of applying for welfare and psychiatric disability, gave Bob an ally in his misery. Although Karl welcomed Bob's friendship and his help in dealing with the welfare bureaucracy, Bob used Karl for the purpose of hostile subgrouping. His seduction of Karl was deliberate, and in its intent, outright sadistic. Since he did not talk about it, and since he had sworn Karl to secrecy, I sensed what was going on but was unable to act on my intuition directly. A few months after Karl's destruction of the frog, Bob visited Karl and after an evening of heavy drinking, Bob called me at 2 a.m. with the message that unless I got to Karl's place immediately, "I would have two corpses on my hands." Obviously, Bob had talked Karl into a suicide pact and then had gotten scared. When I got there, Karl was almost catatonic and Bob, though still drunk, was quite subdued. While I arranged for Karl's hospitalization, I sent Bob home with strict orders to stay put until I could see him early the following morning. If Bob had not shown signs of genuine remorse and shame over his actions, it would not have been possible to continue treatment. His encounter with his own sadism and his irresponsibility, however, had been so blatant that even he was unable to rationalize it out of existence. He had fully expected to be condemned by group and to be thrown out of therapy. When this did not happen, when he had his first glimpse of understanding of the difference between justified criticism and merciless condemnation, he was able to slightly redefine for himself what the terms "help" and "psychotherapy" really mean. Even though he was still craving for unconditional admiration and acceptance, this demand was no longer as unconditional as it had been.

Larry

Larry, after his dramatic first session, applied himself almost for an entire year single-mindedly to the task of dealing with the image of his father. From the beginning, he had defined my office and me as an intensive care unit, the only safe place that he knew. Transferentially, I was the all-powerful mother of earliest infancy, and he projected all her frustrating aspects onto his father. To be more precise, transferentially I was neither a woman nor a person, but an environment. This became so very clear when, after three months of seeing him, I moved my office. Larry's main concern was whether I would take my pillows and my soft rug with me. As long as he was assured that the "playpen" would be restored, he was untroubled by the move.

During each and every session, after first greeting my dog like a long lost friend or a favored child, he replayed the same scenario over and over again: he imagined his father as sitting in my office and he accused him of not having loved him as a boy. Usually, he would do this kneeling on the floor in front of a stack of pillows. Having run through his accusations, he would switch to pleading and he always ended up crying bitterly while embracing the very pillows he had just beaten. During all of these sessions, he was entirely unself-conscious, he merely asked me for a cue with which to begin the sessions and he proceeded from there, asking nothing more of me than my undivided attention. At the rate of once every two weeks, he politely berated me for my power and my unavailability during his times of need, i.e. his sleepless nights. During the entire time, however, he was never late, or missed a session, and he did whatever I told him to do. In short, a model-child, with two exceptions: he refused to approach any of his problems verbally; and he was altogether unwilling to deal with any subject other than his father. The rest of his family was not yet a subject for discussion. Whenever he believed a session had been particularly helpful—as measured by the quantity of tears shed—he would express his gratitude toward me by sharing his luncheon sandwich with Giulietta. As a matter of fact, he solemnly promised, that when I had succeeded in curing him completely, he would buy Giulietta a whole steak.

Although Larry very forcefully determined the content of every session, including its non-verbal nature, he was able, once he was through crying, to absorb many of my suggestions about how to deal with his insomnia and his unruly penis. Instead of fighting the demands of his body, he slowly learned to indulge it, by taking long luxurious baths with lots of bath oil, he bought his own pillows to hug, and spent as much time as possible walking around naked in his apartment since the pressure of his pants was often unbearably painful. In other words, he slowly learned those self-soothing activities that allowed him to function and sleep more peacefully. From the beginning of treatment, he had been unduly concerned about the fact that he needed Valium to go to sleep. Each two milligram tablet required a major struggle that consisted of two components: his unconscious longing for a more empathic mother than the one he had had, and a conscious battle with the expressed values of his father who frowned upon any form of self-indulgence. The fact that each month his father sent him a check to pay for his therapy gave him a profound—though vengeful—sense of satisfaction. At long last, he had the power to "punish the cold bastard for his sins."

Toward the end of the first year, when his hysterical symptoms had receded markedly, and had more-or-less weaned himself from the use of Valium, Larry became somewhat restless. It seemed that much of the backlog of rage against his father had been spent, or rather that his displacement of his rage against the preoedipal mother onto the father, was no longer working for him. One day he announced rather pointedly that even though he knew that whenever I left on a trip where I could not take Giulietta with me, and had to park her with friends, he could never see himself taking care of her. He was too afraid that "something terrible or fatal" could happen to her. Since Giulietta's care had never been an issue, Larry was clearly using this question to tell me something else: namely that the time had come to deal with his real problems. He was letting both of us know, that he had become aware of the fact that he, himself, had internalized the father he had been raging against. This interpretation Larry accepted sadly but without dispute.

Anna

Anna also all but cried herself through the first nine months of therapy. Unlike Bob and Larry, however, she showed no signs of anger against anybody or anything except herself. She was quite clear about the fact that her lover exploited her ruthlessly, but she believed it was she who was to blame for having been involved with him in the first place. Moreover, she was a "home wrecker." She felt enormously guilty toward her lover's "poor neglected wife" who, in reality, conducted a string of extramarital affairs herself and—unlike Anna—enjoyed them thoroughly. Also, Anna had no illusions about her mother's mistreatment of her, which had consisted of two components: a relentless persecution of Anna's physical and emotional needs, her alleged chubbiness, inquisitive intelligence, and later her budding sexuality; and demands that Anna play her mother's confidante and little helper in ways that the little girl was totally unequipped to do. Nothing Anna ever did was good enough. Praise was all but unknown to her. Recalling these injustices—or at least the top layer of them, since the depth and the thoroughness of the persecution did not emerge until later—evoked hurt rather than anger. The profound conviction that somehow she had to be at fault was so deeply ingrained that she felt only pain. Intellectually, she understood that there had to be a great deal of anger but she was unable to feel it. What compounded her misery, was the fact that in her adult life she felt like such a failure. Her marriage had not worked, she knew that she had continuously chosen bad love objects, she often drank alcohol, and at times, clearly too much, she used Valium, and also found herself forever incapable of living a smooth and well-ordered life. Even though she was highly regarded at her job, the actual therapeutic gains that can be made with the families of drug addicts are by definition rather circumscribed. True to form, she blamed herself for that also.

Even though I tried to give Anna what can only be described as wall-to-wall support, she could only accept a tiny fraction of it. During those times where she literally needed a shoulder to cry on, she worried about the effect of her tears on my sweater. Tissues were used as sparingly as possible and she always made sure that she collected all the tissues she had used and put them into her handbag rather than dirty my office. The occasional offer of a cup of tea was welcome; from a therapeutic point of view, however, she considered it inappropriate. The fee she had agreed on was too high since I had made the mistake of not asking her about her actual take-home pay. Thus, she secretly, but bitterly, resented my "exploitation of her misery." It took her almost a year to discuss this point with me. She had also agreed to see me at hours that were extremely difficult for her to keep. This particular secret only came to light when I had asked her repeatedly why she always arrived at my office totally out of breath, and she seemed almost disappointed when I offered her hours that were more convenient for her. Anna's unhappiness was in so many ways circular: she could not break away from her lover, she suffered from his humiliations, and then condemned herself for her moral failings and spinelessness. Step-by-step, however, she succeeded in removing at least some of the sources of her daily harrassments and reluctantly managed to add some creature comforts to her life. Since this process seemed so excruciatingly slow and difficult for her, I decided to give her a female doll with the suggestion that she treat the doll as she herself would have liked to have been treated as a child. She seemed quite pleased with this project, but after several weeks of trying to follow my suggestions, she told me with a great deal of embarrassment that she felt very angry every time she looked at the doll. Consequently, she had locked the doll into a dark closet and tried to forget about the suggestion, which in her mind had grown into an assignment—an additional duty. Compared to Karl's treatment of the frog, Anna's response to the doll was seemingly benign. The difference, however, was only quantitative. When Anna talked about her "failure" to care for the doll, she started to remember that one of her mother's standard punishments of her as a very small child had consisted of either locking her in the basement, or, worse yet, out of the house regardless of the weather and without having dressed her for the cold. Even Anna could see that such treatment borders on child abuse, and for the first time her anger emerged in full force and she was able to attack the pillows. With the recognition of her own internalized bad mother and her (Anna's) rage against her, Phase I came to an end. Anna's life then started to change quite drastically. Within one week of her having beaten the pillows, she separated from her lover.

Chapter 7

PHASE II:

Symbiosis, or: "Make It All Good Again"

The symbiotic phase of infantile development is characterized by the infant's growing awareness that mother and child are not one and the same person. The illusion of omnipotent control is slowly disrupted by the intermittent awareness that the satisfaction of needs is dependent on another who can be slowly substituted by transitional objects. Much of what has been said about ego development in the previous chapter (with respect to the libidinal ego and the emergence of the anti-libidinal ego that develops in response to frustration) also holds true for the symbiotic phase. The gradual awareness of the otherness of the mother, however, now poses problems with respect to the experience of rage at the maternal object—or rather part object—which is in conflict with the fear of losing that part object. This is the central dilemma during this stage and the major source of anxiety. Guntrip (1961) has proposed—though without giving a timetable for this—that the anti-libidinal ego constitutes a fusion of the angry sadistic responses *to* the other and the hostility *of* the other that presumably is introjected or incorporated. In terms of explaining how the sadism of the object becomes the masochism of the subject at this stage of development, it seems sufficient to state that the baby simply has no way of externalizing "bad universe" and "bad me" experiences, and that they continue to reside in the psyche. This process, however, will interfere with the infant's ability to fuse good and bad self and object representations, and will manifest itself later in defensive splitting, i.e. the inability to ascribe good and bad attributes to the same object. The bad universe experiences may or may not result in a physical symptom. If they do, and if the symptom results in intense and pleasurable maternal care, it would be reasonable to speculate that a pattern of somatization is established. We can probably view this as an archaic example or illustration of sensorimotor intelligence—the baby's problem solving ability—one which the body will continue to remember as bringing relief.

Primary narcissism, under optimal conditions, finds its sustenance in the famous gleam in the mother's eyes. In its absence, the grandiose conception of the self finds insufficient reinforcement. To the extent that the mother is experienced as an other, she is idealized as the source of all power and all life giving supplies. If the mother is consistently unempathic, the age-appropiate dependence on the magic of gestures and signals on the child's part will be frustrated, and this will interfere with the development of a rudimentary sense of self. Moreover, the continued absence of maternal soothing prevents the child from internalizing these functions and to slowly learn to soothe itself. The body self is not experienced primarily as a source of pleasure but, very often, as an enemy that will be later consciously or unconsciously attacked in various ways. What Stern (1938) observed and described in his adult patients as "organic insecurity" probably dates to that period of infantile development. What all of this means is that the infant emerges from the symbiotic phase with the dim awareness that survival and pleasure cannot be taken for granted, but that they must be extracted from the environment through manipulation and sacrifice.

The patient who has experienced less than optimal mothering, rejection and neglect during this phase, will be characterized by an ambivalence between the attempt at omnipotent control and the exercise of a form of pseudo-self-sufficiency. Transitional objects tend to be substitutes rather than truly soothing objects. The repertoire of genuinely self-soothing activities is limited or even absent. All psychic structures and the emergent self are vulnerable to fragmentation under traumatic conditions and object hunger is intense.

The patient who has successfully "hatched" in the therapeutic encounter, however, will enter Phase II of the treatment, hopefully with the accumulation of enough "good me" experiences to be equipped to deal with the repair work that is to take place during this phase of treatment. If all has gone well during Phase I, the patient enters Phase II with the following therapeutic gains:

1. A modicum of trust in the therapist has been established. The extent of that trust, however, varies with the degree of ego impairment, the patient's ability to utilize transitional experiences (Modell, 1968; 1963) and transitional objects, and the patient's capacity for maintaining object constancy.

2. The patient believes that since the therapist knows most of the salient facts about his life, he is, therefore, in a position to help.

3. He will have accumulated a small repertoire of self-soothing and anxiety relieving mechanisms that he can call on when he feels badly. This includes phone calls to the therapist and to friends and the ability to risk asking for an extra session. In other words, the patient who previously reacted to traumatic events with despair will now be more likely to turn to others.

The transition from Phase I to Phase II constitutes perhaps the most dramatic shift in the patient-therapist interaction. This shift has the following components:

1. The change from a more-or-less self-absorbed monologue to a dialogue.

2. The recognition that this fixture opposite the patient is a very special and important person to the patient.

3. The patient has begun to trust and depend on this person and has invested it with enormous powers.

4. The awareness of his own potential for sadism has been noted; and

5. The therapist is blamed for these changes and is therefore expected to remedy them, "to make it all good again."

Put in a nutshell, the inner dialogue with which the patient enters Phase II goes something like the following: "You have brought me to this point of questioning my values, my self concept, my fatalism and my identity. Since these changes in my inner life are all *your* fault and *your* doing, you better fix it for me. This is all your ball game."

The recognition on the part of these patients that they, themselves, in many ways have become the parent they have been raging against, is a very painful and often shame-provoking experience. And because of its hurtful nature, this glimmer of insight will increase the patient's dependency rather than decrease it. Although self-doubts are hardly a new experience in the life of such patients, this one is qualitatively different from the ones with which they are familiar. To doubt one's abilities, intelligence, charm, beauty, and lovability is one thing. To discover powerful strange internal objects in one's psyche feels like a betrayal of one part of the psyche for the other, is another. The realization that the mind that one has grown accustomed to as one entity is, in fact, a whole Shakespearean drama over which one has seemingly no control, induces a profound sense of helplessness. Consequently, the patient's feelings toward the therapist are now highly ambivalent and strongly charged with rage, shame, dependency, and object hunger. Thus, the key concepts during Phase II are tact, empathy, and compassion. The main task confronting the therapist during this phase is to convey to the patient that we can deal with *all* parts of the patient's psyche *including* the ugly introjects that the patient would prefer to either disavow, project onto the therapist or the rest of the world. In this process, in which the patient often feels bombarded by narcissistic injuries, the therapist will have to find ways of diffusing the extremes of the patient's transferential love and hate in order to prevent head-on collisions that might prompt the patient to act out or to despair.

One of the greatest difficulties encountered in Phase II is the inevitable power-struggle between the patient who feels that the changes in his self-concept is the therapist's "fault,"—and, therefore, the therapist's responsibility—and the therapist's stance that it is the patient, himself, who has made these discoveries about his parental introjects and identifications. It has been my experience that no matter how tactful the therapist may be in pointing out the patients' contributions to their fate, the struggle with shame and guilt will take a very heavy toll on the patients' still immature ego's, particularly since they naturally assume that nobody else in the entire world has such "dirty secrets." Although I would not go so far as to say that during this phase group therapy is an absolute must, I, for one, have found it the single most useful tool, not only for the diffusion of the extremes of the transferential love and hate, but also because a group can function as a second family and as a social support system. Life in large metropolitan centers is anomic enough even for people whose capacity to relate to others has not been severely impaired. Most important, however, is the fact that for the sadomasochistic patient, shame and guilt are the main stumbling blocks during the symbiotic phase. Consequently, it is immensely helpful for a patient who feels flooded by his encounter with his own sadism, to know that he is not the only "monster" in the room, and that the "monster" is still loved and accepted. Once the patient has understood the difference between "being all bad" and acting badly, he is ready to enter Phase III of the treatment, namely, individuation and separation, which is aimed at teaching the patients to assume responsibility for their own actions and fates.

TREATMENT GOALS AND OBJECTIVES

First of all in order to avoid misunderstandings, it has to be pointed out, that following the transition crisis from Phase I to Phase II, the changes in the therapeutic interaction that take place, drastic as they may be, do take place gradually. The patients, themselves, will see to it that the shift in emphasis remains as gradual as they need it to be. Since I firmly believe that the content of any individual session is entirely the patient's responsibility, the changes that are discussed in this chapter, are changes that essentially the patients, themselves, will make. The therapist, who until then has been essentially a party to a monologue, will now be asked to be more active in his or her investigations of the relationships between the material reported in Phase I and the events taking place in the present. Although we can be more active than before, it is usually the wiser course to take if we can wait until the patient asks us whether we can make any sense out of what is happening in his life.

The treatment goals of Phase II are the following: 1. Since we assume that the age-appropriate attempts at omnipotent control frequently met with failure, rejection, and shame, the patient has to be taught the difference between conscious control of the environment and one's fate and omnipotence. 2. Infantile grandiosity and exhibitionism have to be gradually transformed into the desire for genuine mastery, even though most of that work will be done in Phase III. 3. Patients will slowly learn that life is, indeed, a series of cause and effect relationships; that things never "just happened" but that life events have causes and that actions have consequences. 4. Since self loathing is a highly developed trait in the sadomasochist, the task just mentioned, can only be accomplished, if we consistently attempt to bolster the patient's self esteem by genuine expressions of respect, empathy, and compassion. Solid praise for each step taken and the expression of pride in the patient's accomplishments in therapy are a sine qua non for further progress.

Concretely during Phase II, we should try to teach the patient to examine the arranged victimizations in the present in light of the imposed victimizations in the past and how these early childhood experiences set the patient on the troubled route of recreating them over and over again and each time with the hope that *this time* the object can be forced to react differently. Since each such failure at omnipotent control is experienced as a narcissistic injury, it will, thus, tempt the patient to run his head against the proverbial stone wall, only to fail again because the investment in the perfection of the self or, alternatively, in the changeability of the parental other, is still too powerful to give up. Throughout these repeated cycles, the feelings of despair, helplessness, rage, shame, and guilt have to be counteracted and synthesized. Moreover, the more masochistically-inclined patient will typically react to each piece of insight self-punitively, while the more sadistically-inclined patient will react either with massive denial, projection, or expressions of more-or-less unneutralized rage directed either at the therapist or the people in his immediate environment. After all, it has to be remembered that during Phase II, patients have little or no sense of the fact that they have options—when they reach that point, they have entered Phase III—for the time being and particularly after the transition crisis, they experience their psyche as minefields. Consequently, anxiety will induce them time and again to return to the safe heaven of Phase I. The combination of the insights into their sadistic potential and the sensitization to their own suffering that developed during Phase I, however, will prompt them to go back to work on their troubles. It is usually a disturbing dream or an upsetting event that forces them to do that. A typical sequence may be the following: the patient may start out the hour with complaints about how unappreciated he feels. The therapist who during Phase I would have mostly validated the patient's feelings will now want to determine whether the patient is dealing with a narcissistic injury, i.e. either an unrealistic craving for being noticed and valued, or, alternatively, a pathological hypersensitivity to real or imagined criticisms. The third possibility is that it constitutes a masochistic approach to ordinary life situations. If this complaint constitutes primarily a narcissistic injury, it will have to be dealt with by comparing the ways in which the parents responded to the child's grandiosity and exhibitionism in early childhood. Instead of merely commiserating with the patient, however, the therapist will now take an active stance and suggest ways in which patients can either get some appreciation some place else, or, more important, give it to themselves. The reaction to such a suggestion is usually rage: "You are just as bad as my parents." This turn of events should then lead to a discussion of the ways in which a patient does not hear the positive responses given to him, or how he actively elicits negative responses. Whatever insights are gained, helpful as they may be, they also produce a sense of helplessness and despair. At that point, it is vitally important that the therapist actively tries to intervene when the patient concludes that, "My parents are right—I am indeed no good," by offering compassion for a childhood history that resulted in such self-damaging behavior. Throughout Phase II, the therapist will have to repeat over and over that actions may be ineffective and/or reprehensible, but that what the patient suffers from is not a "rotten soul" but rather, a "poverty of behavioral resources." (Becker 1965) If, however, the original complaint about the lack of appreciation, rather than representing primarily a narcissistic disturbance, is what I have come to call "the harrassed housewife syndrome," namely the man or woman who, "having worked their fingers to the bone" because "If I don't do things, nothing ever gets done around here," and, thus, feel forever unappreciated, then both the desperate need for appreciation and the somewhat sadistic and controlling ways of obtaining it, have to be examined. This will slowly make sense, since patients may have vaguely noticed that their way of functioning will earn them a position of feeling or being indispensible, but not much respect and much less love. Alternatively, the complaint may come from a patient who has done everything in his or her power to appease and seduce a sadistic love object, or one who has provoked a benign one to act sadistically. In either case, the hidden agenda will have to be examined, and it will be traced back to the child's habitual ways of obtaining attention through either suffering or provocation. Furthermore, since self and object representations are still blurred, deliberate efforts have to be made to point out time and again that despite the evidence of interpersonal failures, there are also successes that are not due to the qualities of the other, but the patient's own conscious efforts.

One of the most difficult subjects during Phase II is the relationship with the actual parents. Patients who have had little or no contact with parents when they entered treatment will now turn to them again with a renewed zest. Usually, this is done for the purpose of testing their new insights, to gather more information, and to confirm—or change—their views of them. The testing of new insights, is usually based on the proposition that maybe, if they, with their new insights, and perhaps some newly acquired humility, approach their parents differently, all will be well. Depending on the degree of pathology of the parents themelves, however, two possible outcomes are likely to occur. 1. Patients may discover that nothing has changed, that their parents are just as critical, rejecting, self involved, or double-binding as they always were. 2. Less disturbed parents may respond more positively than they did in the past. Since the quest of patients during Phase II is still one for unilateral love and adulation appropriate for the infant during the symbiotic phase, however, they will not be satisfied. Thus, either way, the encounters are bound to be disappointing, and for some time the patient returns to the victimized position and will probably regress temporarily to the hatching phase.

Similarly, excursions designed to gather information may be equally disappointing. The family who operates cognitively primarily through mystification is still infinitely better equipped to defend their reality than the patient who has just begun to study some of its facets. Thus, they will return from each parental encounter thoroughly defeated and angry because nothing has been clarified. Their feeling, that they have again been had, will probably produce a profound sense of rage or depression since it intensified their sense of utter impotence. In this case, too, regression to Phase I is all but inevitable. The more sadistically-inclined patient who approaches his family in order to indict them and to confirm his negative view of them may wind up finding just that. One of my young male patients, a former alcoholic, approached his alcoholic father with the question, "What did it feel like to have been a child abuser?" and he wound up very abused, indeed, and, in response to the beating he received, went on a drinking binge that later required his hospitalization. The therapist's responsibility here is two-fold: 1. to discourage, if not the visits themselves, at least the unrealistic expectations that accompany them; and 2. to respond sympathetically to the patient's hurt, rage, sense of shame, and defeat. Needless to say, a response which implies "I told you so," can only make things worse and undermine the shaky trust that has been built during the course of therapy. If anything, we should try to counteract a premature devaluation of the parental other, without whom the patient might feel too bereft. Patients' statements such as, "My parents never loved me, they gave me no affection at all" have to be modified with the reminder that they certainly did not get what they needed, but that somebody gave them enough to muddle through. The good memories have to be ferreted out and cherished. Since obviously, they had not died of infantile miasma, the real problem is that they got enough to have had a taste of love, and, therefore, want more. In the case of patients who suffered from an unusual amount of neglect or abuse, and who still came through with less damage than what could be expected, it is important that during Phase II patient and therapist together, search for what might be called "the hidden caretaker." This may be a forgotten maid, an older relative, a sibling, a neighbor, teacher, or even a pet. The fact that patients may not remember having particularly loved these hidden caretakers, does not mean that they did not, in fact, depend on them very much. Their memories are focused on the unavailable or rejecting parent, rather than the steady presence of the accepting caretaker. The enrollment of the "hidden caretaker" is an invaluable maneuver in counteracting premature object loss.

Since shame and guilt play such an important role in the therapy of the sadomasochistic patient, and since they are particularly troublesome during Phase II, it is important that the therapist is fully aware of what these two feeling states really represent. In distinguishing shame and guilt, Alexander states:

> Shame is a reaction to feeling weak, ineffective, or inferior to others. The psychological reaction to shame is the opposite to that of guilt: it stimulates aggressiveness. To get rid of shame an individual has to prove that he is not weak and can beat the person who shamed him. Shame is such a primitive reaction that even animals exhibit it; but guilt feelings can arise only after an individual has acquired a conscience that is to say, after he has incorporated the moral values of his environment. (1924, p. 370)

In other words, guilt is a superego function, while shame is a much more archaic one, that evokes the wish for archaic forms of retaliation, such as plucking out the very eyes which saw our humiliation. It is perhaps the single most powerful emotion in the human experience. Nobody wants to die from guilt, but wanting to die from shame is quite common. Shame pertains to our being, while guilt pertains to doing; consequently as Block Lewis (1971) has pointed out, guilt calls and allows for reparations, although no such recourse is available for the feeling of shame, except to eliminate the person who shamed us or was witness to our shame. Since the rage toward the shaming agent is often blocked by love, guilt, or fear, the person experiencing the shame has no alternative but to redirect the rage against the self. It is the total self, however, rather than an event or an action that is the focus of the shame experience. Consequently, if the full extent of the fury were to be unleashed, suicide (or homicide) would be the only logical outcome. And, indeed, much of the suicidal ideation of sadomasochistic patients during this phase is rooted in shame. This shame is usually evoked by the sense of betrayal, discussed earlier, where the patient experiences his or her sadistic introjects that seem to have a life of their own and which give the patient the feeling that they are no longer in control—they are no longer masters in their own house. The often enormous sensitivity to narcissistic injuries also predisposes the sadomasochistic patient to strong feelings of shame.

The therapist who mistakes shame for guilt, and who reacts to feelings of shame as if they were merely superego functions, will seriously misread the patient who now, in addition to the shame experience, also has to cope with the therapist's lack of empathy, i.e. with feeling truly misunderstood. The resulting rage is not so much an unforgiving reaction to the therapist's mistake but a seemingly legitimate way to discharge the shame-based rage.

In the case of the sexual sadomasochist, it is precisely his ability to suspend or split off the superego functions that allows him to pursue his activities without shame or guilt and to employ the rationalization that since no harm has been done to another person, there is nothing for which to feel guilty. The fact that a patient may not feel any shame over these activities, however, does not mean that no shame is present; it is disavowed and will emerge eventually and forcefully. In fact, one of the common reasons for splitting off the feeling of shame, is that if it were felt, it would be too insurmountable, and it would conflict with the false bravado that is so typical for the sexual sadomasochist. When dealing with shame in therapy, we, the therapists, automatically become one of the objects of the patient's wrath. Block Lewis (1971) made the brilliant observation that:

> The therapist, who cannot help being witness to the patient's shame experiences is automatically an object to the patient's humiliated fury, which is likely to be either bypassed or unacknowledged. It is a repetition of past relationships to parental and other figures who witnessed humiliations. It is, however, not only a repetition of the past, but a concurrent phenomenon of the present artificial, therapeutic relationship. *It cannot be totally analyzed away* by showing its resemblance to the past, and the question 'Why be ashamed of being in treatment?' makes it easier to endure treatment, but can also increase the patient's shame of being ashamed, thereby leaving a residue of unanalyzed symptom source. (p. 58) (emphasis mine)

Although dealing with shameful experiences in group therapy will not eliminate this "symptom source," it can dilute it and thus, make it easier for the patient and therapist alike. After all, to be the sole agent in the provocation of such intensely painful emotions may well induce counter-transferential guilt.

TRANSFERENCE

The major characteristics of the transference during Phase II are the following: 1. Its intensity, the attachment to the therapist as the all-powerful other is profounder than it was before and will be in Phases III and IV; 2. Rapid alternations between transferential love and hate; 3. A power-struggle over the question as to who is now responsible for the patient's life and well being; and 4. Fear of object loss. If we define the term resistance and its corollary, the nature of the transference as the patient's need to maintain the continuity of his or her identity, it would follow that the transition crisis from Phase I to Phase II, mobilizes powerful negative elements into the transference situation. Having discovered their potential for sadism, seriously challenges the patients' familiar identification with the victimized position and it leaves patients with two options: to either devalue the therapist, blame him for this "lapse"; or to devalue the self and cling to the therapist as the magician who can "make it all good again." The more powerful the tendency toward self-blame—the masochistic stance—the more pronounced the sense of helplessness and, thus, the clinging attachment to the idealized therapist. Consequently, fear of loss of love object and/or fear of object loss becomes a very real and sometimes overriding concern during Phase II. "How can you like me if I am that bad?" is the question that crops up over and over again, which forever puts the therapist in the role of the potentially rejecting parent. For example, the patient who during Phase I may have been quite oblivious or "reasonable" about the therapist's vacations as long as standbys were available, now begins to take the absence of the therapist quite personally. "You may need a vacation from me, but I cannot function without you" is essentially the bind such patients find themselves in. They may harbor the suspicion that it is their "badness" that drove the therapist away—their wish for omnipotent control—and they may either try to reestablish the symbiosis by being "good" so that the therapist does not *want* to leave them, or, alternatively, present themselves as so helpless, so surrounded by impending crises that the therapist *cannot* in good conscience leave them to their own devices. Larry, for example, when he realized that he had failed on both counts, finally dealt with my vacation during this time quite ingeniously by sending himself to summer camp as a drama coach. Thus, he could maintain the illusion that *I* stayed home and that *he* was leaving *me* as all normal children do during the summer.

The more sadistically-inclined patients will attack the therapist whenever their identity is challenged or threatened. It is done in two interrelated ways: 1. Devalue the therapist's skill, competence, understanding, and values. Their own sadism is rationalized as self-preservation in a world that is characterized by the law of the jungle, a fact the simple-minded therapist has not yet grasped. 2. If this maneuver fails, attempts are made to entice the therapist to participate in unethical practices that are designed to force the therapist into a twin-relationship. This double-pronged approach is exemplified with the following vignette: Session one: the patient stated that it had come to her attention, via the grapevine, that I often had sexual relationships with my patients. This did *not* represent a sexualization of the transference but an attempt to devalue my ethics and self-esteem. Having cleared this issue up as best I could, she proceeded to provoke a terrible, hair-pulling fist fight with her lover which resulted in a temporary breakup of the relationship. In the next session, she was deeply depressed and despondent and alternately questioned the value of my therapeutic approach and the possibility of ever finding a worthwhile lover in this wicked world. In this hour, I was not invited to participate or help. In the third session, she demanded that I give her a written statement for her insurance company indicating that her emotional troubles were the result of an accident which she had suffered prior to entering therapy. This request represented the kind of dishonesty that was quite typical of her parents' life style. When I refused, she became extremely abusive and spiteful. The impasse was only broken when she could see that the entire sequence of events had been designed to discredit me in order to maintain the continuity of her life experience and her identity. Moreover, I told her that her overt demand for my participation in a fraudulent scheme was really a covert but desperate plea for a trustworthy object to rely upon in order to risk changes in her own sense of self and her expectations of others. A radiant smile confirmed the accuracy of this interpretation, though it did not constitute the last of those kinds of battles.

Since the examination of the family romance and of current love relationships tends to loosen the bonds between the patient and his past as well as that with his present significant others, the dependency on the therapist's magical powers is intensified. Although the analysis of the patient's family dynamics are alternately disturbing and liberating, they are, nevertheless, for a long time quite confusing. Thus, patients hope—and fear—that the therapist knows much more about the actual family dynamics than they do. This assumption produces both trust and distrust. The statement: "I am glad you know what is going on, because I surely don't," is quite typical for the ambivalent relationship to the therapist's real or attributed understanding of the patients internal conflicts and hidden agendas. The underlying fear of course is that eventually the therapist will "unmask" the patient, discover his "rottenness" and confirm the feeling that everything all along was entirely the patient's fault.

What all of these transferential elements add up to is a power struggle that revolves around the concept that the therapist, as the all-powerful other, is capable of changing the patient's life without them really taking responsibility for their lives. Emergency phone calls and demands for extra sessions are therefore quite common and should be responded to non-judgmentally. For one, because patients during Phase II are still quite incapable of seeing us as separate persons with limited schedules and ordinary needs for rest and food, but also because these requests for extra sessions are prompted by two elements: 1. The actual event that triggered the emotional tail-spin in the first place; and 2. The enormous disappointment that even though they are *in therapy* with such an omnipotent therapist they can still get into considerable trouble. The fact that at least some of these emergencies are designed for no other reason than to test the powers of the therapist *in order to fail* him or her is an insight that will take a long time to penetrate. Until patients have achieved a modicum of autonomy and separateness, they can only cast the therapist into two possible roles: the magician who does for them or the rejecting, disappointing parent.

The length to which patients will go in demonstrating their helplessness and the extent of their disappointment varies of course with the degree of ego-impairment. Ambulatory schizophrenics like Karl can respond with escapes into psychosis that may last anywhere from a couple of minutes to several days. The therapist will have to trust that given a consistently supportive but unalarmed response, such patients will eventually find more constructive ways of dealing with their disappointments. Treating psychotic episodes as a matter of choice, albeit a poor one given the general ambience of most mental institutions, is, in my view, the only appropriate response since it does not mystify the nature of the interaction. Moreover, we are saying to the patient that he or she is not "going crazy" but "acting crazy" and, thereby, exercising the only power that they feel they have. If patients truly believe that short-term hospitalization is the only way in which they can protect themselves—and others—from their self-destructive or homicidal impulses, this option will have to be respected.

Although escape into psychosis represents an extreme, the negative transference reactions of the less-disturbed patients are, in their motivation and interpersonal meaning, quite similar: namely attempts to force the therapist into the role of the omnipotent parent who is indicted for failing by the patient's failures. Underneath Larry's and Anna's overt idealization and obedient responses to my suggestions, therapy and the therapist were secretly devalued. Although they seemingly did what they were told, much of it was done to prove that none of it made any difference anyway. More specifically, the conscientious pursuit of one set of goals is often used to sabotage the pursuit of another equally important goal. In a similar vein, suggestions offered by the therapist are deliberately misunderstood and carried out in such a way that they spell failure or injury. One particularly harrassed and overworked young woman who left my office with an extensive list of self-soothing items and activities obediently bought all the ingredients for a luxurious bubble-bath cum snack session that was designed to relieve her enormous inner tensions, promptly tripped on the subway stairs and broke her ankle. With her ankle in a cast she was unable to either take a bath or come to therapy for more than four weeks.

The transference situation in the case of impulsive borderline structures like Bob, is particularly difficult because such a major part of their identity is tied with their need to devalue. If one asks such patients who they are and what they stand for, the answers will be almost entirely in negative terms. They will tell us whom they despise, what people they have nothing in common with, what ideas, political systems, and social institutions they believe should be fought by them, etc. Thus, the constant question put to the therapist is the following: "Are you for or against me? Prove that you are not in the enemy camp." Since that quest can never be satisfied, these patients are singularly handicapped in taking in any of the kind and accepting responses offered to them. This negativistic stance toward therapy, coupled with a readiness to act out impulsively and destructively, produces one therapeutic impasse after another. When Bob during one of his nightly escapades picked up a psychotic sadist who gave him more than he had bargained for, he swore up and down that he had no idea that the man had been so disturbed. Moreover, he believed that this was just additional evidence that in the gay world no love is to be found and therefore, he might as well quit trying. Only several years later, did he admit, that on some level he knew exactly what he was doing—that he had in fact practically "smelled" the psychotic potential. Secretly, and in part unconsciously, he believed that it was entirely within my powers to find him the ideal lover, and to introduce them. During this time, Bob was so conflicted about his need to devalue all objects and to cynically destroy every element of hope. At the same time he conveyed such an extraordinarily intense object hunger with every body movement and with the most devouring looks I have ever encountered, that he created an almost unbearably intense atmosphere in the room. Although his whole body expressed ravenous hunger, every word spoken communicated the opposite, namely the concept that hope in a heartless world is self-destruction. The conflict between his oral greed and his oral rage eventually became so powerful that he could no longer tolerate individual sessions and chose to settle for group therapy only. This decision was, in part, motivated by intense envy; he wanted everything he thought I had, and was terrified of his growing impulse to swallow up or destroy his therapist. Although dealing with an "ungiving" mother was too hard for him, group also represented a major threat, namely his eight hungry siblings. Thus, he was torn between the impulse to contemptuously leave the field and to do competitive battle; fortunately, the competitive side of the conflict won out.

TECHNIQUES

The major therapeutic tool during Phase II is the interpretation of the way in which early introjects and identifications determine the patient's interactions with significant others and the therapist. Depending on the material that the patient brings in, this work will focus on childhood history, current involvements, dreams, and the dynamics of the transference. Although all four subjects are of importance, which one of the four subjects receives the lion's share of attention depends, to a large extent, on the needs of the patient. For example, it has been my experience that the degree to which mystification has been a dominant facet in the cognitive mode of interaction in the family of origin may well make it desirable—if not imperative—that the actual family dynamics are unraveled first. This can sometimes mean an ongoing attempt at unearthing family skeletons through painstaking research on the part of the patient. Not much progress can be made with a patient who is actively engaged in a conspiracy of silence or denies such traumatic events as rape, suicide, or other forms of intrafamily violence. With respect to these traumatic events, we seem to have come almost full circle since Freud, who at first took stories of incest at face value and later concluded that these tales of early seduction or violence were fantasies or screen memories, usually of an hysterical imagination. A perusal of the recent empirical studies on these subjects suggests that the actual incidence of incest and violence is quite widespread, even among middle class families, and we as therapists have to be alert to the possibility that we are *not* dealing with a screen memory but reality. I am not advocating that this kind of detective work, however, should be a number one assignment, forced on the patient; I am merely suggesting that we encourage patients to pay close attention to whatever illuminating information comes their way and for us to convey an attitude of skepticism whenever a family myth clearly appears "fishy." This will lay the necessary foundation for all the subsequent work, namely separation and individuation.

The analysis of an unsatisfactory current involvement with a significant other should lead to an understanding of the origin of that pattern in childhood. However the insight that "I am acting toward myself or toward my lover as my mother acted toward me" is only a starting point. In order to effect behavioral changes, we have to:

1. Mobilize the patient's hidden strength, the capacity for hope, the possibility for more creative solutions and the ability to utilize or develop a sense of humor.
2. We also have to try to give them some awareness that one's identity is not a given but subject to conscious modifications.
3. We should try to provide them with alternatives when it comes to their limited ability to soothe themselves, cope with despair and deal with somatic complaints.

Throughout Phase II, it is our goal to strengthen the patients' inner resources that they, of course, do not feel they possess. And even if they did, the hidden agenda that spells, "If only . . ." or "One day I'll get mine . . ." constitutes a strong, deterrent force. Thus, our goal should always be to be as demanding as possible in expecting the patients to become their own good parents and at the same time, act as facilitators and provide the good parenting when a patient is truly at a loss.

Since I have found the fantasy of being adopted by the therapist a rather common phenomenon, a reversal of that fantasy can be mobilized. Fantasy and play obviously are of an enormous importance in infancy and childhood. The small child literally borrows the mother's ego to try out in fantasy the feats envisioned in later life. Patients who can do likewise, i.e. borrow our qualities and our attitudes toward them, will in that fashion lay the foundations for subsequent mastery. The fearful insomniac, who can visualize us as sitting by his or her bedside like a good nanny or mother, may have an easier time going to sleep. As Modell (1963, 1968) has pointed out, the transference of the borderline patient (and that of the character disorder at times) is essentially a transitional one. Instead of viewing this as a limitation, it can also be built upon to work for us, until the patient begins to truly individuate. What I am advocating is to take the patient's ability to fantasize and to teach him to utilize it in a constructive and self-soothing fashion.

The techniques described below are tools that are to be used *in conjunction* with the standard work of verbal interpretation, useful ways to cut through therapeutic impasses or bottlenecks and ways of dealing with pre-verbal material. Some of these exercises have the function of preparatory of "quasi dreams."

1. Sadistic introjects   The transition crisis from Phase I to Phase II, among the four patients discussed in this book, was precipitated by their treatment of, or fantasy about, a. a stuffed frog; b. a doll; c. a fellow group member; and d. my dog, in other words, all objects which in some way were connected with the therapist and which, at the same time, were self-representations. Obviously, sadism directed at the therapist or the patient's self-representations, if it is acted out is bound to be counterproductive to say the very least. In order to counteract the sadism, what needs to be encouraged is the development of compassion for the infant-self which, way back then, internalized parental rejection, hostility, or outright sadism. Patients who feel particularly helpless in remembering their early childhood and its emotional climate can be greatly helped with the following assignment: "Picture yourself as a child." Once a patient has focused on a particular image of himself at a more or less specific age, I ask him to spend the following week with that child. Patients are then instructed to keep that imaginary child with them 24 hours a day. That means that starting with the end of the session, they will have to hold the child's hand when walking down the stairs down to the street since the steps are rather steep. They have to be very careful when crossing the street. Obviously, meals require special attention, since a cup of coffee and a cigarette will satisfy an adult at breakfast time, while a three-year-old wants corn flakes and milk. Room will have to be found for the child to sleep and a bedtime story might be required before the adult can settle down to read. Even though most patients "forget" the assignment during most of the week, even the short time they are able to carry it out, is usually quite revealing in terms of a. when they remember and when they forget; and b. what fantasies of caretaking activities come easily and what others produce rage. For example, one patient who left the session and went directly to a restaurant for dinner, reported that the thought of ordering an orange juice for the child in addition to his martini was already enraging. When he pictured the child munching a hamburger and mashed potatoes, he felt like pushing the child's face into the plate until it choked, because "I just knew he would dawdle." Assignments of this kind can, thus, neatly reproduce a wealth of information about the ways in which the patients perceived their parents' attitudes toward them. Coupled with a guided regression (see Chapter Five), the man described above got in touch with many memories revolving around his parents' relentless persecution of his "otherness," his typical childlike attitudes toward food, and his attempts to assert his autonomy and receive attention by dawdling at every meal. When a year later he repeated the fantasy exercise, he found himself encouraging the boy to take all the time in the world, and when he could feel that getting dessert was no longer contingent on "finishing everything on his plate," he knew that he had taken a major step in expelling a sadistic introject. Although I generally encourage lonely patients who are thinking of acquiring a pet to do so, this should *not* be done if impulse control is poor, because a serious injury to an animal could be too devastating for a patient whose rage is still mostly unneutralized.

2. *Hope and creativity*   A patient who is stuck in a rut and clearly unhappy about it can be asked, "If you had only one month to live and could spend it any which way you want to, what would you do?" This can accomplish several goals simultaneously. A patient may conclude that she would spend this time in Hawaii, sunning herself and swimming but *without* her lover, or alternatively realize a long cherished dream of driving down to South America by himself. In both of these cases, they realized that there are, indeed, things they would like to do—but that if this month were all that was left of life, they would *not* burden it with an unsatisfactory love relationship. They were also letting themselves and us know that they have specific goals that they have put off for no real reason, for they are quite feasible. In other words, this question puts people in touch with the fact that in the service of their hidden agenda, they are suspending time, treating life as if it were forever, and are postponing choices that they *could* make

now, but have chosen not to. Middle-aged and older patients in particular, need reminding that the life span is, indeed, limited and that although they may not be able to change all of their life circumstances, they can change *some.* For example, one man in his sixties, who had battled for more than 35 years with his wife, came to realize through this question how little time was, indeed, left, and that the financial hardship involved in a separation and the aloneness were well worth the peace it could give him in return. Since many patients tend to respond to questions about how they would like to spend their last month, or a perfect Sunday with fantasies that involve often one impossible element, usually money, the therapist can then rephrase the question: "If you were 10 years old and could spend a Sunday in any way you would want to . . ." The answer would probably involve a trip to Yankee Stadium or a visit to the circus. The next question should be: "Do you still think you could enjoy this?" This may open up an awareness of how much they have impoverished their lives by leaving the simple pleasures and options of childhood behind. Play in childhood, after all, is serious business. Aside from constituting a tryout for adult roles, it is also the arena in which adult professional choices and avocations are tested, where creativity is still uncurbed and where we are not yet cut off from the wealth of our inner resources. Children can create a whole world out of mud pies and they may well be future sculptors, gourmet chefs, chemists, or architects. Thus, it can be immensely helpful to a patient to temporarily return to the world of childhood play and to spend a day on the beach building sand-castles instead of pursuing the singles bars. It helps if we are quite directive in giving these instructions or suggestions, because although patients may comply merely to humor their "nutty therapist," the activity, itself, will unearth forgotten pleasures and creative impulses. It may also generate a great deal of sadness over the impoverishment of their current lives. The more direct the link to the childhood play can be made, the better. For example, an adult who remembers having liked to draw, may not be able to relate to a fancy set of water-colors, but react enthusiastically to the characteristic feel and smell of a box of crayons.

3. Humor   One of the most important facets of therapy—or for life, for that matter—is the development of a sense of humor, particularly for those patients whose propensity toward shame is particularly pronounced, who feel badly for feeling bad, and therefore have developed not just a system of denials but one of secrecy. These were children who experienced their unhappiness as a personal failure that marked them as "ungrateful children," unappreciative of their parent's efforts. Patients who feel ashamed of their troubles and experience the therapist as an inquisitor who will sit in judgment of their emotional troubles, suffer from a double handicap. Therefore, to introduce a certain degree of lightness and bantering into the therapeutic situation—rather than trivializing or minimizing the situation and the communication—may well make the seemingly unbearable more bearable. My most shame-ridden patient has revealed many of her secrets by opening the session with a joke that paralleled whatever her particular predicament was at that time. In a similar vein, Tilmann Moser (1977) in his account of his analysis, must have found the terms "grandiosity" or "grandiose self" too painful and, thus, nicknamed them "the dragon" (*Der Lindwurm* in German is an even less frightening animal). Conversely, a shame-provoking interpretation, if presented in the form of a joke will not only achieve its goal as effectively as it would if it were presented seriously, but it will also allow the patients to stand back and recognize the pattern as not being entirely unique to them. Moreover, it allows them to have a good anxiety relieving laugh in the process. For example, one of my favorite stories for certain sadomasochistic patterns, as for example "in justice collecting," involved two fishwives who had a screaming fight in the village square. Eventually, one of them got so enraged that she picked up a big chunk of horse manure and threw it at the other's face. Since the opponent's mouth was wide open, this was where a good portion of the manure landed. The victim responded by pointing to her full mouth and by uttering, "This will stay here as evidence until the police arrive!" In a similar vein, Kohut (1977) tells the story of a colleague who is alleged to respond to expressions of unbridled grandiosity by simply handing such a patient a scepter and crown.

4. Creativity   The development of creativity often involves nothing more than a person's redefinition of the situation. For example, one young man reported to the group that he had had a wonderful Saturday afternoon letting more sunshine into his apartment by cleaning the windows. He had in that way managed to turn a chore into a pleasant enterprise. The music that he played, while doing the work, was, therefore, not interpreted as a distraction, but as a celebration of sunshine and spring. He topped off the celebration with a good bottle of wine.

Many objects that are broken and, thus, useless for their intended purpose, can be put to use in another way. Thus, the misfortune of having lost one item is offset by gaining another object. This kind of creative use of our ability to redefine a situation or object, if consistently encouraged and rewarded by group and the therapist, can become quite habit-forming and, thereby, effectively counteract the victimized position that is so typical for the sadomasochistic patient's outlook on life. Patients who claim that I am not taking their suffering seriously enough, will have to be reminded time and again that hardship, accidents, misfortune, and struggle are inevitable facts of life for everybody, but that the interpretation of the situation is our choice—and sometimes our only choice. The part-time student who works as a secretary, may chafe under the label secretary. On the other hand, when she labels herself as a student and as an aspiring professional who happens to earn her living and tuition by working in an office, she will see not only herself differently, but also evoke a different and more positive response in others. One young woman, who attributed much of the barrenness in her life to the fact that she lived "in the wrong part of town, where nothing happens," and to the fact that she could not afford to move to where she thought "the action was," came to realize that she had never really lived in her neighborhood at all for a period of more than five years. She had merely used it to sleep in, and had spent her time being deprived and bored. Once she decided—after quite some prodding—to actively explore the parks, museums, tennis courts and side-walk cafes, her boredom and her obsession with moving was replaced with a wealth of satisfying activities and social interaction. She reported to the group that her dry cleaner had lived a very exciting life, was full of anecdotes and had entertained her for the better part of a Saturday afternoon.

In general, patients' convictions that they cannot do what they would like to do, that they are too weak to defend themselves against others should be interpreted as an option not to exercise the strength they actually possess. Since many patients refuse to accept this view and consider it absurd, it is sometimes helpful to demonstrate this fact physically. One technique is to invite the so-called weakling to an arm wrestling match. Almost invariably, they will start out exerting no force at all. The same holds true for a similar exercise where I use one of the lines in the carpet as a border between two territories and I challenge the patient to try to pull me over the line, while I try to do the same. Although none of these patients use all their strength, they may use increasingly more when prodded. When they have used as much strength as they think they are able to employ, I let them win. In the subsequent feedback and discussion about their reluctance to use their natural powers, however, usually childhood memories are unearthed that pertain to having feared their own rage, usually exaggerated ability to inflict bodily harm on parents and siblings, fear of competitiveness, and finally their investment in the victimized position.

5. Self-soothing activities   When it comes to the problem of soothing and parenting themselves, sadomasochistic patients have two problems: "ignorance" of what they can do, in other words a poverty of behavioral resources; and a seeming inability to appreciate what *is* available to them, either in terms of objects or activities or in their utilization of their senses and their imagination. Since all their life they have waited for that soothing to be supplied by all-powerful others, they have had little opportunity to use their own ingenuity. For example, one of my patients who had previously been a fast and efficient shower-taker, on my suggestion switched to taking baths. Then, she graduated to bubblebath and the use of oils and perfumed soaps. Later yet, she added rubber ducks, boats, and countless other floating objects, and eventually she transformed the entire bathroom into a tropical forest by adding live plants and by painting a jungle landscape on the walls and ceilings. Her cats doubled as lions and tigers. Thus, her bathroom became her sanctuary from the world where she could spend many hours as the queen of the Amazon. Patients who habitually eat on the run, can be taught to set a table with a table-cloth, napkin, flower, and a candle. The impoverishment of the senses, i.e. taste, smell, hearing, touch, and sight often requires a very active reeducative effort. Anna, who had forever led an extremely harrassed life, had to be taught that it is perfectly all right to use an occasional session to just lie down on the couch, let me tuck her in with a particularly soft blanket, give her a teddy bear to hold and to turn on some soft and soothing classical music on the radio. At first, she could only tolerate five minutes of such "uncalled-for pampering" but eventually, she managed to enjoy it for as long as 15 minutes before anxiety compelled her to go back "to work." I might add that I usually employed these methods on days when she came in physically ill, but unwilling to cancel. Although Anna never got over her self-consciousness when it came to the enjoyment of the other paraphernalia of the nursery, other patients have been able to utilize a baby bottle and a pacifier at home to counteract anxiety. The ability to extract visual pleasures from one's ordinary everyday environment, can be stimulated by suggesting the use of a camera to capture the first spring flowers, snow drifts or the turning of the leaves. The use of color filters can turn the ordinary photographer not necessarily into an artist but into a person who begins to realize that reality can be manipulated by fantasy.

Of equal importance is the mobilization of discarded soothing memories from the past. The "hidden caretaker," mentioned earlier, can be resurrected and utilized. The patient who is unable to relax and sleep, can slowly learn to picture the benign maid, neighbor, grandmother, or pet as sitting by his bedside and watching over him. If no such hidden caretaker can be found, we have to bank on the fact that in every patient's life, there have been moments of utter contentment and safety. For example, the paralyzed Ph.D. candidate who is haunted by the picture of the critical faces of her thesis committee can be asked to picture a blank screen with a vertical dividing line in the middle. It is then suggested that she project the hostile faces of the committee on one side of the screen. When the picture is clearly in the patient's mind she is asked to picture on the blank side of the screen the proud and delighted faces of her camp-counselors when they handed her the long distance swimmer of the year award. Once the second visual image has become firm, it is then suggested that the good image be shifted until it blots out the anticipated threatening image of the thesis committee. If no memory of kind persons can be found, we have to search for safe places. One particularly anxious patient could not come up with any such memory. Furthermore, during this session she felt extremely uncomfortable sitting on the couch. Thus, I suggested that she make herself comfortable in whatever fashion she saw fit. By arranging the pillows and the blankets for a while, she finally built herself a contraption that she came to recognize as the long-forgotten tree-house that she had shared with her sister. This became her special fantasy place.

The symbolic gift also fits into that category. Someone who faces a particularly frightening event such as an exam, job interview, air travel, etc. can be given a small but personal gift by the therapist that serves as a talisman. Such gifts may be knick-knacks, sea shells, dried flowers, museum cards, etc. In other words, objects that are both meaningful to patient and therapist alike, inexpensive and, depending on their purpose, are small enough to carry in one's pocket or suitable to tack over one's desk or bed. One young woman who suffered from rather debilitating anxiety attacks on awakening, was given a postcard portraying Paul Klee's, "A Guardian Angel Serving Little Breakfast," and it never left her nighttable. And although it did not miraculously cure her anxiety attacks, it did give her the hope that one day the ghosts that interrupted her sleep would fade away, as indeed they did. Anna who always believed that she needed to justify her existence by hard work and service to others, was quite happy about a photo of Giulietta whom she envied as the symbol of uselessness and laziness and a solid "entitlement position."

6. *Somatic complaints*   Psychosomatic ailments require the same attention as dreams or verbal communications. First, they have to be deciphered and, then, have to be attended to by dealing with them directly. Patients who come in with stomach pains, headaches, congested lungs or bronchi, muscular cramps, impaired vision or hearing can be asked to let that part of their body speak. If the muscle spasm, for example, expresses an unwillingness to perform a duty or a task that the patient feels obligated to attend to, a dialogue between the two warring parts should be suggested in the hope that a compromise solution can be reached. If this approach yields no results, patients can be asked to picture themselves as one inch tall. Once they have this image clearly in their minds, they should be invited to let this miniature version travel through their mouth (or ears or nose) to the part of their body that ails them. Once they are there, they should describe what they see and then think of ways to soothe the pain. In this way, the following sequence may ensue: a middle-aged man with a particularly traumatic childhood began the session by telling me that he had been nauseous all day and also that he had dreamed he had chosen four rather ferocious weapons to battle his parents. He then woke up in a cold sweat. Letting first the weapons and then the stomach speak yielded very little except increased anxiety and the recognition that the fourth weapon was not really a weapon but some kind of a tube. The trip inside the stomach, however, revealed that the stomach was in fact a womb and the tube in the dream allowed him to escape from the

womb through the belly button. Having solved the problem of being male and pregnant and by delivering the tiny version of the self via the belly button, in other words without having to give up his male identity by acquiring a vagina, the nausea promptly stopped. The disappearance of one symptom, however, immediately resulted in the production of another. Now, his arms were shaking and his muscles were twitching. In letting the muscles in his arms speak, it soon became obvious that he was debilitating himself in order to keep himself from using the heavy weapons in the dream with which he could kill his parents. Having made this interpretation, his arms relaxed and he could talk about his extreme reluctance to disrupt his current life by opening up the pandora's box of his childhood with all the accumulated rage. In a previous nightmare, it had appeared in the form of a tidal wave from which he had tried to escape on a rickety bicycle and coffin-sized aluminum boxes.

Respiratory symptoms, particularly if they interfere with the patient's ability to breathe properly, often represent the inhibition of screams of terror or rage. Once the nature of the scream has been identified, those screams should be encouraged to come out. Patients who are understandably reluctant to scream, without some way of muffling the sound, should be given a pillow to scream into. All the precautions pertaining to the ventilation of rage described in the previous chapter, however, have to be carefully observed.

GROUP THERAPY

Group therapy, beginning with Phase II, is an invaluable adjunct to individual psychotherapy, and I usually inform every patient from the beginning that if and when I feel that the group experience seems to be beneficial for them, I like to put them into one of my groups. Given the fact that historically group therapy was designed as a tool for the replay of the family dynamics of the patient's family of origin, the preparation of a patient for the participation in the group, should include the information that probably they will at first experience the group as if it were, indeed, their family. I usually explain that *this* family differs from their own in three important ways:

1. Its primary concern is the welfare of the *patient,* rather than

the maintenance of the *family system*. In other words, the patient who has been labelled in a way that prevents optimal growth, will not get the reinforcement for his or her accustomed role and identity. For example, the "crazy person," the "helpless little girl," the "family dummy," the "tyrant," the "troublemaker," the "delinquent," "mother's little helper," the "Wunderkind," etc. are all attributed roles that became the foundation of an identity at the exclusion of all others and which have since become dysfunctional in that they conflict with the stated goals in the present. Alternatively, a patient may have been assigned two conflicting identities, as for example mother's little helper who is also expected to obtain a Ph.D. degree. A family that functions only because every family member splits off their unacceptable qualities and attributes them to one particular child, clearly needs that child to do the acting out for them, and also feels it has to persecute the child for it. Any attempts at "reform" will be actively, but secretly, opposed or undermined. The group will not only actively discourage this self-labelling, it will come to expect an identity that is functional for the goals that the patient now wants to pursue.

2. Once patients have become full-fledged members of the group, the group will be there for them for as long as they want it and in whatever capacity they need it, provided they act in good faith. If a catastrophic event occurs in a patient's life, the group will rally around and give help and support to see this group member through the crisis. Furthermore, short of truly destructive behavior toward other group members, nobody will ever be thrown out of group or be abandoned because of their "sins." Scapegoating is never permitted and all group members are protected from excessive interpersonal aggression and verbal assaults. In other words, group members who feel the need to ventilate unneutralized rage can do so by attacking inanimate objects such as pillows, but never at the expense of a fellow group member. Since many patients associate the group experience with Fritz Perl's famous "hot seat" technique, this fear has to be dispelled before a patient enters group.

3. The group, unlike most families, constantly examines its own dynamics critically. Assigning roles, or accepting dysfunc-

tional behavior patterns or presentations of self that are phony will occur at times, but hopefully they will be analyzed before they have a chance to become institutionalized. The patterns in question can pertain to group as a whole or to individual members. An example of the former would be an unspoken agreement to avoid all interpersonal anger, i.e. the drawing up of mutual non-aggression pacts. An example for the latter might best be illustrated by one of my female group members who assumed a persona of fragility. Having been trained as an actress, she managed to communicate the message so effectively, that whenever she was challenged in the least, she conveyed to us that the subject under discussion pained her far too much to even speak about it by averting her eyes and withdrawing with an expression of utter agony. She did all this non-verbally and soon the guilt level in the room became almost unbearable. In the course of two sessions, this particular con game was dismantled, gently but effectively, and everybody including the con artist felt better.

Having stated how the group *differs* from most patients' family of origin, it is equally important to look at the ways in which the similarity with the family can benefit the patient. For the group experience to be effective in terms of allowing patients to work toward "psychological birth," continuity and integrity are perhaps the single most important factors. For a group to function on an ongoing long-term basis, prospective group members have to be able to honor the necessity for their continuous presence and for their commitment to the group's integrity. A group that has a great degree of turnover cannot seriously function as a second family because, if that were the case, the group would never lose its "as if" quality. Moreover, the fear of losing love objects would be constantly mobilized rather than alleviated. The objection could be raised that by treating patients with such high expectations, we are disregarding their actual psychosocial development and the limitations inherent in it. This argument is only partially true. What is being asked of patients—nothing more and nothing less—is a commitment to a new mode of therapy and to trust the therapist's judgment that they will eventually benefit from it. Put differently, we cannot expect patients at the begining of Phase II to live up to all of these standards, but we *can* expect them to give it an honest try.

Once the initial hurdle of the new group member, namely to provoke failure, has been safely navigated, patients tend to be firmly committed to continuing this new and strange way of being in therapy. Provoking failure often follows the following script: the new patient will listen for the first few hours in order to determine—among other things—what kind of behavior is most unacceptable to the group and then act on it with a singleminded determination and stubbornness. The internal reasoning underlying such maneuvers is that if *they* are the ones who arranged the rejection they have not really been rejected. Thus, it is vitally important that the therapist—as far as is humanly possible—assumes a great deal of responsibility for the new patient until the patient has settled in. Needless to say, the truly determined provocateurs will succeed in alienating the group no matter what we do, but in my experience they are the exceptions rather than the rule. After all, the sadomasochistic patient deep down, is deathly afraid of failure and rejection. Thus, the patient who habitually, but unconsciously, provokes cannot be left to his or her own devices. Until they learn more constructive ways of relating to group, a part of the individual sessions may have to be utilized to discuss the previous group session and how to short-circuit negative interactions in the future. It may be necessary to say directly to a patient something to the effect: "I have noticed that whenever you are particularly anxious you tend to paint yourself into a corner. How would you like it if I called your attention to it the next time it happens and *before* you get too boxed in?" Chances are this suggestion will be welcomed. A patient, who has perhaps for the first time managed to utilize an adult other to help him relate to a group situation, will most likely feel quite elated and the therapeutic alliance will be strengthened. Moreover, a patient who has been introduced to group therapy in this fashion, will be infinitely more tolerant when the next new group member arrives and starts with a similar attempt at self defeat.

CASE MATERIAL

Karl

Phase II of Karl's therapy (approximately 18 months) was primarily characterized by an intense power struggle between Karl and me and Karl and group. He was determined to learn as much as possible about his early history, even though much of the material that was uncovered resulted in psychotic episodes, or psychotic states. After Karl's lover had left him, Karl had stopped making any efforts in his own behalf. As stated earlier, he had gone on welfare and psychiatric disability, that allowed him to eat but precluded the indulgence in even the smallest of luxuries that he had cherished all his life, such as movies, theatre. concerts, or books. He made no effort whatsoever to refurnish or ever rearrange his apartment that his lover had emptied of most of its furniture. Karl shunned people. Although he attended group and occasionally used it to deal with traumatic memories or dreams, he did not really relate to any of the other group members, with the exception of Bob. More often than not, he expressed his rage against the group for not "helping him any more," by sitting through the entire session in stony silence. Since obviously nobody was unaware of how he felt, many attempts were made to draw him out and to mobilize him to utilize his artistic and interpersonal resources. All suggestions were devalued as not being pertinent to his problems. When he was asked a question, his standard answer was "I don't know," or "I don't understand" that exasperated the group time and again, but never really alienated it. The picture that Karl presented, in many ways resembled that of a small child who suffers from a severe infantile or anaclitic depression and refused to be comforted. On some level, he was perfectly aware that the life he led would depress anybody; he held out for a miraculous intervention from the outside, however, to somehow make it all good again. In the meantime, he punished the world with his obvious suffering. In his individual sessions, however, he was more inclined to act constructively by allowing for some comforting. He applied himself diligently to the task of unravelling his childhood history, particularly his identity as a male that had been severely tampered with by his mother's crossdressing him.

During this time, my interpretations of his dreams and memories were essentially geared toward two goals: to help him understand what actually happened; and to point out in each instance that no matter how traumatic his experiences had been, he had been able to draw upon his environment and his own inner resources in order to prevail. Although he had had little choice but to withdraw from the world through most of his childhood, he had never relinquished his hold on his reality—nobody had really succeeded in fooling him. Karl was able to portray his inner world through bizarre drawings, most of which depicted dreadfully threatening female figures with piercing phallic noses. Most of these figures looked more like horse-shoe crabs than persons. Heimann's (1966) contention, that bad internal objects arise during the undifferentiated stage as a result of passively endured intrusions of a hostile and invasive mother, seemed to be borne out by these drawings since the self was missing in all of his group portraits except for self portraits that contained only pictures of him and were devoid of any other objects. Only during Phase III could he portray himself in relationships to objects.

After the suicide pact (see Chapter 6) Karl was hospitalized for 10 days and seemed to relish the experience. It was proof, after all, that he was, indeed, truly insane and that he could not help himself. Moreover, it proved that therapy did not work and that if nothing else he could at least try to make his therapist and his group feel as impotent as he experienced himself to be. Since at no time was long-term hospitalization suggested, he had to deal with his problems all over again after each discharge. In the course of one year where he hospitalized himself five times, his attitude toward hospitalization and medication slowly changed. Piece by piece, he learned to take conscious control over the material that, in the past, had produced psychotic episodes. He became less inclined to dive into it regardless of the consequences. He stopped using his Elavil haphazardously and self destructively. Entering the hospital became a matter of precaution rather than the result of a major crisis. He learned to anticipate and sense the imminence of another tailspin and he hospitalized himself without much fanfare. Although the first time he had involved every person he knew, he eventually reached the point where he could simply and factually inform me—or leave a message with my answering service—that he would spend the next week in the hospital. Group became used to his periodic absences and responded supportively but without alarm. Even though Karl became increasingly responsible in dealing with the more severe expressions of his troubles, he did not yet relinquish his identity as a crazy person, and he refused to do anything that would improve his living conditions.

The transition crisis—confronting self-responsibility—that signalled the end of Phase II and the beginning of Phase III took place in two steps: He requested to see me during my Christmas vacation in order to ask me what I thought his diagnosis was, and I told him the following: "When you first came into treatment, you were a borderline schizophrenic, i.e. a person who *potentially could opt* for the career of a mental patient, either inside or outside of a state institution. *Now,* however, this is no longer true. The work you have done in therapy is of such magnitude, that you may still *choose* to act crazy, but that does not mean that you are crazy. What you do from now on, is strictly a matter of choice; in fact it has always been a matter of choice. Obviously, you must have wanted a full life all along, since for 2 ½ years you have opted for life and for sanity each and every time you picked yourself up in order to come to therapy." After thinking this over, Karl reluctantly admitted, that even at this very moment, he could perceive me normally or as being either two inches or twenty feet tall. In other words, he said, "*I can depersonalize you at will.*" A couple of weeks after this encounter, Karl entered the hospital for the last time. His last stay however, was very different from the previous ones in two ways: a. During each previous stay, the resident social worker had suggested vocational rehabilitation programs, which Karl rejected. This time, he agreed to give it some serious thought. Even though Karl still envisioned himself as a great future author—in fact he wrote up a storm and diligently distributed his manuscripts to many publishing houses and film companies—he did concede, that until he was famous, learning a marketable skill might not be such a bad idea. b. While in the hospital, Karl played the role of the participant observer. During his first session with me after his discharge, he gave me a run down of the psychodynamics of his fellow patients as well as their interactions with their families that he had observed during visiting hours. His analysis of these malignant family systems sounded exceedingly accurate and astute and his delivery of them was hilariously funny. In other words, he suddenly revealed two astounding talents, one as a diagnostician and one as a comic. What was of greatest importance, however, were his conclusions, namely, "Being crazy is really a rather silly thing to do—you have to be embarrassingly simple minded to keep it up without laughing not only at yourself but also at the family system." Since Karl had always been hypersensitive to ridicule, he knew *exactly* what he was doing in telling me the story this way. In effect, he had instructed me to look at his psychotic reactions as pretty ridiculous maneuvers rather than as his fate. Although this new insight needed a great deal of consolidating—and at times almost seemed lost—it was equally clear, that Karl had set it up in such a way, that he could never really return to his previous position. His career as a crazy person was over.

Bob

Following Karl's first hospitalization, Karl withdrew from Bob, and they ceased to be lovers. Although Karl clearly wanted to continue the friendship, Bob felt so humiliated by what he interpreted as Karl's out-and-out rejection, that he pursued him with a relentless hatred. Part of that hatred also served the purpose of covering up his shame over the suicide plot that he had imposed on Karl. Bob must have felt so hurt and enraged that for more than six months, his only contribution to group therapy consisted of attacks on Karl. Every attempt on the part of the group to examine the dynamics between the two would only intensify his hatred to the point where Bob was quite ready to leave the group altogether. He could not tolerate any critical analysis of his self-destructive motivations in this interaction as well as his sadistic provocations. Neither could he own up to his desire to destroy the group as his second family. His enormous propensity toward shame precluded any insight.

Bob's daily life was dismal. He vegetated on welfare and psychiatric disability, and since, unlike Karl, he had no intellectual or other interests, he did not know what to do with himself. His drug use was extensive and he drank frequently, in a fruitless effort to deal with his deepening depression. In his individual sessions, he tried to talk exclusively about his victimizations both in his past and in his present life. The suggestion that he had something to do with his present misery was rejected on the grounds that, given his dreadful past, he deserved a year off; besides being as depressed as he was, *nobody* could expect him to work. Given this unyielding position, an attempt had to be made to reach him in some other way. Dreams and guided fantasy trips proved to be the most effective arena for work. In these fantasy trips, Bob could envision a more benign world without having to admit that his visions bore any resemblance to reality as he knew it. His inordinate craving for admiration and his strong desires for revenge were also exercised in his fantasy life. Although dream interpretation had been productive through most of the first year of Phase II of his treatment, it came to an abrupt halt when he brought in a dream in which he was represented as the ten-year-old Jesus in the temple, with God as his thinly disguised father. This dream also had clear sexual connotations. Bob found his dream abhorrent on three grounds: a. All his rage up to this point had been focused on his father, and consequently, the mere suggestion of a loving or sexual involvement seemed preposterous. b. Bob despised religion, and to discover religious ideation even in his unconscious, seemed too shameful. c. He feared that the dream somehow "explained" the origin of his homosexuality in Freudian terms, theories that he had heard about, but rejected as bizarre. Unfortunately, for many years to come, this session turned out to be the last fruitful individual session that we have had. After Bob had presented the dream, and after he had played the different parts of the dream, there was no way in which he could disown his own production and his associations to it. He responded with rage and shame and finally with complete disavowal by totally discrediting the process of psychotherapy in general and my skills in particular. Attempts to explain to him the choice of symbols in dreams fell on deaf ears. The attempt at unifying the contradictory feelings about his father and about himself was a task his ego was incapable of, since it evoked too much shame and corresponding narcissistic rage. The original developmental arrest did not yet yield to therapeutic intervention. At that time, Bob could only resort to disavowal.

A few sessions after this dream, Bob announced that he could no longer afford both individual and group therapy. This decision was announced as a fait accompli, and I insisted that he choose group rather than individual therapy until such time where he would get a job and, thus, be able to afford both. From that moment on, Bob continued to be engaged in the therapeutic process but to a much lesser degree. A part of his being was withdrawn. Given this partial withdrawal, it is not really accurate, to speak of a transition crisis proper. A significant change did take place, however, which changed Bob's life considerably and helped to lay the foundation for his eventual return to serious work on his psyche. Once Bob's therapy consisted of group only, he dropped his persecution of Karl. Instead, he would rage at his sexual partners, or some real or imagined slight by me or a fellow group member. Almost invariably, he would use the entire 90 minutes of group time. For close to 75 minutes, he raged, complained, and devalued each and every helpful suggestion or interpretation. Only 15 minutes before the end of the session could he allow for the fact that he was deeply hurt rather than enraged. Only then could he allow himself to cry and be comforted. It was as if he had to test the group's good will over and over again, since no insight ever carried from one session to the next. During this period, however, he also became more and more addicted to the S&M scenes in the bars and the trucks. Moreover, his provocations of the law became rather outrageous. One night he barely escaped arrest after having smashed almost every street light on an entire city block, and the ensuing noise had alerted the police. When he finally witnessed the attempted murder of a homosexual couple by a group of Puerto Rican teenagers, he was frightened enough to bring the problem to group. One particularly astute group member elicited the exact times and dates for his S&M escapades and his encounters with the welfare department, which revealed an almost perfect correlation between the experience of humiliation by "some dumb jerk of a case worker" and the subsequent self-inflicted humiliation in the S&M bars, preferably by a young, blond, blue-eyed Nazi representation. It was also pointed out to him, that he had never forgiven his father for not having honored his graduation from college sufficiently, and that his unwillingness to look for gainful employment, might be his form of getting even. Bob, for once, really listened, and he realized that there was no way in which he could continue to escape from dealing with his ambivalence toward his father that had been revealed in his dream. He accepted the fact that for whatever reasons, his malignant involvement with his father was so powerful, that he had been willing to risk his life for it. Following this group session, Bob seriously looked for employment, and checked on the possibility of going to graduate school. It was as if he was saying "if the battle over the question of being taken care of endangers my life, I am willing to temporarily relinquish my position and try to assume the responsibility for earning a living."

Larry

Since the displacement of the rage against the preoedipal mother onto the father was obviously no longer working for Larry, it was now my responsibility to help him cope with the conflicts between his need for and rage toward me. In order to diffuse this rage—without invalidating it—I put Larry into the same group that Anna had become a member of 6 months earlier. For the first few months, as the newest member of group he enjoyed his role as the youngest sibling enormously. He presented himself as even more unsophisticated than he had done with me. He made every effort to downplay his previous professional accomplishments. His favorite place to sit was on the floor next to my chair, and many times, he reached for my hand for comfort.

It took him several months before he was able to talk about his troubles. Although he clearly "took to" group, he found it very hard to accept that he could no longer think of himself as my only concern and that there were others who were also important to me. His vision of me as an extension of himself was shattered; this made him quite angry. He became equally upset, when after the initial settling in period, the group did not permit him to treat them like rag dolls that he could throw around at will. Since group did not allow him to become their little baby-boy, he had to try to come to grips with the fact that the other group members were his peers and that both men and women share similar fears and hopes. For a long time, he found it truly incomprehensible that such formidable creatures as professional women could be fearful of rejection or ridicule by men like him.

In his individual sessions, Larry became increasingly aware of his ambivalent feelings toward women. He had a series of involvements with rather immature, but unusually attractive, and very young women. His explanation for his choice of partners was at first centered on the competitive thrill he derived from being seen with such beauties by other men. But it soon became clear that their inability or justifiable unwillingness to give Larry what he ostensibly wanted, was the element that made these women so attractive. Those women, who were not naturally rejecting, soon became so in the face of Larry's attempts to suffocate them with his insatiable needs and his covert sadism. Through a series of dreams, Larry got in touch with his enormous terror of being laughed at or ridiculed by women. He was sure that if he ever got truly close to any woman who was his equal, she would respond to his needs with laughter. The thought of being ridiculed enraged him so much, that he could not allow any of his dates to sleep over at his house for fear that he might do something terrible to them. In time, Larry was able to recount many childhood fantasies of taking mother away from the family, but those fantasies came to a painful halt when he imagined her ridicule and his father's contempt at the thought that such a puny little boy could take care of his mother. On a deeper level his fantasies and dreams revealed the wish to return to the womb where none of these problems exist. Whenever he fantasized about his prenatal existence, however, he did not seem to be particularly contented. Therefore, I asked him: "Larry, what would make you truly happy?" His response was: "I don't know what would make me happy, but I can tell you what really turns me on." With a great deal of reluctance and considerable shame—mingled with pleasure—he shared with me his favorite masturbatory fantasy: Together with another male, who has to have an enormous penis, they could capture and attack a small, helpless prepubescent girl. After having made her plead for mercy, scream and beg, they would penetrate her first orally then anally and vaginally simultaneously. Larry would have a powerful orgasm and the girl would either choke to death from the sperm in her throat or explode internally from the ejaculation into her anus. Once Larry had given me what on some level he considered to be his dirtiest secret, he was quite surprised that the response was not one of shock, disgust or punishment but the suggestion that his fantasy might have something to do with rage over inadequate feeding experiences, painful and/or humiliating toilet training, and the fact that he was probably less than overjoyed over the birth of his younger sisters. For several weeks, Larry searched for memories that would connect his fantasy with early memories of his mother, but nothing emerged. In his eyes, she was still the saintly perfect mother. He did play out his rage against women in group though, an exchange which marked the transition to Phase III. He skillfully provoked Anna, who at the time was one of the least assertive women in the group, into what for her was a rather uncharacteristic outburst of anger. In response to it, Larry got up, moved across the room like the Tarzan of his childhood movies, seemingly with the intent of attacking Anna physically. Once he was stopped and meekly sat down, Anna a therapist herself, retaliated by reducing Larry to an ugly heap of psychopathology by using every dirty word in the psychiatric dictionary, including the suggestion that "a schizophrenic psychopath" should not be in a group with functioning neurotics. Larry was crestfallen and at the same time triumphant. He had achieved victory through defeat and proclaimed: "See, I told you, I really belong into a mental institution" (his fantasy of being totally taken care of). The group then confronted Larry with his pseudo-innocence, his continuous efforts to reproduce the monstrously frustrating aspects of the mother of earliest childhood in order to vindicate and support his victimized position in life. Although my interpretation of his masturbatory fantasy had not made much of an impression—at least on a conscious level—his acting-out in group propelled him into the slow acceptance of the fact that provoking victimizations by women helped him to relieve his rage, need for retribution and control, but that it accomplished the opposite when it came to his needs for tenderness and being taken care of. Perhaps his profoundest insight gained from this episode was: "Other people have feelings too, if I hit them they will hurt, and then they don't want to have anything to do with me." Although this insight required a great deal of consolidation, the first important step had been taken. Larry thought for the first time about the question how he as a person affected others, and that other people might conceivably have other functions and interests than to be mere need gratifiers or withholders for him.

Anna

Perhaps the most difficult task during Phase II of Anna's therapy was to teach her the difference between responsibility and guilt. When it was pointed out that she herself arranged her life in such a way that it encompassed a maximum of suffering, she felt unjustly condemned and burst into angry tears. I had, in her mind, joined her persecutors. In order to help her with this conflict, I put Anna into group. She immediately made herself "useful" by helping everybody else with their problems. For quite some time, however, she dealt with her ambivalence toward me by relating to the group as the "good" part of therapy and to our individual sessions as the "bad" judgmental part. Thus, in group she relived many of her childhood traumas and she could allow the group to be the good, sympathetic, and soothing mother. All the reparative exercises, such as collective rocking of her, the replay of the "perfect birthday party" and group hugs were freely given to her, time and again. The complaints about her current life, however, were mostly discussed in her individual sessions. There, Anna, too, held out for a consistently supportive therapeutic approach that would miraculously make it all better. As she came to realize that her therapist would not comply with this demand, she went on a campaign to covertly fail the therapist. Anna's most important daily complaint, after she had left her lover, pertained to first, the dangerous subway ride to work and her fears of having to walk to the subway after dark; and second, the possibility of being mugged in the neighborhood where she lived. Slowly, she came to recognize that purchasing a car and moving to a safer neighborhood could eliminate those two very real dangers. (Anna had been mugged once and she had witnessed a second mugging from her window.) Therefore, she bought a car, and six months later found an apartment in what is probably the safest part of town. The purchase of her car and her move, however, gave her no joy, no sense of mastery and accomplishment. To the contrary, she reacted to my suggestions like an obedient but angry child. For when she had completed the move, she informed me that the increase in rent and the car payments used up all her disposable income, and that she was no longer able to afford therapy. "Unlike you," she told me, "I am not a rich shrink." The angry message was: "Now what are you going to do?" "Now are you going to treat me for free?" My response to this question was a major surprise for her. I suggested that she, too, could become "a rich shrink" if she obtained postgraduate training in an analytic training institute. Once the initial shock had worn off, Anna liked the idea very much; not however, because a real inner shift had taken place, but because the prospect of being in school again, the additional work it implied, the additional chores it would add to her life, was most appealing to her. What was attempted in her case was an enrollment of her masochistic defenses toward a non-masochistic self-actualizing end, a gamble that paid off extremely well, since by the time she actually started to practice, she no longer felt the need to undermine her therapy and to fail her therapist.

The inner shift, i.e. the transition from a mostly symbiotic way of relating to an acceptance of self-responsibility, required that she dealt with her choice of love objects. After she had left her callous lover, she dated several men in a row, all of whom were clearly sadistic and distant. Finally, she settled for a young man for whom she clearly felt contempt. He seemed to be immensely immature, lived in constant fear of his family, and required a great deal of babying. Unlike her previous lovers, this man was never mean to her outrightly, he only complained that Anna was not more available and that she had no intentions of marrying him. In the course of 10 months her complaints about her lover and her boredom with him became more pronounced and she discussed this involvement in group. To her surprise, the group, instead of commiserating with her, critically examined her investment in this particular relationship. In Anna's view, her mother was a mean persecuting shrew, and her father was a charming, warm, lovable man who was victimized by her mother. All through her childhood and young adult life she had felt nothing but compassion for her father's lot in life. Although she was not able to see her idealized father realistically until much later in treatment, she suddenly saw herself as the shrew in relationship with her current lover. With the help of the group, she came to realize, that all her relationships with men were, in fact, rather sadomasochistic games, and that the only difference between her past and her current involvement was that for once she had turned the tables—*she* was now the unavailable, critical partner. These insights came slowly and painfully. They were possible, because Anna had learned to utilize me and the group as supportive agents who could be critical of her *actions* without comdemning her *being*. She had learned the difference between responsibility and guilt, and she was willing to test her capacity for choosing love objects and relate to them on a more equal basis.

Chapter 8

PHASE III:

Separation and Individuation

The major difference between Phase II and Phase III of the treatment process is to be found in the patient's attitude toward therapy and therapist. While during Phase I, therapy is experienced as something that is happening *to* the patient, and Phase II constitutes a power struggle in which the therapist is expected to do *for* the patient, Phases III and IV increasingly become a joint enterprise. As therapists, we feel more and more that we have a partner in our work and, at the same time, a very powerful opponent, who will engage us in belly button to belly button combat.

The separation and individuation phase roughly corresponds to Gedo and Goldberg's (1973) phase of castration anxiety and phallic narcissism, encompasses Kernberg's (1976) self and object differentiation and the consolidation of good and bad self- and object representations, Kohut's (1971) formation of a cohesive self and Mahler's four sub-phases of the individuation and separation process: a. differentiation; b. practicing period; c. rapprochement; and d. the beginnings of the fourth sub-phase.

After the stormy struggles over the question of self responsibility, or rather the failure at exercising omnipotent control, patients will now begin to relive what Mahler has so aptly called the toddler's love affair with the world, which among other things, literally means the joy that is derived from standing on one's own feet and moving under one's own steam. Among the patients I have treated, usually the greatest progress during this period is made in the area of professional pursuits. Typically, this is the time when patients return to school or to work and when jobs turn into careers. During Phase III, patients learn the skills that enable them to become their own good parents rather than depend on their environments to do it for them. These developments prepare them for Phase IV, the establishment of permanent love relationships, super-ego integration and the formation of a sound ego identity. The most commonly encountered pitfalls during this period are: 1. Premature separation, manifesting itself in flight or "escape into health"; 2. Premature or excessive disillusionment with their own abilities and the effectiveness of their therapy; and 3. Massive narcissistic disappointments resulting in a reactivation of archaic narcissistic strivings and corresponding shame.

TREATMENT GOALS AND OBJECTIVES

Developmentally, Phase III encompasses an enormous amount of infantile development; the entire period from the beginnings of upright locomotion to psychological birth at age three. It includes the growth of complex cognitive and motor skills and sensorimotor intelligence, and entails the experience of having a will of one's own, having it actively opposed by the will of another person, and finally, the discovery of the genitals and of sexual differences.

If all goes well, *optimal frustration* will result in the consolidation of good and bad object representations and to a reasonably stable differentiation of self and other, and object constancy—both ego functions. *Optimal disillusionment* will result in the transformation of primary narcissism into a cohesive self composed of healthy self-love and love for others. Infantile grandiosity, which reaches its height during the differentiation phase and a corresponding deflation during the repproachment phase, has been replaced by a sense of mastery. Identification has replaced idealization.

The parents of the future sadomasochistic patient failed their children in several ways during this period. The child's attempts at individuation and separation were not properly welcomed as steps that were seen as beneficial for the child and as a source of pride for the parents. To put it in the most simple framework: those aspects of the individuation and separation process that were considered to spell trouble for the parents were usually frowned upon, while those which relieved the mother of burdens were usually welcomed. In each individual case, however, it has to be ascertained precisely, what the experience was like for a particular child. Although patients can not always be able to reconstruct these early experiences, the reconstruction of "analogous telescoping experiences" will give us a fairly clear indication of what must have gone on.

I have found the following interactive constellations to be common in the history of sadomasochistic patients during this developmental phase: 1. Premature loss of maternal assistance; 2. Premature disillusionment with the primary caretaker; 3. Role reversal between parent and child; 4) Harsh and punitive discipline; and 5. Ridicule for the toddler's love affair with the world, and its own abilities. Even though these different interactive patterns usually overlap, we will, for the clarity of the argument, discuss them separately in order to delineate the different treatment goals and techniques.

1. The parent who perceived the infant primarily as a burden, and who during the symbiotic phase responded to the child with a minimum of care, will react to the child's growing independence with a great deal of ambivalence. Any newly acquired skill that relieves the mother of tasks that previously she had to perform for the baby, will be encouraged and welcomed. She reasons that if the child can pick up a toy once, there is no longer any reason for her to continue doing it for the child, particularly if there is a younger sibling who requires attention or, if she wants to return to her previous professional or other interests. Thus, the child takes pride in its accomplishments because they bring praise, but at the same time, pays the heavy price of being prematurely deprived of many aspects of maternal caretaking. Moreover, the increased capacity for locomotion on the part of the child, for this type of mother, is a source of irritation and additional work—rather than a source of pride—since the child ceases to stay in its crib. The toddler is experienced as being constantly "underfoot" because it still needs to cling to the mother and, at the same time, wants to exercise its newly-acquired skills. Thus, instead of being allowed to crawl

around, these children are either restrained as if they were still babies, or, alternatively, left to their own devices and then severely reprimanded when they touch something they are not supposed to touch, fall, or otherwise hurt themselves. In short, the child's love affair with the world is not reflected by a corresponding gleam in the mother's eyes, but a barely concealed expression of exasperation and very little genuine admiration. The children of such rejecting mothers usually also suffer considerable damage during the rapprochement phase when, in response to their need to "refuel," they are told to stop being such babies. In other words, these children experience growing up as a very mixed blessing, since some aspects of it are responded to warmly while others, constitute a source of parental annoyance with the child, without the child being able to tell them apart. These infants have reason to be volatile and cranky, a behavioral response that intensifies the negative aspects of their interactions with their parents. Usually, toilet training for those infants tended to be early, harsh, or persecutory. Again, the parental attitude can be summarized by the statement, "If you can do it once, there is no excuse for subsequent lapses." Some of these children were either left in their dirty diapers as punishment, kept naked for hours, kept on the potty until they "produced," or were yelled at or spanked. The emergent sense of self of these infants, from very early on, becomes tainted with a sense of badness and shame that is connected with their bodily functions as well as with their wish to actively explore the environment.

2. Premature disillusionment in the goodness and omnipotence of the parents is part and parcel of what we have just called "premature loss of maternal assistance" (or excessive frustration) since the mother cannot be counted on to be there when the child has fallen, wets its diapers, or needs her for other reasons. These problems can be compounded, however, as in the case of a depressed mother who cannot deal with the active attempts on the part of the child to engage in its games and explorations with her. Such a mother may actually shrink away from the infant. The same is true for certain narcissistic mothers who want to play with the child when *they* are in the mood and rebuff the children when they take the initiative.

Thus, the experience of children of depressed and narcissistic mothers during the individuation and separation phase differs from that of the rejecting ones because they carry with them a constant undefinable sense of dread, the expectation that something terrible will happen either to themselves or to significant others if they exercise their newfound autonomy and interest in the outside world. At the same time, they will later in life exhibit an enormous object hunger, a craving for admiration and a form of pseudovitality to cover up a profound sense of inner emptiness. They cannot trust any object to reliably be there for them since closeness spelled withdrawal on mother's part.

3. Role reversal means that the mother looks at the child as a substitute parent and will react violently to the child's separateness and individuality if, and when, it does not benefit her own infantile needs. The children of these mothers will subjugate their sense of self and their self interests to the real or imagined needs of the mother. They soon learn that their value as little persons is contingent on anticipating their parent's wishes and expectations and, chameleon-like, they turn themselves into whatever they think their parents need them to be. Karl, for example, according to his mother, offered sound marital advice at the age of three, and Anna, at the same age, was already helping her mother take care of a younger sibling.

4. Parents who view their child's willfulness as a trait that should be eliminated as quickly and as effectively as possible, will react punitively when the infant moves, eats, and generally responds in a way that is age-appropriate. Food preferences are not permitted and the child will have to stay at the table until it has eaten everything on its plate. Thus, aside from inflicting inappropriate frustrations on the child, its autonomy and ability for self-regulation are actively attacked. Even under optimal conditions, the relationship between the mother and the toddler is—among other things—a battle of wills. The harsh and authoritarian parent, however, will turn the normal battle of wills into a persecution of the child. Should—for reasons that we do not fully understand—these battles become sexualized, the basis for sexual sadomasochism has been laid. Even if there is little or no sexualization,

however, a reservoir of profound hatred and sadism is established that will be reactivated in adult life.

5. Ridicule of the child's first steps and its attempts to seduce the parent into recognition, positive mirroring or play, coupled with parental contempt for the child's failures is a particularly pernicious parental response to the toddler's love affair. It undermines not only his pride and sense of self, but also precludes any kind of joyful learning experience. Fathers and siblings in this respect can be as cruel, if not more so, than mothers. The message: "Who do you think you are, you little twerp?" will induce children to pretend to know rather than risk asking for help. They would rather injure themselves time and again in their efforts to walk and climb by themselves than to rely on parental assistance. As adults, their sense of shame and corresponding secrecy, particularly for their failures, can be so pronounced that they will deprive themselves of the most ordinary forms of human support. Therapeutically, they pose particularly difficult problems because typically, they do not approach their therapists with questions but with solutions, and they present the outcomes of their actions rather than their plans.

In the light of what has just been said, our adult patients, depending on the particular constellation of parental and interactive traits, approached the chronological age of psychological birth with considerable structural defects. As a result, they never had a chance to develop a superego proper, since we assume that the development of a sound superego is contingent on the development of a cohesive self. What these patients do have are the rigidly introjected attitudes of their parents with respect to what constitutes good and bad behavior.

Patients enter Phase III with the following liabilities and assets: During Phases I and II, they have hopefully accumulated a sufficient amount of "good holding" experiences to counteract the more traumatic aspects of earliest infancy. They are able to trust their therapists, at least most of the time, to truly work in their behalf. Their failure at omnipotent control of their therapist, *and the transition crisis* has resulted in a first glimmer of understanding that the therapist can not, and will not, give them what they did not get in earliest infancy. Consequently, they will consciously set the goal to assume self-responsibility and to autonomously take care of themselves. The combination of ego-impairment, self-pathology and their early experiences of premature loss of maternal assistance, disillusionment with the mother and consequently the self, ridicule and/or persecution, makes this an exeedingly difficult proposition. Thus, the therapeutic climate has to be one of optimal acceptance of a *gradual* learning process. Patients will have to be taught that this time around they will not be kicked out of the nest before they are ready; they are bound to make mistakes that have to be understood rather than ridiculed or frowned upon, and that their therapist will respect and honor their autonomy and individuality. Most important, however, is the therapist's ability to communicate pride and joy when the patient does move forward in spite of his or her inner difficulties.

In order to delineate the treatment goals and objectives for Phase III more clearly to the patient who is now a full fledged partner in our work, we have to ferret out what the various hidden agenda's are that motivate the patient to hang on to his old and familiar ways of operating. This is the time when the secondary gains of the syndrome have to be examined over and over again in order to give the patient the opportunity to truly chose between autonomy and mastery on one hand and helplessness, sadistic suffering, emotional blackmail, and a *perverse* sense of specialness on the other. It is very important during this time to be aware of the internal consistency of the patient's script, which means that giving up one facet of it endangers the whole. Positive willing has to be encouraged while negative and counterwilling will have to be presented as possible—albeit unrewarding—options.

In other words, working through Phase III constitutes repeated cycles of examining behavior, ferreting out the hidden agenda, tracing it to its origins, ventilating repressed feelings, supporting attempts at mastery, and responding to and analyzing the resistance to individuation. Rapproachment maneuvers have to be distinguished from resistances. For example: a patient who is doing well in school or at work may come in with no real complaints, stating that all has gone well but that he is feeling terrible. Usually, in these instances, there is nothing manipulative about the patient's complaint and, therefore, there is nothing to interpret. Chances are, that what the patient has come for is "refueling," i.e. being with an accepting supportive other. But since the sadomasochistic patient has had no good refueling experiences, they must make themselves feel terrible in order to "deserve" or "justify" their quest for mothering. Karl, during a severe rapproachment crisis was miraculously "cured" after he spent 45 minutes sitting on the floor, chitchatting, listening to music, and demolishing an entire box of penny candy that I had given him.

Another form of rapproachment maneuver consists of the display of pseudo-maturity, with the implication that therapy is finished and that the patient should terminate. Underneath that message is the yearning to be talked out of leaving and to be welcomed in their wish to resume the therapeutic work. Some patients can, in fact, go so far as to arrange their work lives and schedules in such a way that therapy is, indeed, impossible. If not too much negative pressure is put on them they usually return a few months or a semester later and the work can be resumed. The purpose of these maneuvers, and their variations is usually to test whether we care enough to protect them from their attempts to "run away from home" or from another maneuver that I call "playing in traffic" i.e., the senseless exposure to danger.

In sum, the treatment goals for Phase III have to combine the following components: 1. We have to facilitate individuation and separation the exercise of mastery and survival skills. 2. We have to analyze and counteract the early experiences that produced the development of the negative and the counterwill; and 3. Strengthen the patient's autonomous wish for positive willing as opposed to the hidden agenda. As a result of this process, self-other differentiation will proceed and the major ego-defects will be repaired. Pathological narcissism will be slowly transformed into healthy self-love and regard for others. Mastery will replace grandiosity, and identification will replace idealization. The propensity toward shame will recede and gratitude will take the place of envy. Though superego integration essentially takes place during Phase IV, superego modifications have to be undertaken throughout Phases I through III, whenever an archaic and sadistic superego forerunner interferes with the patient's functioning and hampers the patient's ability to internalize and exercise self-soothing activities or functions. Alternatively, if we deal with a patient who has suspended his superego, and whose sadomasochism manifests itself in overt delinquency or sexual acting out that impedes further growth, the therapist—at least in part—may have to assume the function of an auxiliary superego.

TRANSFERENCE

The shift toward the felt necessity to assume self-responsibility results in a series of changes in the transference, and, as we will discuss in the next section of this chapter, the interpretation of it now becomes one of the most important therapeutic techniques. In the case of a schizophrenic or borderline schizophrenic, Phase III revolves primarily around the choice between sanity and craziness. Consequently, if the life-jacket transference described earlier has been sufficiently strengthened, it will provide a strong positive transferential undercurrent that allows the patient to test his powers of fragmentation and psychotic distortion and subsequent "putting the self and the therapist back together again." In other words, setbacks will mobilize psychotic transference reactions, but now they have a different quality. They are exercised in the service of the emergent ego, and in that sense, are semi-controlled.

With the borderlines and the character disorders, where psychotic fragmentation is not really an issue, the transference is quite stormy with constant vascillations between idealization and disappointment and concomitant devaluation. The borderline structures with a vertical split will continue to demand from the therapist a mirroring of grandiose and exhibitionistic strivings, and if anything less than wholesale approval is given, it will result in the projection of the shame-inducing qualities of the early parent onto the therapist. Since it is our goal during Phase III to strengthen the compensatory structures of these patients, the helpful solution is if the therapist is cast in the role of the helpful father, who, after all, in the traditional families these patients grew up in, assumed (or should have assumed) the role of teaching their children the skills that would have enabled them to deal with the "world out there." Thus, it is by no means therapeutically contraindicated to assume, at times, the role of the kindly mentor to facilitate the learning experiences of dealing with the demands of the real world. The inevitable lapses in empathy, however, together with the provocations on the part of the patient, will reactivate expressions of unforgiving rage to cover up shame. When Bob had become a therapist-in-training, he came into group shaking with fury, since his supervisor had pointed out to him that in relation to his patients, he had given some indications of countertransferential problems that seemed to be based on overidentification. In other words, he had been told that he had exhibited a shortcoming that *every* beginning therapist shares to a greater or lesser extent. To Bob, this message meant total devastation and an attack on all his abilities and talents. The supervisor had devalued what Bob considered to be the most valuable aspect of his work, namely the identification and the empathy with his patients.

Thus, he came into the session with the demand that we restore his self esteem by judging his supervision report as the vindictive nonsense that he had to see it as. The challenge was clear: "If you agree with *me*, all is well. If you agree with *him*, I have to devalue the both of you." This is the tranferential challenge that this kind of patient will pose time and again and it takes an enormous amount of tact and humor to put things into perspective. In this particular instance, the crisis was weathered when I told him "In other words, you are doing with your patients now, some of the same things that five years before, I slipped into doing with you, when I supported you in your wish to quit your job, which we both know was a mistake. Welcome to the club of humanity that only learns by making mistakes." Thus, confidence was restored and he could ask me for some suggested readings that would help him to understand the problems of countertransference. Since in the same session Bob was also reminded of the enormous progress that he had in fact made, the transferential balance was at least temporarily re-established, until he came across the next critical comment by an authority figure.

In the case of the borderline structure with a horizontal split, the major transferential problems revolve around the persistent demand that the therapist make them feel good, since they have a hard time dealing with the frustrating aspects of the therapist and the therapeutic interaction. "Prove that you love me by giving me your qualities that I admire so much" is the persistant demand, which of course, meets with consistent failure. Only in this instance, however, the failure results in depression, despair, and suicidal ideation. These patients see us as monstrous withholders when their merger wishes are not met. Their demands and neediness appear at times bottomless, and they will create one crisis situation after another to prove their entitlement for total care. Like starving and neglected children, they will crave and cling; the disillusionment in the omnipotent therapist will produce despair and futile attempts to get their merger wishes met elsewhere, usually by a string of short-lived but extremely intense love affairs. In short, the transference is characterized by persistent object splitting that gives it its pronounced yo-yo quality. When one such patient, Maria, learned that I had decided to add a new member to the group, (she was not yet ready to relinquish her position as "the youngest sibling") she experienced that decision as such a powerful assault on her concept as a person whose needs mattered, that after she left that session, she promptly smashed up her car. It took a great deal of soothing to convince her, that *this* therapist-mother, unlike her real mother, could care for more than one sibling.

The better structured personalities, the character disorders, represent a very similar transference problem, with one major difference, however. The effects of the necessary disillusionments with the omnipotent therapist are less profound. Ego and object splitting, instead of being the predominant response, only occur under extreme crisis situations. Consequently, their ability to incorporate some of the good aspects of the therapist is less impaired. They are emotionally the "better eaters." Since their interactions with the early parents, however, were somewhat more benign, they also incorporated their frustrating and forbidding aspects more thoroughly, and they will continue to project them onto significant others. Although the transference situation is less stormy and more stable than that of the borderline, it is, nevertheless, quite solid and pervasive and less easily penetrated. Given their more elaborate and socially acceptable defensive systems, they are in a better position to rationalize their masochistic interpretation of life and their sadism is expressed more subtly. Anna, for example, turned me into her frustrating, persecuting, and hateful mother, but at the same time, resisted and devalued my supportive responses as being therapeutically "unsound." Only in jest could she ask me to borrow my ego, or for me to go and confront difficult people for her, in order to set boundaries. But these requests were always presented as a joke. In the process of becoming a therapist in private practice, Anna had to leave the clinic where she had worked for many years and which she profoundly disliked. Instead of looking forward to the prospect of leading a better and freer life, she secretly blamed me of depriving her of a bad home situation and for forcing her to go out into the cold cruel world. Thus, she acted on the basis of a life-time habit of being a good obedient girl who did what she thought she was being told. Being also exceedingly polite, she did not express her rage openly, but turned it into obsessional concerns over the details of this impending move. The unexpressed rage manifested itself in insomnia.

The more openly narcissistic patients will also express the craving for admiration and their narcissistic rage in terms that are much more covert. They will develop symptoms not to be found in any psychiatric textbook, and then poke fun at the therapist for looking somewhat bewildered. With a great show of benevolence, they will then enlighten the therapist as to what this symptom is all about. Also, a contemptuous display of esoteric knowledge is designed to put the therapist in his place, and keeps the patient emotionally empty. Some of them can be extraordinarily witty in recounting their calamities, particularly in group, and while they cherish the audience appreciation for their wit, they bitterly resent the absence of concern that the story should have elicited had it been presented differently. Only a consistent interpretation and active intervention will reach the empty, unappreciated child underneath and provide them with a sense of being understood without being put down for their calamities.

TECHNIQUES

During Phases III and IV, the entire repertoire of interpretive and ego-building techniques has to be used and often in the course of a session. The process of growth, in terms of separation and individuation, allows for, and demands, regressive moves that previously might have been too frightening for the better functioning patients. The formerly psychotic patient who is now afraid of regressions will have to be taught that they can regress in the service of the ego without fear of irreversible fragmentation. Our thrust during Phase III is three-fold: 1. We have to chip away at the hidden agenda; 2. Strengthen autonomous functioning; and 3. Uncover those infantile experiences that impeded emotional growth in the first place. The "good hour," or, more likely, sequence of hours, will contain all three elements. The starting point may be a complaint about the fact that the therapy is going nowhere, since the patient is still in the same dead-end job or marriage as before and that he hates every minute of it. Thus, the transferential meaning of the complaint has to be explored. We may ask the patient what a successful therapy would consist of. The answer to this question, usually, has two components: a fantasy of having a therapist who can magically do for the patient; and rage at the therapist for not doing it. Thus, the complaint to the therapist is an attempt on the part of the patient to make the therapist feel as impotent as the patient considers himself to be. This is a maneuver that could be called "passing the emotional buck" instead of assuming self-responsibility. The next step is aimed at the patient's resistance and hidden agenda. An invitation to fantasize what would happen if the patient picked himself up and pursued, for example, that course of study that could result in the kind of career that the patient has always dreamed of, will probably reveal the interpersonal objective behind the patient's failure to do for himself. When we ask patients to fantasize it is very important that we encourage them to really spin out their fantasy tales. Every time the patient stops, he should be egged on with the question, "And then what would happen . . . ?" In these explorations of the anticipated consequences of behavioral changes, the entire cast of characters of the patient's past and present life will probably play a role and with it, many different layers of hopes and fears that are attached to these significant others. Consequently, these excursions into fantasy have to be repeated over and over again to uncover the various layers. What has to be conveyed to the patient is our belief that at the bottom of their defensive maneuvers was never anything other than the wish to survive and that the present behavior represents survival techniques that once were essential, but have since outlived their usefulness and have become dysfunctional. This basic faith in the origin of the deepest motivation must be expressed repeatedly, to counteract the patients' profound fear that if they allowed their psyches to be fully explored, they would reveal monstrous human beings. If that fear of their monstrousness were allowed to persist, it would be paralyzing at best and, at worst, could easily result in premature termination. Thus, a first exploration as to what would happen if the patient would allow himself to succeed professionally may elicit nothing more than the fear that the spouse, lover, or therapist would lose interest in him. This fearful anticipation has to be explored further to determine whether competence and autonomy represents primarily premature loss of maternal assistance, fear of ridicule, i.e. assault on the infant's self-esteem. Alternatively it may indicate the introjection of a parental message of the child's basic badness and stupidity, i.e. the projection of the parental sense of incompetence onto the child. Finally it can represent a defense against the mother's narcissistic use of the child's accomplishment which induced fears of incorporation. Usually, rather than decide for ourselves what motivates the patient's negative response at *this particular moment,* it is better to ask the patient a question, such as, "When was the first time you felt this way?" Chances are, the patient will come up with a particular memory that encapsulates one of the psychotoxic elements that was just enumerated, or alternatively, a combination of several of them. One patient, Maria, remembered that at age seven, she still wet the bed occasionally. This particular girl had grown up essentially neglected since her father had focused all his attention on the oldest daughter and her mother paid almost exclusive attention to the younger brother. Thus, this child, who had started bedwetting at the age of four, was told in harsh and no uncertain terms that as long as she acted like a baby, she would have to wear diapers every night. This she did with a great deal of resentment. The real injury—and her sense of specialness—consisted in her father's habit of asking her at bedtime, and in front of company, whether she had put on her diapers. Needless to say, in adult life this young woman thrived on humiliations, which she obtained through seemingly indiscriminate sexual acting out with a host of clandestine and degrading love affairs, obesity and a marital relationship in which she played the role of the sick, but delinquent, little girl. If we look at this woman's particular memory, two elements stand out: premature loss of maternal assistance and persecution; and severe narcissistic injuries, i.e. the infliction of shame. Thus, paternal care and a sense of specialness was bought at the expense of baby-like behavior and consistent humiliations. Therefore, the interpretation had to be offered that without her bedwetting, she would not have had a sense of mattering at all, of having a distinct sense of self, and of getting attention. Therapeutically, the following cycles were repeated: 1. Conscious attempts to get her parent's attention just for being the way she is, which in her fantasy dialogues always resulted in failure. As Larry had done so often, she imagined her parents as being in the room with her but preoccupied either with each other or with the other two children, and she tried to interrrupt them to get their attention without being yelled at. 2. Ventilation of rage over her father's shaming of her which put her in touch with her profound yearning for her mother's care at a much earlier age. 3. She shed many angry and self-depreciating tears. When she had cried herself out, I would ask her if there was anything I could do to make her feel better. It took her almost six months to work herself up for what in her eyes was the most outrageous request, namely that I brush her hair. Having done this slowly and carefully, we spent the rest of the session in companionable silence. The real therapeutic breakthrough in this instance, consisted in her ability to formulate a concrete request, which was entirely realizable since no magic on my part was involved, and to use it constructively, as indicated by her need for silence afterwards. She seemed to really digest the experience, and in the month following this incident her sexual acting out decreased and her autonomous functioning increased. In the group, where at the beginning she had established her role as the "depraved one" she replayed several times her role as the neglected middle child who is again made the target of ridicule. In the reversed script, i.e. Maria's direction of the same scene but this time with a good ending, the therapist was cast in the role of the kindly aunt who persuaded the mother to set specific time slots aside which were exclusively designed for her to be alone with this child. The rest of the group remonstrated with the father for not understanding the real meaning of the bedwetting. In time, Maria learned to internalize the soothing functions of the therapist and the group; she learned more constructive ways of feeling worthwhile and functioning autonomously and her rage against her younger brother, older sister and her father, whom she had blamed for depriving her of her mother's love, slowly receded. Thus, she could stop punishing men with her contemptuous affairs and give up the need to devalue women as the great deprivers. It should be noted at this point, that the decision to honor her request for having her hair brushed rested on the evaluation of the dynamics of this particular patient, and at the timing of the event. A patient who was overindulged during the symbiotic phase and infantilized during the individuation separation phase should *never* be indulged in this way. The hidden agenda of this particular woman had read as follows: "If I cannot get all of mother's love, i.e. return to the time before the brother was born, I shall accept nothing, I will devalue all positive responses. Instead, I shall keep myself a helpless delinquent vis-à-vis my husband, an interaction which demeans both of us but frees me from self responsibility. Furthermore I will continue to punish my father by picking up lower class brutes who slap me around and whom I can then despise." In other words, what she was saying was, "After all my parents have done to me, how can I be anything but an incompetent, contemptuous slut?" The request for brushing her hair came only *after* she had given up some of her magical expectations of her therapist and *while* she was in the process of applying to college; in other words, it had a preparatory function, namely, to allow her to risk autonomy without fears of losing all maternal care.

In other words, the concept of optimal disillusionment, technically, always has the following components:

1. In order to overcome the resistance toward individuation and separation, i.e. autonomous ego functioning and mastery, we have to ascertain what a particular behavior pattern is supposed to convey to the therapist; the interpretation of the transference.

2. A connection has to be made to a significant memory that contributed to one or several aspects of the hidden agenda.
3. More suitable resolutions to the internal conflict have to be searched for which are *realistic* in terms of what the patient *can* and what the therapist *cannot* do.
4. Preparatory exercises have to be devised in which patients explore in fantasy, on one hand, what positive and negative consequences a specific change would entail, and on the other, whether, even if the worst anticipated outcome came true, if the patient would still be able to survive.
5. A patient who needs an active soothing experience or a transitional object should be given one.
6. The new and more constructive mode of functioning has to be acknowledged, praised, and exercised over and over.

In these cycles, positive and negative regressions have to be distinguished. A patient who has moved rather rapidly in a short span of time, may experience two phenomena: fear of object loss, and reactivation of narcissistic rage. Most patients take a step forward after they have had sufficient preparation, and we should help them to take those steps as gradually as they need to be.

The more masochistically-inclined patient, however, will use the progress, in order to defeat himself and the therapeutic alliance. Anna, for example, would plan changes in her personal or professional life in such a way that they exhausted her to the point of collapse. She would come to her session looking dead-beat tired, harrassed, dissheveled, and on the verge of hysterical tears over some infuriating, but inevitable, aggravations of city life. Then, she would set out to explore through what fault of her own the superintendent, plumber or electrician had fouled up her plans for meeting her already hectic schedule. The overt message was; "Look how hard I am trying, but nothing works out, because I am really not competent to hold it all together," i.e. omnipotence in the form of self-blame. The covert message was, "I am an obedient little girl, consequently I am doing what you tell me to do, but as you can see, it is going to kill me, and then you will be sorry." An immediate interpretation of such a covert message would only result in a stalemate and produce justifiable rage on the part of the patient, since it would be truly unempathic. Although an understanding of the situation and its interpersonal intent is the ultimate goal, a patient who has experienced depletion will first have to refuel regressively before an interpretation has a chance to be heard. Thus, at these junctures, I usually invite patients to take off their shoes, lie down on the couch, cover them with a blanket and put on some soothing music with the suggestion that they use the session to just plain rest. This suggestion tends to result in angry protests that they do not intend to spend that much money for something they could do just as well at home—the accusation that their unhappiness is exploited by the therapist. If the patient goes along with this suggestion—and they almost always do—rapid regression to the symbiotic phase will ensue. It encompasses the experience of neglect during the first year of life and a soaking-up of the soothing and participating silence of the therapist in their attempt to rest and sleep and block out the internal and external turmoil. This has to be accepted as a healthy regression for these reasons: 1. It tends to eliminate the need for an interpretation since the patient usually offers it without prompting, 2. The patient will get in touch with pre-verbal experiences and mourn the permanent loss of that kind of good mothering. Thus, the detour through the therapeutic modes of pacification and unification brings about further disillusionment with the mother of earliest infancy, the gradual internalization of the empathic mothering in the therapeutic alliance which prompts the renewed attempt at autonomous functioning with less of a punitive hidden agenda.

An unproductive regression, based on the reactivation of archaic, narcissistic rage can occur when the initial attempts at autonomy are unconsciously tinged with too grandiose expectations. In this case, a profound experience of anticipated shame tends to produce a need for secrecy that shuts the therapist out. No active immediate intervention into that type of self-destructive isolation is known to me. Empathic interpretations of the need for admiration are experienced as patronizing by the patient who has boxed himself in in that way. The patient has to be allowed to rage about his fate until he sends out a disguised cry for help. For example, Fred (See Chapter 2, page 63) who had dropped out of college at 20, returned to college at 27. He did extremely well and he surprised me with his seemingly flawless acceptance of the role of the lowly undergraduate student. All his previous intellectual arrogance seemed to have disappeared, and he completed all his course-work with excellent grades. His group celebrated his graduation, and he was torn between the choice of going to graduate school or looking for a job. After he had asked his family to also give him a graduation party, all his previous joy over his success vanished since the party had been extremely disappointing. His family had been essentially unimpressed. After a month of total inactivity, depressed brooding and a great deal of masochistic sexual acting out, Fred revealed his plans for writing a book which in terms of subject matter seemed to be very similar to this one but much broader in scope. Subtle tactful hints that a direct progression from writing excellent college term papers to a major work in the social sciences was perhaps too ambitious and difficult an enterprise, produced intense rage. He was convinced that I was out to crush all his newly acquired self-esteem and he increasingly saw me as his mortal enemy. His sexual acting out escalated further, and he was secretly quite pleased every time he picked up a case of V.D. Interpersonally, outside of therapy, his demanding behavior, his "entitlement position"—"my special suffering in the past now entitles me to special privileges, and what is more, only the best is good enough for me"—and his need to devalue everything good that was given to him became more and more pronounced. He refused to do anything in his own behalf. The regression seemed impenetrable. His archaic exhibitionistic and grandiose strivings and the anticipation of humiliation kept him in a state of perpetual rage, alternating with depressions and a profound sense of inner emptiness. The therapist was kept impotent. Therapy could have ended at this point—or at least been interrupted for quite some time—if the grandiosity as expressed in the book-project had been explored further. Instead, after having discussed the impasse, we decided to bring the problem to group. Fred set out to utilize the group as his defense attorneys to expose my vindictive and competitive stance, since he had reached the point where he believed that his rage had reached such proportions that he felt that he could easily kill me in his individual sessions and was quite afraid of it. When in group, in response to his accusations, he got warmth and acceptance—though no validation of his interpretation of the impasse—he burst into tears and he had to be rocked by the group for some comfort. Only after this session could he apply himself to the systematic exploration of this regression to earliest infancy and to his paranoid ideation. It was then that he discovered through the examination of family photographs that he had been born with slightly defective legs which were corrected through plaster casts and various orthopedic contraptions which made standing and walking extremely difficult. Apparently his handicap was a source of embarrassment for his family and his vigorous attempts to stand up and to walk with his orthopedic bars caused a great deal of laughter but very little empathic and supportive assistance. At that age, his parent's shame over his condition, and his being shamed by them were not yet differentiated in his mind and he settled for two sets of options: 1. If I cannot move like Tarzan, I will not move at all; and 2. If I cannot obtain total admiration I will arrange for constant humiliations and, thus, be in charge of my fate.

GROUP THERAPY

The role of group therapy during Phase III is of special importance. It has several functions: 1. For those patients who are still solidly rooted in the symbiotic phase, watching the "older" group members struggle with individuation and separation problems has a preparatory effect. In a well-run group, members are astonishingly tolerant of those group members who are functioning on a more primitive level of psychosocial development, and they can genuinely indulge these "younger siblings" until they, too, reach the point of having to assume self-responsibility. 2. Group members who have interacted for a long time and on a continuous basis, know a great deal about each other's family history, defenses, hidden agenda's, and sadomasochistic maneuvers. Consequently, they can in fact be quite effective in interpreting each other's behavior. If one member has not yet established enough awareness of his or her defensive style, if experiences and interpretations do not yet carry over, the other group members will remember and establish the link between the hidden agenda of a past experience and the complaint in the present. We can, and I think we must, establish a group climate where in the identification with others, the compassionate component, is stressed, and the wish to destroy and attack the negative mirror image is curbed. A patient who watches a group member displaying very similar defensive maneuvers, i.e. his own interactions with the group the year before, may well wish to attack the new member because the memory is shameful; and the newly-acquired modes of interacting are still, somewhat shaky. When this happens, the identification has to be dealt with immediately. Usually, the invitation to look at the new member as if he or she were a mirror establishes the points of similarities as well as differences. Thus, the attack, which is really a disguised form of self-loathing, is short-circuited, slowly replaced with compassion, and the new patient feels a sense of belonging, i.e. some understanding that his problems are not all that unique and that, obviously, they can be helped.

In those instances where shame is an outstanding feature of the pathology, a patient may be able to reveal shameful actions, thoughts, or fantasies to their therapists, but very often this is not sufficient because, in a way, the therapist is not seen as a real person, his responses can always be interpreted as constituting the "proper professional stance" rather than a genuine reaction. A patient can go on for a long time assuming that underneath the non-judgmental stance, the therapist is really horrified. A patient who can bring himself to reveal his shameful secrets to the group, however, is less likely to interpret the group's accepting responses as a fake. Moreover, the admiration for the patient's courage in revealing shameful material is a definite bonus for everybody since it allows the others to deal with their own shame barrier, secrets, and the subject of trust which is the prerequisite for overcoming the need for secrecy. Since, for obvious reasons, much of the work done in group therapy is painful and shame-provoking, I have found it extremely helpful to start each group session with a procedure borrowed from Re-evaluation Counseling (Jackins, 1964 and Somers, 1972) which is called "New and Good." Each group member can bring in one or several instances in the past week where they overcame a particular difficulty of theirs, "starved a pattern" so to speak, or otherwise did something that they take pride or joy in. This procedure has several advantages:

1. It may make it easier for group members to later deal with those instances where they were *not* able to drop their old ways of relating.
2. Admiration for positive steps taken facilitates further growth.
3. The more quiet or less troubled group members—or those who are still very new in group—get a chance to let the others know what is happening in their lives.
4. Those group members who habitually claim that absolutely nothing new or good happened to them all week will eventually have to ask themselves whether something is not drastically wrong with their way of looking at their life.

5. The wish to bring a "new and good" may, at times, motivate a group member to *make* a move that otherwise they might have delayed for some time.
6. Sharing progress in this way produces a collective sense of pride in the effectiveness of the group's interaction and, thus, solidifies the group's cohesiveness.

No matter how supportive, empathic and compassionate a group may try to be, the process of optimal—and sometimes massive disillusionment—is constantly at work, however due to both the normal and the pathological limitations of the various group members. Lillian, for example, who was quite articulate and insistent upon her request that due to the fact that her parent's comings and goings had been entirely unpredictable during her childhood, she should never be disappointed when it came to keeping a date or social arrangement. She was certain that if anybody ever forgot an appointment or kept her waiting unduly, she would never be able to trust that person again. Thus, the first time someone did indeed forget, all hell broke loose and it took her a long time to digest the fact that others have their own needs and shortcomings and that her very insistence on this particular "proof" of trustworthiness would be an invitation to disappoint her, particularly on the part of those patients who had grown up with the constant maternal demand that the child "prove" its love and devotion. When she finally came to understand the difference between trustworthiness and dependability, she could drop her demands for that type of perfection in others.

A continuous attempt to resolve conflict between group members by having them reverse roles deepens the understanding of how family members can affect each other positively and negatively. Also, group members who come to realize that they are now almost exactly as old (or even older) as their parents were when they raised them in the way they did, must eventually make a choice between indicting the parents and consequently, themselves, for having similar shortcomings, or, alternatively, begin to extend their newly found compassion for themselves to their own parents. As this understanding grows, they may be able to relate to them with a much greater degree of tolerance for their inability to change. As the hidden agenda loses its compelling power, patients will relate to their parents differently and, therefore, at least in most cases receive a different and more positive response. In some instances, however, the separation from the parents due to the parents pathology has to be rather total and permanent, a process that is usually only completed during Phase IV. The reenactment of the relationship between siblings in group is at least of equal importance to that of the interaction between parents and children. The grievances of the younger sibling for having been tortured by an older one, if it is played out against the grievances of the first-born who saw the second-born as an invasive intruder and depriver of maternal love and attention, brings out the problems of envy, guilt, and competition and underneath it, frequently a passionate involvement between those siblings who ostensibly hated each other.

In fact, it has been my impression that the *first full-fledged sadomasochistic reenactment* of the relationship between the child and its preoedipal mother as well as the relationship between the parents, very often *takes place between siblings*. What I am referring to in this instance is far more complex than simple sibling rivalry. An analysis of one particular sibling constellation may illustrate the general point: the relationship between an older brother and a younger sister. Three of my women patients have shown an almost identical pattern: the first-born son—seemingly the apple of their mother's eyes—received the lion's share of their mother's attention while the fathers either ignored or persecuted them. As these boys grew up, they developed into a chronic schizophrenic, a career criminal and an alcoholic respectively. During their childhood, however, they seemed to have been the adored narcissistic extension of their mothers and at least in part, substitute husbands. When the girls were born, their mothers showed little interest, and in two instances showed considerable contempt for their daughters. As these girls became toddlers, they quickly realized that the only way to the mother was through their older brothers, whom they idealized. They tagged after their brothers and willingly put up with teasing and torturing, in other words anything that would keep them in their brothers' good graces. One of those girls voiced her envy of her brother's perferential treatment by her mother continuously, only to have it invalidated by the mother as an indication of the girl's badness, ingratitude, and competitiveness. The other two disavowed their envy and imitated their mother's adulation of their brothers. The older boys, all being subjected to an equally pathological treatment by their mothers—albeit of a different kind—quickly learned to use their sisters as the recipient for their frustrations. They needed their sisters badly. Consequently, their mistreatment never reached the point where the younger sisters would relinquish their bond; to the contrary, occasional indulgences, even acts of outright generosity served to intensify the love-hate relationship. As young adults, these women all disclaimed *any* affectionate ties with their brothers, even though the quality of their relationships with men, at the beginning of therapy, resembled their relationship with their brothers *more*, than they did that with either their fathers or mothers. In group therapy, they encountered a very guilt-ridden older brother, who had tortured his younger sister—kept her crazy as he put it—in order to remain the favorite child. As the woman just mentioned learned to empathize with the suffering that this young man had gone through, and the horrifying aspects of what they considered a privileged position, they slowly relinquished some of their profound rage and envy and their need to attach themselves to men like their brothers. The process of disengagement from their brothers, however, was hard and protracted. For several years, the sister of the schizophrenic boy continued to envy his position, because the mental institution where he was kept was exceedingly expensive and the cost was borne by her mother, an arrangement which entailed no financial hardship whatsoever for that particular family. The fact that for all intents and purposes, this young man had ceased to live at 17 when he was hospitalized, was something his sister chose to disregard for a long time. In other words, group therapy can be a uniquely effective tool for the working through of one of the earliest manifestations of sadomasochism—namely that between siblings which evolves as a powerful secondary formation in response to a less than optimal parent-child relationship.

CASE MATERIAL

Karl

For Karl, the working-through process, essentially revolved around his testing out the merits and disadvantages of sanity and craziness, respectively. After his last hospitalization, a program of vocational rehabilitation was proposed that would train him as a paraprofessional in the mental health profession, and which included the utilization of his artistic skills and talents. Karl, very reluctantly agreed to give it a try. He had very little confidence that he would be able to deal with his emotional turmoil successfully enough to put in a full day's work five days a week. He gave the impression of someone who was willing to temporarily suspend the option of becoming a career patient—but only under protest. For a long time, he acted as if his counselor, his therapist, and his group were forcing him to do this and he very often relied on outside pressures to get up in the morning, to talk him into staying for the entire day. Many group sessions were spent in an effort to keep him from dropping out of the program. At times, we all felt as if we were trying to shove a gigantic elephant through a narrow front door. He strongly held on to his self-concept as a great critic and writer of fiction. His negativism psychodynamically, however, made a great deal of sense to me and to group. Although the group often felt exasperated, they never ran out of patience. They sensed what was at stake. Karl was mortally afraid of being set up to fail, and then being told, "I told you so." After all, from an early age on he had been burdened with tasks that were impossible and their inevitable failures had built up an almost bottomless sense of shame. Thus, he had become determined to avoid commitments to the autonomous pursuit of scholarly or professional success in order to avoid failure, humiliation, and shame, and his corresponding propensity to react with overpowering rages or depressions. His ability to function in this program in a sustained fashion—and without a commitment to sanity—was his test of the integrity of the persons who urged him to do it. Put differently, if he were to find out that the transferential parents were not setting him up to fail, then he could make a commitment to give it all he had and to do his very best. As it turned out, despite his occasional attempts to fail, despite his complaints and very real terrors, he was soon recognized by his superiors and teachers as one of their most promising candidates, and this evaluation was communicated to him. Even though this positive feedback frightened him, he also began to like it, and reiterated his opinion that this was not going to commit him to finishing the program. In the course of a year, however, it was clear to everybody—including Karl—that he was going to go on voluntarily and that his interest in the field had been aroused. He was hooked. At this point, several changes took place. First of all, Karl started to neglect his writing without missing it at all. Second, he took a lover, much younger than himself who seemed to encompass on a smaller scale many of the attributes of his former self as well as some of the characteristics of his parents. Bernie, aside from his charming qualities was also a spoiled prince, exceedingly immature, dishonest, greedy, unemployed, and determined to be taken care of. He was also a not-so-petty thief. He appeared like a disarmingly charming and seductive overgrown puppy dog, whom Karl indulged with great pleasure. Third, Karl slowly gave up his belief that I had forced him into something that made no sense in terms of his real ambitions. Instead, he became quite interested in learning from me how to deal with crazy people in his job. His initial encounter with patients involved dealing with a population that was both disturbed and senile. Their manipulative behavior of this fresh student in the beginning resulted in Karl's feeling and acting like an octogenarian after his first day on the job. He came to my office looking ancient and he complained about a raging headache. In the course of 10 minutes listening to his tale of woe, I started to develop a headache myself. Therefore, I suggested to Karl that I would play Karl if he agreed to play my part. Reluctantly, he agreed. When he saw himself—and his patients—mirrored in his therapist's caricature of a whimpering angry child, he suddenly came to life, burst out laughing, and both our headaches cleared up. He could take his own self back, without merging it with that of his charges. In the course of his training, we repeated exercises of this kind whenever his self-other differentiation had become blurred. Karl learned rapidly and willingly. Since his on-the-job training also entailed working with elderly schizophrenic women, some of whom were overtly seductive to the point of exposing themselves to him, and some who were either incontinent or deliberately smeared their feces all over themselves and their beds, Karl faced what must have been the ultimate challenge. Suddenly, he found himself the adult caretaker of seductive mother-figures and of grandparents who were not toilet-trained and who seemed to take great pleasure in having Karl clean them up and change their beds. Thus, he had only two choices; to give up or to learn something about schizophrenia. He was after all, confronted with adult versions of his own five-year-old self, which he understood only too well, and he had to figure out the psychodynamics of his mother's sexual seductiveness, against which he had tried to wall himself off all his life. These women, however, did not appear monstrous to him, but merely pathetic. Soon it became crystal clear to Karl, that he was going to understand crazy people and that he would never again be able to even *contemplate* joining them.

His relationship with Bernie was an equally important arena for Karl's growing up. Originally, these two men acted in a highly symbiotic fashion. Many of the split-off unacceptable parts of Karl's psyche were relegated to Bernie. Thus, Karl worked responsibly in the adult world and Bernie stayed in the playpen. Bernie was the demanding child, Karl the exasperated parent. A great deal of emotional growth took place, however, in the time they were together. Although in the past, Karl's behavioral resources had been limited to either idealization or total devaluation, total love or total rejection, he now began to talk about problems in the relationship without flying into rages, immobilizing himself through depressions or simply leaving the field. He learned to sort out what were his problems and to differentiate them from Bernie's complaints. One incident was particularly instructive. On their first New Year's day together, Bernie told him, "I want you to make this the best New Year I have ever had." Karl's immediate response was to run and to never want to see Bernie again. The echo of his mother's imagined demand that he stop the Red Army single-handedly, almost overwhelmed him. Upon reflection, however, he recognized his own propensity toward magical thinking mirrored in Bernie's infantile longings and realized that he could simply say "no" to this global request. Karl's wish to discuss his relationship with Bernie in therapy fluctuated. As long as he needed Bernie to act out his own infantile patterns, the interaction was not discussed in therapy. Only when Karl outgrew the vicarious pleasure of indulging the other, did Bernie's demands and his negativity become enough of an irritant to be brought into therapy. Unfortunately, although Karl continued to grow up at an amazing speed, Bernie became more and more threatened, and seemed to react regressively. In a last ditch effort to preserve the status quo, Bernie engaged in rather serious theft which stood a good chance of discovery, and Bernie engaged Karl in a conspiracy of silence, very similar to the one Karl's family had engaged in after the war when his father regularly stole food for the dinner table. Thus, burdened with a shameful secret that he was not allowed to share with anybody, including group and me, Karl temporarily slipped back into the only too familiar pattern of self-isolation. He was depressed and his enthusiasm for work disappeared. Suddenly, everything seemed to be too much, and he sat in group in stony silence. Finally, when the group and I had grown sufficently alarmed to confront Karl, did the ugly secret come out, and together with it, Karl's profound rage at Bernie and at his own weakness that had prompted him to participate in these games. Although the relationship lasted a good while longer, this incident represented a real internal breaking off of an interactive pattern that no longer served his inner needs. When they finally did separate, it was with sadness and regret on Karl's part, but there was no longer rage and, consequently, no depression.

As Karl's training program came to a close, Karl knew he had found a career that truly suited him, and decided that he wanted to become a professional rather than a paraprofessional. To this end, he enrolled in college where he performed brilliantly so that he knew that in a few years time he could enter graduate school. After graduation, he took a job where he performed so well that this agency, where the turnover of the paraprofessional personnel is exceedingly high, decided to promote him with a hefty increase in pay in order not to lose him. Phase III came to an end when Karl had reached the point where he was sufficiently confident that his professional and academic success was not a passing thing but an integral part of his self, and when he realized that he no longer needed a lover-twin to carry his infantile longings. Thus, he fully committed himself to life, sanity, and autonomous functioning. Yet, despite his progress, there was still a major source of discontent in his life: namely the relationship with his children, whom he had in fact abandoned, and his relationship with his father. What Karl was saying in effect was: "In order to become the man I want to be, I have to come to grips with my real father first and to start actually acting the part of the responsible father to my sons." What differentiated Karl's thoughts about his children and his role as a father at this point from his earlier tortured ruminations about the subject was the emergence of an ego ideal and a superego proper. He was getting ready for the transition from feeling "I ought to" to truly wanting to act in a way that feels responsible and ethical.

Bob

Following the transition crisis at the end of Phase II that had convinced Bob, for the first time, that he had been willing to risk his very life in order to maintain his malignant bond with his father, he decided to put the initial complaint, which had brought him into therapy, on ice so to speak. He decided that his wish to be able to combine love and sex was out of his reach—probably forever, but that he could at least achieve professional success, social recognition, and interpersonal power. He decided to become a psychologist and to work as a practicing clinician. Although he never articulated this, he must have realized on some level, that without the rehabilitation of his compensatory structures, he would not be able to deal with his primary defect in the self. For the time being, external admiration had to serve as a substitute for genuine self-esteem. He insisted that he could not afford—or wanted to—be in individual therapy, but he faithfully attended the group sessions.

His return to work and school reactivated all his old problems with male authority, and to a lesser extent, female authority. It also brought back his intense envy of my position and the wealth and power which he ascribed to me. School work was exceedingly difficult for Bob: he procrastinated; he handed in what could have been an excellent term paper if only he had included a chapter of his summary and conclusions; he lost grade points by submitting his work one day after the deadline and he manifested every other self-defeating pattern known to graduate students. Criticism of his exams or papers and of his work performance refueled his chronic narcissistic rage. It seemed as if every step along the way was a life-and-death struggle between his wish for adulation and his fear of being criticized. Unfortunately, criticism to Bob meant everything short of receiving an instant Ph.D. degree. Thus, he compromised by creating situations where he did indeed not have sufficient time—or access to reserve books—to receive more than passing grades. Thus, he settled for a secondary sense of grandiosity: to have gotten passing grades, given the circumstances he himself created—did indeed take a lot of doing and demonstrated a very keen mind. The constant anticipation of humiliation and denigration that he had experienced at the hands of his father and grandmother made it impossible for him to ever do his best and to receive an objective evaluation. His paranoid ideation was quite apparent in his relationships with his co-workers who were perceived as constantly plotting injustices, slights, and expressions of contempt for him.

His determination to succeed with his goals was strong enough to see him through school with a masters degree. Had his grade average been higher by one decimal point, however he would have been able to enter the Ph.D. program. This he had avoided carefully. Given the insignificance of the difference between the grade average he obtained and the one required for admission to the Ph.D. program, it was quite clear to him and everybody else, that he could have done better had he chosen to.

A similar pattern of compromise emerged in his pursuit of sexual humiliations, his drug abuse, and alcohol consumption. For the most part, his nighttime escapades to the S&M bars were confined to the time between handing in a term paper or taking an exam and before receiving the grade for his work. Aside from that, only an unusually stressful day at work resulted in the pursuit of that particular remedy. His drug abuse followed a similar pattern. Instead of using them primarily to anesthetize his internal conflicts, and to escape from the problems of living, he depended on amphetamines to see him through the various deadline crises, and their escapist function was restricted to occasional binges.

The most promising sign of progress, however, was Bob's slow but steady shift in attitude toward group, which correlated with his tentative attempts to reach out for his siblings. On some level, Bob knew that his survival depended on his connection with the group and their unwavering support. This he dared not jeopardize. In the past, he had made every attempt in group to engage me exclusively and to block out the other group members. He seemed to aim for an individual session with group merely as an audience. He did this by only addressing me, by never looking at anybody but me, and at times by literally turning his back to his fellow group members. As this was pointed out to him, time and again, he could slowly abandon his competitive stance and involve the entire group in the discussion of his problems. Although on the surface his level of insight into his provocative interactive stance did not seem to increase, something very positive did happen. He lost his sense of shame in the group situation. He could state positively: "This is the only place in the world where I don't feel I have to be ashamed." Three elements seem to have been responsible for this shift: 1. Despite his protests to the contrary, the cumulative effect of testing the group over and over again, and finding them accepting and supportive, convinced him that there were at least eight people in the world who had no investment in attacking his self esteem. In this environment, he felt valued enough to let go of his most self-defeating defensive maneuvers. 2. Those group members who exhibited similar defensive patterns had originally evoked murderous rage in him and he feared them as potential attackers. Through repeated role-reversals, often supplemented by other group members joining the dialogue as alter egos, he slowly understood the process of projective identification, and he became more compassionate toward the split-off parts of himself. Compassion for the self allowed for more compassion for others and the first expressions of generosity toward them. He saw "younger" group members struggle with some of his old problems, and instead of plotting vindictive schemes, he often held out a helping hand that earned him a great deal of gratitude and admiration. 3. Finally, in the course of three years, there had been four group members whose basic character structure was very similar to that of Bob's. All four of them had dropped out of therapy but had kept contact with Bob. Thus, he could watch them play out their hidden agendas and getting very badly hurt in the process. He came to realize that given sufficient determination, people can indeed wreck their lives to the point where changes into more positive directions become more and more difficult, if not impossible. While these patients had been in group, Bob had perpetually sided with their victimized position. Once they left and felt free to act on their impulses, Bob was forced to do some serious rethinking of his previous loyalties. Fear is a poor motivating force, however, and in and by itself, it would have accomplished nothing. But a continuous re-evaluation of the position of the steady group members, his own stance, and that of the ones who had left, did contribute to a growing sense of who Bob was and, more importantly, who he wanted to become.

Following graduation, Bob's self esteem suffered some serious blows, due to the scarcity of jobs in his field open to new graduates with no experience. It reactivated his conviction that hard work and honesty get you nowhere, and he played around with the idea of falsifying his resume by inventing some bogus jobs. For those plans he encountered nothing but opposition by group and by his therapist. But instead of flying into one of his rages, he started to deal with his enormous fears of being unloved, unwanted, and worthless. In the course of these discussions, he could for the first time share with the group many of the miserable aspects of his childhood, something which in the past shame had prevented him from doing. Thus, group came to see a side of Bob, that they had sensed, but had never really seen. Underneath the callous cynical delinquent was a frightened little boy, wanting to be honest, but too terrified of absolutely everything and everybody, to act on his real wishes. These revelations strengthened the protective stance of group toward him, their ability to truly empathize with his torments and to extend a degree of support to him that enabled Bob to get through the rough process of job hunting without falsification of his resume, and the pursuit of post-graduate education that would eventually enable him to become a practicing psychotherapist.

Probably by a combination of accident and design, Bob finally found a job working under the auspices of the Catholic Church, a tragi-comical arrangement for someone with Bob's history. Although the work proved to be a unique challenge since he worked with young-sters with problems very similar to the ones he had encountered in adolescence, having to work within the authority structure of the church, brought back his old conflicts with the church, father figures, religion, and authoritarianism. In discussing his various run-ins with his superiors, it became very clear that as much as he ostensibly hated the job, he was also extremely determined to keep it, with the hidden agenda of replacing his superiors. Since Bob has become much more open about his not so unconscious fantasies, he has also developed a sense of humor about his more irrational aspirations. Thus, he could finally own up to his secret hope of becoming the next pope, and he managed to have a good laugh at that fantasy. In deciding whether and when he should look for other employment, he also exhibited, for the first time, a very genuine concern for his clients. He began to realize, that even though he could not work miracles for them, he would also feel thoroughly unethical if he left in such a way that they would suffer unnecessarily. In other words, the only two options that he had known—battling and overthrowing authority and identifying with it—suddenly yielded a third alternative, to act as responsibly as possible toward those who depended on him, and at the same time to work toward a position that would do justice to his own needs and desires. While this does not yet represent a true transition to phase IV. i.e. readiness for superego integration - we can nevertheless detect the rough outlines of a positive ego ideal.

Bob is now in the process of pursuing this third alternative and his work is becoming increasingly a source of genuine satisfaction. Since he has thrown all his energy into his profession, however, his social life has become almost barren. In the few private sessions that Bob has requested, it has been pointed out to him that nobody can work as a therapist or counselor who does not also have a satisfactory personal life. Bob knows that in order to obtain that goal, he will have to resume the therapeutic work that he abandoned when he left individual therapy. He has taken the summer months to think this over, but I am quite convinced that in the very near future he will work up the courage and the desire to take the steps that are necessary and will allow him to finally live a full life.

Larry

Following the transition crisis, Larry attempted to set up a rather rigid "mental health" plan, a set of rules that distinguished between "good," i.e. sane, and "bad" symbiotic behavior patterns. In the process of doing so, however, he had a series of dreams that started out with images of murdering my husband, and led to a battle between the two of them, and finally ended in a dream where the two of them formed a homosexual union, with my husband cast in the role of the seducer. These were clearly *not* oedipal dreams, since the transference to me had never become sexualized. This series of dreams had two functions: 1. The first set, that revolved around the murderous encounters, was designed to slowly accept the fact that even though there was a significant other in my life, I would not deprive him of my attention, thus, there was no need to eliminate the competition. 2. The second set of dreams had a different function. Since he unconsciously perceived that the process of individuation and separation meant two things, giving up some of my caretaking functions as well as opposing me, he secured for himself a male ally, just in case things got to be too rough, a second line of defense so to speak, just as he had done in childhood so unsuccessfully. In view of the presenting problem, it is interesting to note that in the transference, the rage against the preoedipal transferential father, was of relatively minor importance. In fact after these dreams, in his fantasies about my husband, he always cast him in the role of someone who truly could and would value his artistic performance, and who would be very proud of his accomplishments.

Having understood these dreams as preparatory for his separation and individuation process, Larry set the following goals for himself: 1. He decided to make enough money to pay for his own therapy, rather than collect war-reparations from his father who, up to this point, had paid for his therapy. 2. He set out to establish "a mature relationship" with a grown woman like everybody else in group. 3. To restrict his therapy strictly to verbal interactions—no more pillows. 4. To cut down his individual therapy sessions from twice per week plus group, to once per week plus group, and most importantly, 5. to return to the stage.

The implementation of his mental health plan, radically changed the transference situation. After he had found a girlfriend, Christina, an actress who appeared to be his peer, and who was pretty but did not look like his fantasies of *Playboy* centerfolds, he spent a rather blissful honeymoon period with her. In many ways, she assumed many of the emotional functions that had previously been mine. She mothered him, played therapist, and adored his talent and his previous accomplishments. Thus, having established her as the good preoedipal mother, he could turn me into the bad mother, the depriver and withholder, and the strict disciplinarian. First of all, the frequency of their dates was rigidly confined to no more than three times per week, with only two sleep-overs. Meeting more often, was considered "bad" i.e. symbiotic, and *not permitted* by his therapist. In this way, Larry protected himself from his merger wishes and at the same time, could blame *me* for his deprivation. Any suggestions that it was he after all who had set up these rules, went unheard. Larry was determined to recreate in me the monstrous mother of his toddler years and he proceeded to do so with a deliberate and protracted campaign. In his individual sessions, he became increasingly withholding. When before, he could not possibly cram enough into his sessions,—every minute counts—he complained now that he had nothing to say, that he did not know what I wanted him to talk about. He began to be late, and he was at times quite hostile. When these maneuvers failed in terms of making me angry, he proceeded to try to bore me to death by endlessly obsessing about professional concerns, the interpretation of plays, acting techniques, etc. He kept asking me repeatedly whether I was not growing disgusted with him, and I told him over and over that how he chose to utilize his sessions was entirely his decision, not mine.

His next campaign was the attempt to provoke me into losing my temper and to finally "show my true colors" which he was sure I would do one day. He watched me carefully in order to catch me in a bad mood, acted contrary, spiteful, and condescending. He portrayed me as the exploiter of human misery and himself as the captive of such an inhumane set-up. Eventually, Larry did succeed. He was lucky; he caught me right after we had moved to a new apartment, and five minutes after a department store had notified us that even though we had already discarded the old kitchen stove, we would not get the delivery of the new one for six weeks. Larry, on entering my office, immediately sensed my rage and sweetly asked me what was wrong. After he had briefly commiserated with my predicament, he proceeded to redouble his efforts at provocation and I did, indeed, lose my temper. Somewhat against my better judgment, I told him that he acted like a nasty brat. The display of my frustration and anger, however, proved exceedingly disappointing to Larry. The outburst was short, to the point, and did not deter me from picking up where we had left off in the previous session. Larry had to conclude that 1. I was human like everybody else; and 2. That even his most skillful provocation did not turn me into a monster he could truly devalue. Although on some level he had to test my limits and his powers in order to feel safe, he also felt slightly ashamed of himself for the very way in which he had gone about it. Following this episode, Larry felt relieved and ready to resume the work he needed to do, namely to deal with his fear of returning to the stage, and to resolve some of the conflicts with Christina that had emerged once the honeymoon period was over. After he had been able to give me back some of my good aspects, I was again allowed to be more of his therapist. Up to that point, Larry and Christina had analyzed each other, and he had merely informed me about his conclusions. Expanding his coaching jobs, in order to be economically self-sufficient, turned out to be the easiest part of Larry's mental health plan—clearly a conflict-free sphere of the ego. In addition to it, the people he worked for valued him and his work so much that they not only made the work pleasant for him but the couple who ran the acting school "adopted" him as a family member, fed him meals and gave him presents. The other part of the program, his preparation for his return to the stage terrified him so much that by merely thinking about it seriously, some of his old hysterical symptoms reappeared, and Larry spent a great deal of time reapplying his old remedies of indulging his painful penis with leisurely baths, oils, and by practicing his parts in the nude. The fantasy of freezing up on the stage terrified him to the point of despair. Eventually, in a group session he was able to go with the fantasy that went as follows:

"In the middle of my act, my body goes completely rigid. I have to sit down and I freeze up in that position."

My question: "Then, what would happen?"

Larry: "The audience would laugh";

"And then?"

"They would have to carry me off stage, sitting on that chair, totally frozen and stiff."

"And then?"

"They would not know what to do; I remain stiff."

"And then?"

"They would have to put me on a plane, take me to my parent's house and my mother would have to put her arms around me, warm me with her entire body, until I am all thawed out."

"And then?"

"I can either stay home forever, or I have to come back to New York and start all over again."

At the end of that fantasy excursion, Larry finally realized two things: 1. Nobody in group at any time during his fantasy-tale, had been inclined to laugh—if anything they admired him for being so clearly in touch with his secret agenda; and 2. That even if his dream could come true, it would not really solve anything since he had no intention whatsoever to leave New York and to live at home. Armed with these two insights, he proceeded to enroll group and his friends to give him moral support and to hold his hand while he prepared for his first stage debut, consisting of a small, but important, part. He had asked Christina to buy him a pair of red underwear that he believed would keep him warm and safe. In his performance, he had now decided to be good for *himself* and for his *new family*. With the entire group in the audience, plus three former group members, my husband and myself at opening night, Larry performed superbly. From that moment on, Larry knew that he was back on the road of making acting his vocation. Having survived what he considered an audacious display of maturity and the shift from the adored child prodigy to a hard-working adult actor, he was now faced with the problems of resuming his career in earnest, to make up for the years he had lost and to work through the resistances against autonomy, i.e. his rage-dependency conflicts with his mother. Through his relationship with Christina, he had managed to circumvent some of those problems. She was clearly very gifted, but no real competition. He had been her drama coach and he kept that role for a long time. Since she was also quite repressed sexually, he acted as her coach in that area also; he actively drew her out and arranged settings where sexual play and sexual abandonment became possible. As Larry started to make a serious attempt to return to the stage, Christina for reasons of her own, pursued a course of professional withdrawal, self-destructiveness, and depression. She also became increasingly withholding. Despite Larry's alleged disappointment with this development, he seemed to be secretly pleased. He could be the responsible adult, while she did the regressing for both of them. He, in a manner very similar to Karl and Bernie, could play the role of the indulgent but disapproving parent, while she played the helpless incompetent child who basked in his reflected glory.

At the beginning of his relationship with Christina, Larry had also been involved with another woman, Lisa. He liked her, but the only thing they really shared was good sex. Since both of them were beginning to get seriously involved with their own partners, Larry continued to fantasize a great deal about her but he never acted on his fantasies. Larry's sexual frustrations with Christina and her general tendency to withdraw, were counteracted by Larry with his sadistic sexual fantasies. As his first recollections of his mother's unavailability and her sexual seductiveness emerged in therapy, and as Larry developed a stronger sense of himself as a person, his favorite fantasy underwent a transformation. Now, he, alone is in a large warehouse where hundreds of grown women are chained to the walls. He would take a great deal of time choosing among them. When he found the right one, he would again humiliate her and have her plead for mercy. Eventually, he would penetrate her anally and she would die from his orgasm. With that fantasy as a starting point, he spent many sessions developing scripts about tying up his parents, punishing them, putting them on a leash, walking them around the house, etc. It is noteworthy, however, that his sadistic fantasies about his parents were entirely devoid of sexual content. Food, toilet training, mobility and restraint, the exercise of power to give and to withhold, and to punish were the central themes. Phase III came to an end through four interrelated events: After Larry had gotten a second and bigger part in an important play, his complaints about Christina's failures, and sexual performance, or rather the lack of it, emerged with a real desire for change on Larry's part. This time he was willing to accept and to utilize my interpretation of their interactive games. He could see that he had delegated his own angry withholding child—part to her. As he set out to change some of these interpersonal arrangements, his sadistic fantasies reemerged. The transition crisis signalling Phase IV—the emergence of a true superego was quite dramatic for Larry: when I invited him to spin one of his sadistic fantasies out in my presence, he chose his old sexual partner, Lisa, as a target. He was able to fantasize with great gusto. At the end of it, however, when he pictured this woman as dead, he was, for the first time, overcome with a genuine sense of guilt and remorse. He kept saying over and over, "I don't want her to die, she has done nothing to deserve this, I want her to come back to life." He threw himself on the floor and he wept bitterly. His destructive sadistic impulses had clearly become ego-alien. Following this session, Larry had two nightmares: 1. He was lying on his back in his bed and an enormous woman lay on top of him. When he was on the verge of suffocation, he woke himself up, trembling. During the next night he dreamed that he and some of his friends had commissioned someone to capture a five-year-old little Nazi, chop off his head and stuff the body into a garbage can. Larry, in his dream was quite surprised that the body was covered with sperm. After having played out the different parts in both of those dreams, it seemed that Larry was getting ready to let go of the preoedipal little Nazi in himself, whose early dreams of revenge and role-reversal had become sexualized. He then started to realize that the overpowering preoedipal mother could no longer overwhelm him. One last score had to be settled, before Larry could really devote himself to the task of growing up, namely his need to be taken care of which he played out dramatically. After a group party, which was designed to celebrate his latest professional success, he went home, quite contented. He sat on his bed, listened to some music and fantasized about having a good mother around the house. Soon, he felt a stong desire to defecate. He held off as long as he could thinking about how nice it would be if someone picked him up and carried him to the bathroom. Finally, he chose quite deliberately to defecate right on his bed. He sat for hours in his own feces, pleading with his imaginary mother to come and to clean him up. At around 3 a.m., he gave up. He did the job himself and he cried himself to sleep. When he woke up late the next morning, he felt better than he had in a long time and when he came to his session he announced, before he was even seated, that he was now ready to stand on his own two feet.

Anna

Enrollment in postgraduate work gave Anna's life a very clear and gratifying focus since she had always excelled in school. Besides, it satisfied her masochistic impulses, since in addition to her full-time job and her therapy, she spent most evenings attending classes or doing homework. Needless to say, she arranged her schedule in such a way that it spelled a maximum of harrassment. On the other hand, she would utilize me as a mentor, as someone who could guide her in terms of what courses to take, what books to read, etc.—in other words, to take over some of the fathering functions that her real father had never assumed. Her mother, too awed by the complexities of the real world had moralized but had never offered the children any real help. As Anna progressed in her training program, doing extremely well, the inevitable question arose as to how she could use her newly acquired skills. Ostensibly, the goal had been for her to leave the job where she was overworked, underpaid, and harrassed. The institution where she worked was so badly run, that little therapeutic work was possible. Moreover, the physical setting was such, that offices were overcrowded with insufficient air conditioning in the summer and so little heat in the winter, that for many months the entire staff had to work in their overcoats. Anna, with her early experiences of being locked out in the cold, suffered enormously during the winter months. Yet the prospect of leaving the place, to look for a part-time job someplace else, and to build up her private practice, was something that Anna fought strongly. To her, it spelled three dangers: 1. The agency had become "home" for her; living with a bad mother seemed infinitely preferable to having no mother at all. She was extremely angry at me and at the group whom she perceived as depriving her, of pushing her out of the nest without offering her a new home. 2. Fear of failure. Even though Anna got plenty of confirmation that she was doing very good work, she feared that her excursion into private practice would reveal shortcomings that previously had been hidden and that would expose her to ridicule for having reached too high. Her mother's voice that said, "And who do you think you are?" was constantly with her. The grandiose strivings that underlay these self-doubts were still too firmly repressed to be interpreted. 3. Her identity as "staff" as opposed to that of a serious professional and as an entrepreneur, was not easy to give up. She knew that if she succeeded as a private practitioner her days as someone to whom work was assigned, someone who assisted and took orders, would be over. So would be her poverty and her victimized position. In order to risk these inner changes, she had to go through a real process of grief and mourning before she could leave the agency. Even though she joked about her attachment to the bad mother, she wept many angry tears before she could hand in her resignation.

Once Anna had reached the point where half of her time was taken up with private patients, she delegated many of her longings for the "all good mother" to her patients who were not subjected to the "harsh" standards that she felt I subjected her to. Her patients had the freedom to switch appointments at will, pile up debts; they did not have to pay for broken appointments and many of them paid fees that were well below what they could have paid, given their incomes. Thus, work retained some of the familiar harrassments for Anna, and it also kept her reasonably poor. Moreover, it was her way of indicting me, of keeping me bad, greedy, authoritarian, and ruthless. Her message to me was: "I am showing you how a "good" therapist operates, so why don't you change and become more like me?" Any attempts to interpret this behavior to her, produced rage and the need to devalue her therapist by attaching herself to some seemingly powerful male professional in the field whom she idealized and to whom she could attribute the perfections that I was obviously lacking. In the course of this particular power struggle, there were also moments when she was overwhelmed by her schedule, felt thoroughly depleted, and needed just plain comforting. Much of that comforting had to be forced on her, since she had an exceedingly hard time taking it in without putting it down as coddling or as a waste of time. As she came to realize more and more that her rejection of compassionate responses was a holding out for total caretaking, however, she could allow herself to take more and to value it. Each session with good mothering produced childhood memories of neglect and abuse and the experience of utter loneliness. Her accomplishments had never been valued at home, if anything, they spelled more responsibilities. The parental message had always been: "If you can do this much, you can do more." Successes were never celebrated; to the contrary, they were put down as a countermeasure to the sin of pride. Thus, a great deal of reparative work had to be done to teach Anna how to enjoy the exercise of mastery and how to cherish the rewards.

Anna's social life was divided between her mostly good and rewarding relationships with her women friends, many of whom shared her victimized outlook on life, and her involvements with men that were invariably disappointing. The men she went out with were either cold, rejecting, and sadistic or, alternatively, kind and adoring, but in her eyes "dull as dishwater." Good enough love objects were devalued, the mean ones she pursued with a great deal of excitement and inner turmoil. Although she could joke about the fact that the ideal lover in her eyes would probably turn out to be an ax-murderer, there was more than a trace of pride in her pronouncement.

Anna never had had male friends and she was quite aware of the fact that she feared men greatly. In order to feel a little bit more comfortable around men she accepted the suggestion to study them— not as potential love objects—but simply as fellow human beings. This she managed to do with a modicum of success, at least on an intellectual level. Eventually, she fell in love with a man who was not even finished obtaining his divorce and who cleverly used women to soothe his bruised ego. He promised undying love, and at the same time, double-crossed Anna with several other women, including his ex-wife. The humiliation of having been played for a fool, produced such profound rage in Anna that she sank into one of the deepest depressions since she began therapy, and following it, a genuine shift in her relationships with men. Her outrage at the narcissistic double-blow was directed primarily at herself, and secondarily at group and her therapist. Since she had been introduced to this man by a fellow group member, there were several weeks during which Anna was the only person who did not know that her boyfriend was sleeping with somebody else, and nobody knew how to tell her. When she was finally given this information, her rage was vitriolic in quality, pointing to some very early shaming experiences. It took many months to restore her confidence in all of us, particularly me, and for her to accept the fact that there had been no way with which the situation could have been handled painlessly, and that the mistakes as she perceived them, were due to concern for her, and not designed to trick or shame her. Although her forgiveness was still only partial, it did put her in touch with memories of having been scapegoated by her entire family, of having been the butt of jokes, and having her confidences betrayed over and over again. There had been times where she felt so humiliated by her parents and her siblings, that she would have gladly killed them all. In the course of these explorations, she also came to realize that her lifetime habit of poking fun at herself was designed to a. forestall humiliations by others; and b. act as a coverup for her self-loathing.

The transition to Phase IV began when Anna, after her last fiasco with a sadistic love object, decided to have a second look at Peter, one of the kind, adoring but boring, men she had dated. To her surprise, she found him to be quite pleasant, even lovable at times. By that time, she had already progressed to having a full-time private practice that was clearly flourishing. Peter, much less accomplished and ambitious, was for quite some time devalued as not being worthy of her, and she quite clearly communicated her expectations that he do better, with the hidden agenda that he should fail. Only Peter did the opposite, and met in time each and every one of her expectations since he was quite determined to marry her. Anna cautiously allowed herself to fall in love and finally decided to live with Peter. Instead of being blissfully happy, however, she experienced an enormous let-down. She discovered her capacity for shrewishness that she had hated so much in her mother. A yet untapped core of self-loathing emerged, memories of maternal persecutions that shame had prevented her from remembering. This shame was so archaic that it went back to the time when shame for the self and shame for the parental other cannot yet be distinguished. Moreover, her family had lived in virtual isolation, no outsiders were allowed into the house in order to hide the pathological family interactions from the outside world. Thus, it seemed quite ingenious on her part, to contact this core of self-loathing at a group party where she had become quite drunk. During the next group session, she was confronted quite gently with what she had revealed during that night. Her response was again vitriolic rage at the group for having seen Anna so down and out. In the course of several months, where she had almost half the group-time all to herself, she slowly and painfully unburdened herself of her early memories and the monstrous practices of her mother's treatment of her. It seemed that her mother had projected all of her own "bad" qualities onto Anna, and then persecuted them relentlessly in a way that can only be described as child abuse. In facing this horrible truth, Anna finally separated from her mother. She could accept the fact that maternal assistance and support had been all but absent and could never be regained.

From that moment on, Anna's relationship to her therapist and to her own patients underwent a dramatic change. Instead of envying and devaluing me for the way in which I run my practice, she decided to identify with me. She could accept that there is nothing wrong with making a decent living and that ultimately, patients are *not* helped if they are allowed to run up debts, pay too little, and switch and cancel appointments at will. Having given up a major chunk of her own infantile merger wishes with an "all-good mother," she could accept the good enough mother in therapy, and in her relationship with Peter, and confidently play the role of the good enough mother with her own patients. Anna now had a much clearer vision of what kind of therapist she wanted to be. Confusing her own needs with those of her patients now appeared unethical and unprofessional. This shift represented the emergence of a realistic and sound ego ideal, very different from her self-sacrificing stance of a few years ago.

Chapter 9

PHASE IV:

Maturity and Superego Integration

If we consider Phase I to have been essentially an objectless stage, Phase II as the stage where the patient's primary quest is to do for him because he can't or rather won't do for himself, and if Phase III is the attempt on the part of the patient to find out what he can do for himself, then Phase IV becomes the stage at which the patient comes to ask what he can do for others, *without* sacrificing the integrity of the self. During Phase III, the balance between the therapeutic opposition and resistance and cooperation was heavily skewed in the direction of opposition; the opposite is true for Phase IV. The major power struggles are essentially over, the appreciation of the therapist takes on a new valence since the capacity for gratitude is replacing envy, and patients are now in a position of preparing themselves for their role as responsible citizens in the society of which they are members. Perhaps the most important development however, is the gradual acceptance of—if not delight in—life as it is rather than a holding-out for a glamorous version of human existence, one which is free of ordinary human misery. If all goes well, termination will constitute a parting of two equals, each with their own identity and both appreciative of therapeutic work well done.

Developmentally, Phase IV represents the whole line of development from Mahler's fourth sub-phase to the entire process of secondary socialization, i.e. the formation of an adult identity. Thus, it entails the unfolding of more complex cognitive functioning, reality testing, psychological birth as well as the establishment of a repression barrier (Gedo and Goldberg, 1973) the development of a superego (Gedo and Goldberg, Kohut, Breger). Since the major battle of wills between toddler and mother are over, love again, supersedes negativism (Breger, 1974). Incorporation and introjection are replaced by identification (Mahler, Kernberg, and Erikson). It also includes the oedipal phase, sex role learning—or in this context the modifications of sex-role stereotyping—the establishment of a sense of inner integrity, and finally, the consolidation of an adult identity that is in keeping with the patient's inner needs and his or her sense of connectedness and responsibility to others and the community at large. In short, this should ideally be the phase of self actualization (Maslow, 1954) and true maturity. The therapeutic mode is one of the interpretation (Gedo and Goldberg).

TREATMENT GOALS AND OBJECTIVES

The four treatment goals during Phase IV are: 1. The consolidation of the gains made during Phases I, II and III and a movement toward the exploration of oedipal and sexual problems. 2. Implementation of positive willing and the emergence of a sound superego as part of an adult identity. 3. Acceptance of life's limitations and 4. Preparation for termination. Since during Phase IV all the techniques listed in the previous chapters come into play, with an ever increasing emphasis on interpretation, however, no separate section on techniques appears necessary. The same is true for the subject of the transference and its interpretation. Whenever special recommendations appear desirable, they are worked into this section. What is of greatest importance during Phase IV is the therapist's ability to hear the truly individual wishes on the part of the patients and to be able to shift treatment modalities in accordance with the inevitable regressive swings.

Patients have reached Phase IV essentially screaming every inch of the way. What made growth possible, i.e. the repair of the major ego defects and the transformation of pathological narcissism, was a consistent balance between support and optimal disillusionment coupled with optimal frustration. The *resignation* to the belief that we must do for ourselves—even though in and by itself, mastery during Phase IV begins to be experienced as fun—is still quite a way from the *wish* to be one's own person, and to truly relish the creative freedom that may entail. Moreover, therapy up to this point, has focused very heavily on the major traumas and the defects in the parent-child interaction which produced the pathology in the first place. Thus, the struggle between "I must" and "I want," and "I can't" and "I won't" will continue for some time. At the same time, the conceptualization of life as a series of options, within the limitations of social life, becomes more and more ego-syntonic. Vestages of resistances to the abolition of hidden agendas and fantasies of revenge will have to be chipped away at gradually. These battles cannot be explained merely in terms of just plain stubbornness, even though they are that, too, but by the fact that inevitably some infantile traumas were left untouched by our therapeutic explorations up to this point.

In some instances, the patient's ego, until now, was simply not strong enough to risk confrontation with very early and very destructive experiences. Thus, during Phase IV, we will encounter two types of regressive swings. One, the need to return to Phases I and II for refueling and the reassertion of negative and counterwilling and the regressions to crucial parts of infantile development that the patient can now risk without fear of fragmentation. With regressions of the second type, the patient may need encouragement and support as well as an explanation that these regressions are *not* an indication that all the previous work has been undone, but that there is simply a piece of unfinished business that needs attention. Under such circumstances, it may even be wise to increase the number of sessions as a strictly *temporary* measure. Regressions of the first type have to be dealt with patiently, by, on one hand, giving the patient what he needs and thereby acknowledging the patient's autonomous decision to set his own pace and, on the other, with a consistent appeal to the patient's ability to get on with the business of living and the suggestion that there is more to life than "ordinary human misery."

The consolidation of the patient's newly acquired autonomy also requires that the patient slowly learns to make peace with those significant others that have been the subject or the target of his or her hidden agendas or vendettas. This means grief and mourning for parental attentions, ministrations, and recognitions that should have been given at the age-appropriate time but were withheld and can never be regained. The same objective holds true for persecutions that were inflicted needlessly and sometimes even viciously and can never be undone by retribution. When it comes to grief and mourning, however, we have to be aware of the fact that many sadomasochistic patients are particularly handicapped in that respect for a number of reasons. For one, the experience of love withheld often preceded their birth. Deprivation on the oral level, so commonly encountered among such patients, gives them much to give up and grieve. In addition, the very process of crying was often not permitted in infancy. The parents either ignored the child's crying until it had cried itself out, or reacted punitively. One family, customarily shoved the crib with the screaming baby out onto the porch in freezing weather with the reasoning that the cold winter air would not only shut the baby up, but would have the additional advantage of strengthening the baby's lungs. Crying toddlers were often slapped around, sent outside, or locked into basements, attics or other isolated places until they were ready to stop crying. In the battle of wills, crying was often responded to with humiliations, the accusation of being a cry baby, and a nuisance. Worse yet, the parent who regarded the infant's crying as an indication of disobedience, of "being sassy," may well have continued to beat or berate the child until it stopped crying and acknowledged the parent's superior wisdom and power. Such children soon learn to equate pain and sadness with humiliation, and they may make secret vows to themselves never to cry again, no matter *what* the provocation. Although they may not succeed with this promise to themselves until they are well into their teens, I have encountered one man in his mid-fifties who had, in fact, never cried after age five. When in therapy he was finally able to cry again, only a few trickles of tears were available to him; it took him a long time to learn the process of crying all over again and to connect it with the actual experience of sadness and pain. In other words, the problem of shame, proves to be an additional obstacle in the difficult process of grief and mourning over the loss of old love objects and fantasies.

Guilt can also play a role. By that I mean the old remnants of infantile omnipotence, where the child learned to associate its crying with parental displeasure, aggravation, and somatic or psychiatric complaints: "If you don't stop crying you are going to give me a migraine or you will drive me crazy." They can be a powerful message on the part of parents who are, indeed, prone to migraine headaches or visible depressions. Although the child might have received some enjoyment out of that dubious power, and at times might have relished his angry tears and their effect, it, nevertheless, can contribute to the disassociation between genuine sadness and healthy tears as a way of coping with loss.

Finally, a child who early in life lost a significant other, or a beloved pet, may have been deprived of the experience and expression of real grief and mourning either because the family chose to deny the event, to mystify the occurrence, or to invalidate the child's feelings. This can be done either by not acknowledging the meaning that the object had for the child—"Why are you crying over the dog, you never treated it well anyway!"—or to quickly replace the object. Alternatively, in the case of the death of a family member, the child may have been excluded from the mourning process either emotionally or physically by being sent away to stay with a relative. In other words, the resistance to proceed with the necessary process of grief and mourning during Phase IV may be due to a considerable extent not to the unwillingness on the part of the patient to relinquish dreams and objects, but to a poverty of behavioral resources in terms of the lack of being attuned to true sadness and the disassociation between the expressions of pain, anger, crying and recuperation that includes the ability to accept comfort.

For the patients with a pronounced difficulty or inability to cry, it is often not sufficient to interpret to them that they are covering their feelings of hurt with either rage or withdrawal. The sadness, the pain, and the hurt have to be *felt*. Therefore, it can be quite helpful to ask the patient to mechanically repeat a statement such as "I am feeling very sad" over and over, and to go with the feelings as they come. This technique can be particularly effective, if patient and therapist face each other and loosely hold hands. (Jackins, 1965) Alternatively, the feelings of hurt—if they are better located in the past through a guided regression—may focus on a particular event, in which case the cue given by the therapist may go something like the following: "My dog died and I feel terribly sad." The dog should be visualized as it was when it was still alive, what it looked like when it was dead, and how it was buried. Finally a reenactment of an actual funeral in group therapy frequently reconnects the patient with the finality of the loss, and grief is facilitated. In these instances, too, it is important that the patient recreate the scene as closely as possible to the way it actually happened. One group member is to play the mother, another is to play the father and so on, until all the significant others are assembled, including the rabbi or priest. The patient plays him or herself. When the loss is finally acknowledged, and the patient can cry, the experience is usually more effective if the patient can also tolerate physical and verbal comfort to reinforce the concept that grief, if it is shared with others, produces compassion rather than pity, ridicule, scorn, or rejection.

For the patient who suffers from a structural neurosis, the oedipal conflicts are *the* problems to be worked through in therapy; the less-structured personalities arrived at the oedipal scene with such a fragmented sense of self, and such massive ego impairments including insufficient self-object differentiation and incapacity for object constancy, that a romance involving differentiated others was all but impossible. What we do find is, in lieu of a better term, a romance between part objects, ego nuclei and powerfully idealized self-father and self-mother representations, including phantom fathers, i.e. imaginary fathers who have no relationship or resemblance to the actual fathers. Typically, the child, disappointed in the mother, turned to the father, often prior to the oedipal period, in a desperate attempt to get some mothering and in order to partake in the imagined greatness and omnipotence of the father. Although typically, the fathers of these patients also disappointed them, given fathers' greater distance from the daily life of the child, the following options were open to the infant: projection and projective identification of the disappointing qualities of the preoedipal mother onto the father—with a subsequent intensification of the hateful feelings during the oedipal period, commonly encountered among heterosexual males (Larry) and some homosexual women. Alternatively, all the bad parental qualities are attributed to the mother and all the good ones are attributed to the father or an idealized image of him, a constellation more typically found among heterosexual females (Anna) and some homosexual men. The failings of the father, that even the desperate child can't disavow or deny, are attributed to the mother and later rationalized as the result of the mother's provocations. The father's unavailability during the oedipal period and later in life is also blamed on the mother who is seen as keeping the child from the father. In all of these oedipal scenarios, however, the child may act out more the incorporated attitude of the mother toward the father, which is usually ambiguous to say the least, rather than its own impulses and desires. Thus, the following pattern may emerge: the girl turns toward the father, with her mother's ambivalence redirects her own and her mother's negative feelings back to the mother, and then parasitically, lives off the idealized father as a self-object. The homosexual boy may undergo a similar development with two possible deviations. 1. either the father is devalued from the beginning and burdened with the child's and the mother's negative view of him; or 2. after the child has turned toward the father with his sexualized desires for mothering and the need for compensatory structures and has experienced a severe rebuff, he may then settle for a life-long, love-hate relationship with the father who remains the prototype of the rejecting but exiting love object (Bob). The even less structured personalities may actually have two fathers, the real one who is hated, and the good and perfect one with whom they have a secret bond and who usually constitutes their unavailable *and unobtainable* ego-ideal (Karl).

Thus, during Phase IV, the father has to be re-evaluated. Among these patients, typically the men, where the brutal father and his mistreatment of his son was the original complaint, the son having separated from the mother will now be able to see the father in a new light, and will slowly learn to see his father through his own eyes—not his mother's—and evaluate him accordingly. To the extent that the father was, indeed, benign, his attitudes and good attributes can become incorporated into the patient's identity as a male, while the negative aspects can be discarded. If the paternal other was too destructive or too absent, the son will actually have to go out and search for role models and mentors from whom he can learn what maleness can entail and whose qualities he can fully or partially emulate.

The girl, who devalued her mother and idealized her father, will have to re-evaluate her father in order to relate to men in a realistic fashion. After all, no mortal man may be able to live up to the image of her idealized father, which the little girl needed to survive. The disillusionment with the father, can, in extreme cases be a seemingly insurmountable task, since it may spell the loss of both parents. After the separation from the bad mother representation, the woman patient now fears that if she finds out that the father was as bad as the mother, that he colluded with her rejection and persecution of the child, she will find herself alone, and deprived of all inner objects from which to derive pride and nurturance. In that case, she will have to return to her relationship with her mother, in order to ferret out some more of the good parts of that relationship, which after all, allowed her to survive, and learn to own and truly cherish those interactive gems.

Perhaps it has to be stressed again that I am not trying to imply that the working through of the relationship with the father begins at Phase IV; to the contrary, this often constituted the starting point of the therapy, and certainly gets a good deal of attention during Phases II and III. The father that is dealt with during Phase IV, however, is a different person from the one that was worked on earlier. He is an object whose representation is no longer contaminated by the mother's attitudes toward him, her idealizations, devaluation, denials, or projections. And it is primarily with respect to the patient's uncontaminated perception of the father figure, that the work done during Phase IV differs from that done during the previous phases. The actual oedipal strivings now encountered in therapy manifest themselves primarily in the patient's attempts to play out male authority figures against females and vice versa. In my experience, the actual sexual incestuous interactions are more likely to be found in the patient's relationships to his or her siblings—or in the case of only children, their peers—rather than their actual parents. The sibling of the opposite sex may easily become the target of the child's sexual striving and the interaction between them is often a caricature of their parent's actual marriage including those aspects of it that were carefully hidden from the children. The adult female masochist, for example, who continuously attaches herself to sadistic men, may not be reaching for a replica of her father at all; she may, more likely, reenact her relationship with an older brother, which mirrors her relationship with the pre-oedipal mother and her mother's relationship with her husband.

Among sadomasochistic patients the emergence of adult sexuality and the development of a sound gender identity was interfered with. We may find confused identifications with parental objects or rather part objects. The fusion with sex with non-sexual aims prior to the Oedipal period or the retreat into asexuality are also quite common. In terms of the real meaning of sex, two constellations stand out. 1. Sex that is primarily oral in origin, a substitute for feeding and a replication or denial of early feeding experiences expresses itself in an often indiscriminate "consumption" of sexual partners who are used and then discarded. In the extreme, as many as 10 partners per week are utilized in this way with a constant craving for more—more variety and greater thrills. Needless to say, the personal characteristics of these partners, aside from possibly their physical appearance, are of no importance. 2. Sexual partners who are chosen to relive and defend against the power struggle with the pre-oedipal mother—or sometimes father—is the more common phenomenon. Giving and withholding, trading sex for caretaking, power and submission all get mixed up with sexuality, resulting in an almost infinite variety of symptoms. The question of power, however, is the most central one, whether the power is exercised or enjoyed vicariously by delegating it to the partner. In these instances, partners *are* chosen for their attributes, mostly their negative ones in order to magically change them, either by suffering or by vengeful attacks, but most often by a combination of both. Whichever way the scenario is played out, it is of utmost importance that mutuality is avoided, so that both partners can retain their grievances in this exchange. Given the lack of identification with parental others, sex role learning was confused from the start, and compounded by sex role stereotyping.

Thus during Phase IV, three components in the sex life of the patient have to be distinguished: 1. pre-oedipal patterns masquerading as sexual problems, i.e. the manifestation of negative willing and counterwilling; 2. faulty identifications with parental others with respect to sex roles; and 3. actual sex role stereotyping. Asexuality or frigidity in women, as Robertiello and Shadmi (1968) have pointed out, can have its origin in the young girl's rage at the mother which results in her interpretation of the sex act as the father punishing the mother. In that way, the father is doing the "dirty work" i.e. the expression of rage, toward the mother for the child. Later identification with the mother, and the attachment to the father following the oedipal period, seals the fate of her adult sexuality, since for her, too, sexuality now means punishment.

If, in addition to that, for example, the girl does identify with the meek and self-effacing aspects of the father, and has her meekness reinforced by her mother, peers and the culture around her, as constituting a proper way of being a "good little girl," then we have a three-layered problem: in the interaction with men, her asexuality serves her own masochism as it protects her from symbolic punishment, and expresses her rage against her partner through her withholding. Thus, we have to work on the problem of oral rage, faulty identification with a meek father figure, sex role stereotyping in the direction of meekness and masochism, and the sadomasochistic repetition of these archaic identifications with current partners. Until all of these layers are worked through, adult sexuality and sex role behavior will be problematical. In other words, during Phase IV when the question, What does it mean to be a humane and sexual man or woman? is to be resolved, the meaning of the sex act per se, the partial identifications with mother and father and the cultural forces that contributed to the faulty conceptions of maleness and femaleness, have to be analyzed and repaired.

The implementation of positive willing—truly growing up, in addition to the consolidation of the previous gains—will have to cover a wide range of interrelated subjects, which taken together, will determine what kind of adult person the patient will turn out to be. First of all, we will have to deal with the remnants of repressed grandiosity. In some cases, during Phase IV, the grandiosity comes to the fore for the first time. The predominantly masochistic patient, whose grandiose and exhibitionistic strivings were so thoroughly repressed that they never became an issue during the previous work, may suddenly discover that the only stumbling block to their exercise of mastery on a wider scale, is shyness, fear of public appearances, perfectionism, and other rationalizations for low levels of aspiration, a pronounced dislike for healthy competitiveness, and a host of similar complaints. Such patients may sound quite convincing in their claims that, even though they have undergone major changes in therapy, they are simply, from a characteriological point of view, not cut out for competitive pursuits or leadership positions. After all, they will tell us, the world can't consist of chiefs alone without also some Indians. A very persuasive argument indeed, and it may in fact be true enough in some cases. More likely than not, however, the shyness and reserved attitude may be a strenuous attempt on the part of the patient to keep the archaic and exhibitionistic strivings repressed at the price of only modest achievement. Thus, it may be enormously important to investigate the true meaning of these inhibitions so that the patient gets a chance to work them through and set realistic goals for himself corresponding to his real talents. A similar approach will have to be used for repressed remnants of oral rage and greed. The patient, who during this time appears too modest with respect to the pursuit of material possessions, may unconsciously be longing for the status of a millionaire, and should be helped to find an appropriate level of material rewards that is satisfying enough and allows him to curb the underlying greed. In other words, the goal is *not* to groom all patients for wealth, status, and power; to the contrary. But unless a patient has fully explored repressed grandiosity and greed, the choices that will determine the adult life style of any given individual cannot be genuine. In order to truly determine where one's talents are best applied, what goals and rewards to give up in exchange for others, the hidden roadblocks must be removed. For example, a gifted teacher with a graduate degree, may well reach the conclusion that even though other alternatives are open to him, Hoboken needs good grammar school teachers more than most places, and the difficult working conditions and the low pay are more than compensated for by the worthwhileness of the task and the fact that it offers him the opportunity to study and write about learning disabilities among the poor. For this particular man, this choice represents an *optimal* balance of all his needs and assets although it may have been quite wrong for somebody else.

In order to arrive at such an optimal balance, a realistic re-evaluation of the patient's professional and academic choices has to take place, both in terms of wanting too much and wanting too little. Although it is certainly true that it is never too late to learn something new, major changes past a certain age may be plainly impractical, particularly during times of economic upheavals. Also quite often, family responsibilities may limit a person's ability to abruptly leave a job and go to school; compromise solutions will have to be found. The librarian in her 50s may be able to obtain a Ph.D. degree in literature, and, thus, realize a life-long dream, but if it is done only with one goal in mind, namely to obtain a college teaching position, the stage for failure is probably set. If the graduate training is pursued, for its own sake, and with a flexible attitude, which aims at some integration of library science and literature, either as a profession or as an avocation, we have again an optimal balance.

Since during Phase IV, superego integration, the basis for adult morality is one of the crucial issues, success and failure per se is only *one* issue that needs re-evaluating. The value and the meaning of one's work can also become a major problem. For example, a career which to a large extent is based on the exploitation of others or a general disregard for the common weal may have presented no moral dilemma for a patient at the beginning of treatment. To the contrary, he may have taken great pride in its social and economic rewards. During Phase IV such a person will probably face the moral dilemma of recognizing that while this work may have been highly rewarding for himself and his family, it has been useless or even destructive to the rest of society. Although it is clearly impossible to come up with a set of solutions as to how moral dilemmas of this sort can be solved, the problem cannot be brushed aside as immaterial to the therapeutic process. If these questions are ignored, invalidated, or shelved indefinitely, much of the previous work may be undone and further growth is inhibited. The older the patients, the more difficult it will be for them to honestly look at the life they have lived and the effect—or lack of it—that their lives have had on the lives of others. If nothing else, an honest validation of the patients' doubts and scruples are called for, as well as grief and mourning over mistakes that are irrevocable. Probably the key concept for problems of this kind is compassion for the self and corresponding compassion for others. The patient who can slowly learn to forgive himself, will on the basis of that forgiveness, find his own resolution of his particular dilemma. The parent who comes to realize, that aside from having *been* a mistreated child, he has also produced two neglected or abused children who are now grown, and essentially on their own, will need a great deal of therapeutic assistance to make his inner peace with past mistakes, to help those children to the extent that they are willing to accept it, and respect the fact that these children are now on their own and must be trusted to repair themselves, just as the parent has done. During Phase IV, almost all relationships with significant others will undergo changes that may range from subtle to drastic. The patients whose morality until then was essentially determined by more-or-less archaic forerunners of the superego, knew only simplistic concepts of crime and punishment, and incorporated parental do's and don't's; obedience to authority will now have to acquire a sound superego. How is one to bring this about? The rehabilitation of the major structural defects, i.e. ego- and self pathology should result in the capacity for object constancy, object love and self-esteem. Egocentrism should give way to concern with others. If these internal changes have indeed been accomplished, it would logically follow that exploitation, immorality, etc., will increasingly be experienced as ego-alien and in conflict with healthy self-esteem. Moreover, as the vengeful components of the hidden agenda are disappearing, the pursuit of inner integrity becomes more rewarding than the continuing indictment or punishment of a love object. What I am saying is that a sound superego should *logically* emerge; it does not mean, however, that it will come *automatically*. A constant questioning on the part of the therapist as to the consequences of every action in terms of its effect on others and on the patient's own inner integrity and dignity, is called for. The patient, who has cheated on his taxes, his business partner or wife all his life without giving it a second thought, must now be asked whether he can really in good conscience go on doing it. Although in the past such questions might have struck this person as moralistic or prissy, he will now with his newly-acquired sense of separateness, give these questions serious consideration. The following vignette may illustrate how the variables discussed so far interrelate: A middle-aged woman who all through 20 years of marriage had felt chronically victimized since she essentially supported the family and had coached her young daughter, who seemed to be an extremely gifted musician, made the following discoveries during this phase of the treatment: 1. From the beginning of her marriage she had subtlely undermined and infantilized her husband in the guise of helpfulness. 2. Giving and withholding of sex was one of the weapons used in this exchange. 3. Her daughter's talent was something she had simply taken for granted; she had never asked herself whether the child actually wanted to pursue a musical career. 4. By creating an almost exclusive bond with her daughter, she had, in effect, prevented almost any closeness between her husband and her child. Needless to say, insight into these patterns came slowly and painfully in the course of Phases III and IV of the treatment process. During Phase III however, the emphasis for her had been on the ineffectualness of her behavior. During Phase IV, in contrast, she became increasingly concerned with the moral aspects of her relationship with her family, in other words with the impact her way of acting had on the lives of others. Though I have at this point no way of knowing whether this marriage will survive, it is quite clear that this woman has undergone the following inner shifts: 1. In terms of ego development: Seeing herself as a person, clearly delineated from her husband and her daughter, and being in the process of giving up her merger wishes with them, she can now test her love for them not as an extension of herself, not as need-gratifiers but as autonomous others. The undermining of her husband and the coaching of her daughter—representing devalued and missing parts of the self—have become increasingly unnecessary. Being able to give more freely of herself, including sexually, and without the pricetag of martyrdom, she is now in a position to test the bond between her husband and herself in a new way. She can do so with the understanding that her husband may be incapable of effecting corresponding changes in himself. It is quite possible that he can only tolerate a merger-wife, a fellow sadomasochist. Should this be the case however, she is slowly becoming strong enough to face the prospect of leaving the marriage with the knowledge that she will survive. 2. In terms of her superego development and the need for inner integrity, there is on one hand a recognition that in order to feel good about herself she must respect her needs and those of others *equally*. She knows that she has never allowed her daughter to be an autonomous little person, that she has always burdened her with her own needy infant. To remedy the situation as best as she can has now become a moral imperative as well as an expression of genuine maternal love. In other words, the growing recognition of separateness on the part of patients, coupled with a corresponding increase in ego strength, enables them to evaluate the ethical and moral aspects of their behavior. Now such considerations are no longer based on fear of punishment or thoughtless obedience to real or internalized objects.

Typically, the relationship with the real parents also undergoes a major transition. Once the hidden agenda has been abolished, and once the patient has reached the point of truly letting the parents "off the hook," a friendship may or may not develop depending on the emotional make-up of the parents. The almost inevitable problem of caring for aged, but difficult parents, is no longer based on the futile question as to what the patient "owes" them, but rather, on the question as to how much a person can and needs to do for them given the parent's needs, the patient's resources, and the demands of simple human decency, divorced from infantile omnipotence and grandiosity.

Among the younger and the middle aged patients, their growing capacity for generosity and the transcending of the self, often involves the wish for parenting, either by having children of one's own, or by "adopting" other people's children who may be in need of greater care and attention than they are presently getting. Community service, volunteer work and the like, may serve a similar function, since giving of the self is no longer blocked by envy and the need for "repayment."

In sum, the adult identity, that is the goal of Phase IV, has to comprise the following facets: 1. The exercise of mastery to the fullest possible extent, and within the confines of the patient's actual life situation and talents. 2. A sound sense of self and its relationship to significant others and the community at large that no longer permits the abasement of the self and the exploitation of others. 3. Finally, and this may seem more of a philosophical point, though I don't think it is, patients will have to come to terms with the fact that "mental health" does not mean the absence of troubles or even major disappointments. What I am saying is that in order to enable a patient to terminate, we have to deal with the hidden agenda that patients harbor with respect to the *therapeutic process itself*. Patients quite commonly assume that life—or rather their glamourized version of it—will miraculously begin *after* termination. This life is often thought of as being almost entirely "wrinklefree," a fantasy which one of my patients has nicknamed the Smirnoff ad. What he means by that is this: To be part of an obviously devoted couple, engaged in fascinating though not necessarily gainful work. Timeless youth, beauty, wealth, slimness and contentment are all part of the picture; dirty socks, loneliness, death and old age are not. In other words, even though in the course of therapy, a great deal of effort has been devoted to affect real life changes, it is part of the termination process to pose the following question: "What you have and what you are right now, essentially *is* your life. Can you wholeheartedly say 'yes' to it?" This line of inquiry comes as a shock to most patients and the therapist will have to deal with this particular hidden agenda in the same way that he or she has done with all the others.

Given such an optimal and ideal development, the termination of the therapeutic process will develop naturally. A patient may want to linger a bit more, postpone the grief and mourning that are involved in separating from the therapist, but the rewards of, and the pride in "being all grown up," usually propel the patient to get this process over with and to let us go as separate individuals with our own lives and foibles.

CASE MATERIAL

Karl

During Phase IV, Karl truly blossomed out in every direction. His performance in school and at work improved further; so did his social life. His excellent performance in school frightened him, simply because he had no previous experience with devoting all his energies to school work without the concurrent wish to undermine it while ostensibly working for it. The anxiety following each grade of A or A+ received in school, were seen as indications that the loss of his negative identity was a threatening experience that had to be interpreted as a loss of a part of the old self. As his new identity as a successful student became more and more integrated, however, he became capable of expanding his professional and academic horizons accordingly. At first, Karl had a very difficult time asking questions in class for fear of ridicule—and a covert need to devalue the importance and the competence of the teacher—his need to be invisible in class vanished rapidly after he had taken the risk to point out to one of his professors that some of the exam questions had been worded so ambiguously that the seemingly "wrong" responses were in fact as accurate, if not more so, than the "right" ones. The fact that this criticism was responded to with interest and concern, and that on the basis of that question several exam grades, including his own, were readjusted upward, powerfully bolstered his sense of being a serious student—a person that others took seriously and one who had no need to suffer injustices in silence. This incident brought into focus the remnants of his old grandiosity. On one hand he had a difficult time accepting the fact that being in his late thirties, he still only occupied the unglamorous position of being one of thousands of undergraduate students, years away from a professional career. Seen in this light, his grades had to be devalued as meaningless. As he learned to value his academic successes however, he slowly let go of his grandiose expectations of himself. This was evidenced by the fact that his plans for graduate school were essentially based on practical considerations, balancing his aspirations and his responsibility toward his children. Karl wants to become a psychotherapist.

The question was still open, however, whether it is better to pursue his goals via a masters degree in social work or a doctorate in psychology. Although previously "The Doctorate" was dreamed of as a personal ornament to impress his family and his peers, and as a necessity to be taken seriously by himself and others, he now looked at it in a totally different light. His ability to realistically evaluate the strains of working full-time and going to school had taught him that he could do this quite readily and for almost any length of time. After the first semester when he had consistently overprepared himself for every exam, he had finally learned to focus on the essential tasks and to do them well without staying up all night to prove his conscientiousness. Thus, the choice of two academic careers was no longer contaminated by either grandiosity, his doubts in his intellectual capacities, or his ability for endurance, but by two principal questions of an entirely different nature: 1. What educational background is necessary and most desirable for a psychotherapist?; and 2. How many years should I invest in preparing for a profession, given the fact that I will be 40 by the time I enter graduate school? What is most important with respect to the time-question, is the fact that Karl can no longer see himself as an isolated individual who is only responsible to himself, but as someone who has two children and, therefore, has obligations to them.

The major obstacle to Karl's ability to deal with his children had been shame. He experienced his past as a monster that would go on haunting him for the rest of his life. He had feared that he would never be able to interact with strangers without having to explain why he had lost almost 20 years of his life. The very thought of having to reveal the failures of his past, including his "craziness," had kept him socially isolated for a long time. Thus, the compassion for the self had to be worked on for a very long time. It was exceedingly difficult for him to accept the fact, that on one hand, life is always a series of choices, that he had indeed consistently failed, and that on the other, given the parental input, it was a miracle that he had survived as well as he had. The abandonment of his wife and children had become a human mistake that was, indeed, injurious to others, but probably the only choice for survival he and the children might have had. As he got a clearer picture of what his married life had been like and what emotional shape he had been in, he increasingly realized, that if he had stayed he would have probably provided a parental atmosphere that would have been as pathogenic as his parent's home had been. In the process of integrating his past and present, a great deal of new material emerged. Some of it pertained to his early childhood and its traumas, and some with his actions as a teenager and during his early 20s. Much of it he had been too ashamed to reveal to me and to group. His investment in the victimized position had not allowed him to see himself as a perpetrator of clearly indecent and immoral deeds.

Karl also read every important book about the period of the war and the post war, and he also saw as many movies and documentaries on the subject as possible. Much of that material served as a cue to the emergence of repressed material, or more correctly, material that he had perceived but disavowed as unreal. Some of these memories re-

sulted in severe regressive swings and required a great deal of pacification, unification, and the integration of other actual historical events,
his parent's pathological responses, and his own inability to cope with
both. In the course of these explorations, Karl asked his mother for an
account of his early life. She obliged and wrote him a very long and
detailed letter that must have taken her days to complete. It did
confirm many of Karl's seemingly impossible memories, and the conclusions we had reached together, and it also added an important
ingredient: It portrayed his mother as a person who had experienced
herself as utterly helpless and incompetent with respect to the task of
rearing two children by herself, coping with the war and its terrors, and
who had, therefore, turned to her children for support and help.
Although it was quite clear that the effect of her helplessness and
disorganized mind must have been devastating for the children, it was
also a very humane and tragic document, since it revealed severe
pathology but no intentional or conscious malice.

With this understanding, Karl could focus on his own responses,
his need to wall himself off against the mother of his early childhood
and her seductiveness, his withdrawal into his own world, and also his
survival skills in an almost unmanageable environment. The insights
gained by these explorations, finally allowed him to disengage from his
mother. His father was still an enigma for him, however, and much of
the old rage and the old terrors were still operating and contaminating
his relationshps with heterosexual men. In the process of preparing
himself for a visit home, another memory slowly emerged as a result of
a series of guided fantasies revolving around the question what kind of
father he would like to encounter. For as long as Karl could remember,
he had had a secret phantom father. This was an urbane, witty, tweedy
scholar, a wise and gentle man, a perfect mentor capable of guiding
Karl in his professional and academic pursuits. He was someone who
was even-tempered and strong without being authoritarian, who could
be truly depended upon in times of crisis, and who would deal with
Karl respectfully and in a dignified manner. This phantom father was
unlike anybody Karl had ever known. He did recognize several traits
that he had dimly preceived in some of his teachers, the fathers of some
of his friends and other male adults not belonging to his own family.
More importantly, however, he recognized in that father figure the
clear outlines of his own ego-ideal, the man Karl wants to become and is
clearly in the process of becoming. Karl slowly learned to actually

fantasize himself as that kind of a man and as that kind of a father. His determination to disengage from his real father and to look after his own children, grew. The grandiose belief that he could appear at the house of his ex-wife like a *deus ex machina,* and miraculously rescue the children, had essentially vanished during Phase III, but he was tormented by guilt and his inability to see any alternatives to his fantasies of total rescue. After his visit home, Karl came away with a rather clear perception of his children's emotional state. He felt that even though their behavior was anything but normal, they were also not "crazy" and doomed to repeat his own sorry adolescence and young adulthood. They are children who are reacting to the psychotoxic elements in their environment, i.e. their mother and grandparents. On the other hand, Karl also saw that when he had the children to himself and related to them warmly, openly but firmly, their need to act out and act up would soon diminish. In other words, he is coming to realize that the children are not hopelessly lost, they can greatly benefit from his letters, his phone calls, and yearly visits. He also knows that he can't "make it all good again" for them either; he can only do the best he can, and hope for the best. The newly-established relationship with his children now also implies a heavy financial burden, compared to his still meager salary. Thus, his plans for graduate school are heavily influenced by his need to earn a middle class salary as quickly as possible and he knows that he will have to find an optimal balance between his academic and professional aspirations and the needs of those who depend on him.

Karl's identity as man is still a little shaky and in need of firming up. Since he separated from his lover, he has not become romantically involved with anyone. Fear of rejection, fear of men in general and fear of misjudging potential lovers are still operating to some extent. His attitude toward love is still more typical of an adolescent or very young adult than that of a grown man, and it has a slightly righteous and victorian tinge that is rather charming. One-night stands are inconceivable for Karl; his pronounced sense of dignity does not permit this. His next lover will have to be his peer in every respect, as he put it: "No children and no father figures need apply."

In group Karl can ask for help and comfort when he needs it, but by and large, he has assumed the role of a responsible older brother and has generously extended himself to new group members who needed a helping hand in settling in. Karl's pronounced teutonic preoccupation with the tragic aspects of life has been superseded by a delightful sense of humor. His compulsivity—the need to work three times as hard as a task calls for—is lessening. He leads a rather satisfying social life and enjoys the cultural events in New York City as fully as his time and budget permit; his parties have become legendary among his friends. The subject of termination had been raised by me eight months ago. At first, this suggestion excited and delighted him, but he soon reacted with a rather pronounced depression. Even though he had been determined to find a lover who was truly his peer, he suddenly associated himself with a man who seemed to exhibit a considerable amount of psychopathology. Although this was not a love relationship, it was, nevertheless, intense and it seemed to contribute to Karl's depression. Karl felt very strongly that he had to know this man in order to find out something about himself. This did not work out, however, since a friendship with this person entailed too many insults to Karl's sense of integrity. Once he stopped seeing this man, he began to search for that part of himself that he felt had been embodied by his friend. Karl agreed that the meaning of this friendship had been a message to me. He had wanted me to know that there was an unfinished piece of business that he could not articulate except by demonstrating it by this strange and intense friendship. Although Karl had spent a great deal of time examining his sexuality, it seemed that his core-gender identity had not received the attention it deserved given the fact of his mother's crossdressing of him as a child. By asking Karl to observe his reactions to other men, in terms of activity and passivity, Karl found in himself a very strong female identification, a little princess that co-existed with a male identification. They seemed to live side by side, like identical twins. By studying his sexual responses in minute detail and in slow motion, Karl discovered that these two identifications worked at cross-purposes. Active and passive impulses cancelled each other out, and the result was frustration and inhibition. Karl concluded that if he wanted to enjoy his sexuality and a firm male identity, the "little girl" in him had to be given up. This, he is now in the process of doing, and I am convinced that when this work is done, the phasing out process will begin.

Bob

Bob has begun his training as a psychotherapist, enjoying it and judging from the feedback he is receiving, his performance is much better than it was in graduate school. For the first time in his life, Bob is experiencing a learning situation as truly enjoyable rather than shame provoking and is increasingly taking pride in his work.

The wish to get more out of life than happiness with his career, namely the desire for a more satisfying personal life, has motivated Bob to return to individual therapy. He is giving every indication that this time around he will work through his unresolved difficulties. The prognosis is excellent.

Larry

For Larry, his first performance on stage was a major triumph, because for the first time in years, he was able to act on stage and in front of an audience without his old hysterical symptoms. In other words, his success was primarily a psychological one. Compared with his previous accomplishments, his part in the play had, in fact, been minor, and being an off-Broadway play, it had not been reviewed in any of the major newspapers. Although Larry had always been superbly confident about his capacity for real greatness in his calling, his subsequent work on stage brought out serious self-doubts and corresponding grandiosity. Larry worked extremely hard, auditioned for countless plays, always aiming for the top. Although overtly he seemed to enjoy the positive notices, and accepted the congratulations from friends, colleagues and fellow-group members, he, himself, did not take any of the reviews seriously, since secretly he devalued the plays, directors, and reviewers who were not the elite in their profession. He had set one particular goal for himself—the lead in one of the most important plays of the season. When he was informed that he had been accepted as one out of two understudies, he became utterly enraged and he tore the letter that informed him of that decision to shreds. His grandiosity and his capacity for unmitigated narcissistic rage emerged for the first time in full force. For several sessions, he had to return to his old habit of punching pillows and to cry copious tears, in an attempt to cope with his sense of shame and humiliation. Until all that anger had been expressed, he was totally incapable of realizing that the acceptance as an understudy in that particular instance was, indeed, a major honor and that with more work, acting lessons, and probably some luck, he stood a very good chance of making it if not to the very top, at least to a position of considerable success. Up to that point, he had only been able to envision playing the lead in a major play or being a total failure, who could only teach acting. He had to slowly learn to appreciate that there are many gradations of success and acclaim that might be worthy of his talents. When he reached that point, he spent an entire session reconstructing the letter that notified him about his acceptance as an understudy and he asked me to sign it. Once the document had been written up with as close a resemblance to the original as possible, Larry crumpled it again and tore it to shreds. Then, he applied himself diligently to the task of putting it back together again with Scotch tape. Symbolically, it seemed of enormous importance to him to do this job slowly and carefully until almost every wrinkle had been smoothed out and every edge lined up with every other edge. Having completed the job, he asked me for a manila envelope to take his letter home. He hung it in his study.

Following this episode, Larry more-or-less abolished his rigid time-table for the attainment of his success, and started to truly enjoy his work, acting lessons, performances, and the positive reviews he received. Instead of only living in the future and the anticipation of acclaim, he has begun to enjoy and value his present life and current stage roles. His self-esteem is no longer contingent on being the best, and perhaps not so paradoxically, his actual success in his field has taken a rather dramatic turn for the better. Larry has also taken notice of the fact that his teachers have not been so helpful to him because they were in love with an irresistible child prodigy, but that they value him as a very gifted senior student and junior colleague, who merits their help and encouragement. Thus, his teachers' generosity slowly enabled him to feel a sense of gratitude, instead of his old entitlement position. These new insights and their integration into Larry's self concept soon manifested itself in his relationships with his own students, most of whom were children or adolescents. Although previously his coaching jobs had been essentially ways of making money, situations where he basically saw himself as "one of the kids," he now started to take his job more seriously. He saw his students as little people with varying degrees of talent, their often-troubled relationships with their ambitious parents, and instead of identifying with them, began to see his role as the adult and teacher in a different light. At the same time, not surprisingly, Larry started to look at his therapist and at the rewards and responsibilities of the profession in a new way. Instead of

taking my presence, interactive responses and relationship with patients for granted, as a phenomenon not to be comprehended or
questioned, he proceeded to study me quite overtly and he began to ask
questions. He greeted me one morning with the statement that had just
occurred to him on his way to the office: "You know, I just realized *I am*
your work." Having dealt with the "work" aspect of therapy, Larry now
wanted to know several things, such as how one sets an appropriate fee
for one's services, what to do if a patient or a student runs up a bill, what
constitutes gratification and success for a therapist, how many hours a
week are required to do justice to all aspects of this profession, etc. In
other words, he no longer saw us as living in two totally separate and
unrelated worlds, but as two adult professionals facing similar reality
problems. In a very real way, I became a person he could learn from
and identify with, something he had not been able to do with his father.
He had missed this thoroughly. But Larry could also see that even
though his father had been unusually cold and aloof, and disinterested
in his children's problems, Larry, himself, had been far too enraged
with his father to allow him to teach Larry anything. He realized that
the wall he himself had erected, was much more impenetrable than the
one he felt his father had put up. Also, in looking at his relationships
with his very young students, he realized that playing the role of a
parent is not necessarily everybody's cup of tea. With that understanding, his relationship with his parents improved vastly. Once they were
no longer subjected to Larry's covert rage, they responded quite warmly and generously.

During Phase IV, Larry's relationship with group also slowly
underwent a significant shift. Although he had always been a full-
fledged member of the group and was very attached to everyone, he
also rightly felt somewhat of an outsider. He felt accepted but not
loved, admired and envied for his professional struggles and successes,
but not needed or wanted as a person to turn to in times of emotional
crises. Larry's sense of specialness, his self-absorption, had kept him in
a position of being the slightly odd one, the one that group members
had the greatest difficulty to identify with. The fact that Larry defended his stance of being the simpleton in matters unrelated to
literature and acting, that he knew or seemed to know absolutely
nothing about psychology, added to his difficulties. To a large extent,
his need for specialness was due to shame. He felt that his sadistic
fantasies, his acting out of infantile dreams set him apart and would be

ridiculed by group if they knew about it. Being aware that his mas-turbatory fantasies were not only sadistic but also extremely sexist made him very afraid of the women in the group. Eventually, however, his need for a more genuine connectedness won out over his shame. Piece-by-piece, he was able to reveal his "dirty secrets" in group and he saw them accepted as human problems no different from those of other group members. After six months of turning it over in his head, he finally shared with group his most shameful secret, namely his defecation on his bed and his yearning for his mother. This revelation produced an enormous amount of admiration in almost everybody. He was told that no group member had the courage to do something like that in the first place, much less to talk about it in group. Though still also a manifestation of Larry's specialness, the "confession" in group was a very positive act and it accomplished two goals. Once the shame barrier had been broken for good, Larry could be more open about his other problems, particularly his relationship with Christina. More im-portant, however, his presentation of self, his ability to genuinely understand the psychodynamics of others, blossomed. Instead of al-ways being the one to make the most irrelevant comments and to ask about the external aspects of a given problem, he developed into an astute observer and his analysis was often one of the most penetrating offered in the group. Although Larry had always tried to be helpful to others, the help he was able to offer *now* was that of an intelligent adult rather than that of a needy and self-absorbed infant. In short, he was no longer an outsider but a valuable member with an amazing amount of psychological knowledge and understanding. His pseudo-stupidity had clearly outlived its usefulness. Coupled with his greater self-acceptance and his capacity for empathy vis-à-vis other group mem-bers, Larry also made a very real effort to reach out for his younger siblings who are now facing problems that are very similar to those that he had faced when he was their age. Instead of seeing himself as an only child, Larry is now able to look at the family as a whole, an interrelated system to which everybody contributed. In his eyes, they are no longer isolated individuals but a set of interrelated psychodyna-mics, similar but separate. It is only now, since Larry has begun to look at the entire family, that many of the missing links in his earlier history have emerged: a set of rather self-absorbed and symbiotic parents for whom the children represented an often unwelcome interruption of their adult concerns, their marriage, and their professional pursuits, that produced a considerable amount of oral rage in all their children. Since also all of these children were unusually gifted, self esteem seems to have been based almost exclusively on artistic accomplishment. Larry's relationship with his girlfriend—or adult love objects in general—will still require quite some work. The competitiveness as well as the symbiotic elements are still pronounced. The unspoken division of labor that allows Larry to succeed professionally and for her to fail, for him to play the father and for her to be the child, and the considerable resentment that such an arrangement is bound to generate, is now being examined. Larry has reached the point where the disadvantages of this type of interaction outweigh the gains that it spelled previously. With his greater awareness of interactive systems—as distinguished from individual pathology—I have no doubts that he will soon reach the point where real changes in his way of relating to women will become something that he truly wants, rather than an expression of conformity to "mental health rules." He is increasingly becoming conscious of the fact that the sadistic gratifications derived from this set-up are in conflict with his wish to be a humane male.

Anna

As Anna's confidence in her skills as a therapist became more consolidated, I asked her whether private practice was all she wanted, or if writing or otherwise expanding her professional life was part of her long-term goals. At first, Anna insisted that doing good clinical work was perfectly sufficient and that she was really not an intellectual at all. Besides, she pointed out, an attempt to write could be interpreted as an attempt to compete with her therapist. The problem of competition, and her seemingly enormous fear of it, was taken up first without producing a great deal of insight. I suspected that underneath her pronounced avoidance of any overt expression of competitiveness, there was a great deal of it. Although these explorations did not result in much understanding of her fears, it did give her the impetus to try writing. This was partly due to the fact that she felt she had received permission from me and partly by the fact that she had managed to turn a suggestion into almost a duty. It took Anna very little time to write the basic outline and a first draft of the paper. She gave the material to many of her colleagues for critical appraisal. The response she received from almost everyone who read her first version was identical: it was an excellent paper. The only suggestions for revisions pertained to the deletion of certain clinical examples that took away from the incisiveness of her argument. There were also a few comments that implied that she may want to underline some of her points a bit more forcefully. Anna, who had been so petrified of her colleagues' responses, should have been very happy over their critical appraisal. She was not. She had, again, succeeded in turning helpful comments into attacks. Moreover, the time and effort that went into making these revisions were totally out of proportion to the actual size of the task. She went into a veritable frenzy of revisions, consulted more and more colleagues, without really making any more major changes. As the day of the presentation of her paper drew nearer, she was endlessly obsessed over every phrase. She visualized an audience highly critical of her every word, her appearance, her voice, her pronunciation, and so forth. It was only, when in the context of her worrying, I asked her whether she was revising a paper or whether she was polishing a monument, that insight finally emerged. The hidden grandiosity was no longer so hidden, even to Anna. Hers was going to be the ultimate paper, the most polished performance ever given in that context and nobody would find the least fault with her. To the contrary, she hoped to be the star of the entire conference. Now it became clear to her that her fear of competitiveness really was a defense against her unconscious grandiose and exhibitionistic strivings that had been so unresponded to in childhood. On the basis of that insight, a flood of new shaming memories emerged, and with it, regressive experiences of self-hatred and shame. Together with her exploration of her grandiosity, she also came in touch with a considerable amount of oral rage and oral greed. Her difficulties with earning and spending money, revealed among other things, the wish for unlimited wealth and utmost luxury. What she experienced was a sense of utter boredom with life, even though her paper had in fact been very well received, her work with patients was entirely satisfactory to her and her relationship with her lover Peter gave her nothing to complain about. In fact, she seemed almost disappointed that the relationship with Peter was so pleasant and that he seemed to blossom in his own emotional and professional development. Even though the protracted work on her grandiosity and her oral rage was productive, in that it relieved some of her boredom and made life a little bit more exciting, there was still a core part of herself that had not yet been touched by therapy. The fact that Anna's fear of rejection by men had turned into the persistent question: "Is my lover good enough for me?" and Anna's continuous habit of idealizing male authority and of devaluing women finally convinced her that she had to re-evaluate her father. Her identification with an idealized father figure, was clearly an obstacle in her ability to enjoy the relationship with Peter. At the same time it represented a life line that she felt she had to hang onto. On an intellectual level, Anna had always "understood" that her father was irresponsible, immature, incapable of listening and responding and that none of her mother's mistreatment of her children could have taken place without his consent or even collusion. Every time this was pointed out to her, or every time she spoke to him and saw that he related to her like a needy self-absorbed child, she would burst into tears and then ruminate about the question of paternal duties. "Who ever said a father should listen to little kids, answer their questions and concern himself with their troubles?" She rationalized his failures and when this became increasingly difficult, she created two father figures; one, the actual person, and two, the dashing prince-like figure of her childhood dreams. For a while she felt truly stuck. Only when she saw how closely her boredom, her attacks of self loathing, and her unhappiness with Peter correlated with our attempts to critically analyze her relationship with her actual father, did she resolve to really delve into the subject. She temporarily increased the number of individual sessions, and the process of grief and mourning began in earnest. The way in which she utilized her time in therapy was quite ingenious. She made heavy demands on group to be valued in spite of her occasional expressions of hostility and contempt and despite her attempts to provoke group into being critical of her. For quite some time she generated a great deal of what she perceived as assaults and attempts at scapegoating. She needed to test her specialness, practice her ability to deal with criticism and express a considerable amount of narcissistic rage when her provocations were responded to negatively. I also suspected that in part she was also tempted to provoke group into dealing with her so unfairly that she could feel justified in leaving the group and thus avoid the problem of dealing with her self-pathology and her narcissistic rage altogether. Thus, it was vitally important to protect Anna from the consequences of her provocations in the group situation which required a great deal of active intervention on my part.

During that time, Anna's two individual sessions were neatly divided into one session for grief and mourning over the loss of her idealized father, and the second session for internal reconstruction and comfort. Anna's unusual reluctance to deal with her relationship with her father, can only be explained by the fact that analyzing her relationship with her mother had resulted in such massive disillusionment, that she could only do it by retaining the idealized father figure. Thus she had to begin with the search for the good, internalized mother and to look for good mother substitutes in her daily life in order to let go of her father. This process is now almost complete. One of the ways in which Anna has used her second session, aside from integrating the insights of her grief session, has been by what appears on the surface as shop talk, even supervision and some female concerns such as fashion and housekeeping. Clearly, for each renunciation, a new identification was needed and the therapist became one of the role models to identify with. What might have sounded at times like a conversation between two suburban housewives, was in fact a crash-course on the subject of being female, competent and proud of it. In this process Anna has also done a great deal of work on her external presentation of self. She dresses more elegantly, she is beginning to take some pride in her body and she enjoys looking pretty rather than ratty and pathetic. The little match-girl of Andersen's fairy tale is rapidly disappearing.

Anna's moral superiority, her Catholic values of virtue and sin, are steadily being replaced by a sound sense of ethics. She is beginning to truly value the life she *now* has instead of living in fantasies about some happy future. By being able to say yes to what is and what she now has, gratitude for the positive aspects of her life is taking the place of envy for those who were born more privileged. Though minor disappointments and disillusionments have yet to be worked on, a termination date has been set.

REFERENCES

Adorno, T. W., Frenkel-Brunswick, E., Levinson, D. and Sanford, R. N. *The authoritarian personality.* New York: John Wiley and Sons, 1964.

Alexander, F. *The psychoanalysis of the total personality.* New York: Nervous and Mental Disease Publications Co., 1924.

Alexander, F. *The history of psychiatry.* New York: New American Library, 1966.

Aschaffenburg, H. Relationship therapy with a homosexual: A case history. *The Pastoral Counselor,* 1966, *4:* 4–12.

Avery, N. C. Sadomasochism: A defense against object loss. *The Psychoanalytic Review,* 1977, *64:* 101–109.

Bak, R.C. Aggression and perversion. In *Perversions: Psychodynamics and therapy,* ed. S. Lorand. New York: Random House, 1956.

Balfe, J. H. Shame, guilt, and the development of mariolatry. In *Psychosexual imperatives,* M. Coleman Nelson. ed. New York: Human Sciences Press, 1979.

Balint, M. *Primary love and psychoanalytic technique.* New York: Liveright, 1953.

Balint, M. *The basic fault: Therapeutic aspects of regression.* New York: Bruner and Mazel, 1968.

Balter, L. The mother as source of power. *Psychoanalytic Quarterly,* 1969, *38:* 217–274.

Baptiste, D. A comparative study of mother's personality characteristics and

275

childbearing attitudes in husband-present and husband-absent families *Dissertation Abstracts International,* 1977, *37* (Purdue University, Lafayette, Ind.).

Becker, E. Mill's social psychology and the great historical convergence on the problem of alienation. In *The new sociology,* I.L. Horowitz ed. New York: Oxford University Press, 1965.

Bemporad, J. R. Review of object relations theory in light of cognitive development. *Journal of the American Academy of Psychoanalysis,* 1980, *8:* 57–76.

Berliner, B. Libido and reality in masochism. *Psychoanalytic Quarterly,* 1940, *9:* 322–333.

Berliner, B. The concept of masochism. *Psychoanalytic Review,* 1942, *29:* 389–400.

Berliner, B. On some psychodynamics of masochism. *Psychoanalytic Quarterly,* 1947, *16:* 459–471.

Berliner, B. The role of object relations in moral masochism. *Psychoanalytic Quarterly,* 1958, *27:* 38–56.

Bernstein, I. The role of narcissism in moral masochism. *Psychoanalytic Quarterly,* 1957, *26:* 358–377.

Bergler, E. *The basic neurosis.* New York: Grune and Stratton, 1949.

Bergler, E. and Kroger, W. S. *Kinsey's myth of female sexuality.* New York: Grune and Stratton, 1954.

Bergler, E. *Counterfeit-sex.* New York: Grune and Stratton, 1958.

Bergler, E. *Principles of self-damage.* New York: Intercontinental Medical Book Corporation, 1959.

Bettelheim, B. *Symbolic wounds.* Glencoe, Ill.: The Free Press, 1954.

Bettelheim, B. *The informed heart: Autonomy in a mass age.* New York: Macmillan, 1960.

Bettelheim, B. *The children of the dream.* New York: Macmillan, 1969.

Bibring, E. Psychoanalysis and the dynamic psychotherapies. *Journal of the American Psychoanalytic Association,* 1954, *2:* 745–770.

Bieber, I. Sadism and masochism. In *American handbook of psychiatry,* S. Arieti ed. New York: Basic Books, 1966.

Blanck, G. and Blanck, R. *Ego psychology: Theory and practice.* New York: Columbia University Press, 1974.

Blanck, G. and Blanck, R. *Ego psychology II.* New York: Columbia University Press, 1979.

Bloch, D. Feelings that kill: The effect of the wish for infanticide on neurotic depression. *Psychoanalytic Review,* 1965, *52:* 51–66.

Bloch, D. The birth and death of a defensive fantasy. *Psychoanalytic Review,* 1979a, *66:* 358–366.

Bloch, D. *So the witch won't eat me: Fantasy and the child's fear of infanticide.* Boston: Houghton and Mifflin Co, 1979b.

Blumstein, A. Masochism and fantasies of preparing to be incorporated. *Journal of the American Psychoanalytic Association,* 1959, *7:* 292–298.

Boehm, R. The femininity complex in men. *International Journal of Psychoanalysis,* 1930, *11:* 444–469.

Bonaparte, M. *Female sexuality.* New York: International Universities Press, 1953.

Bowlby, J. *Attachment and loss. Vol. 1.: Attachment.* New York: Basic Books, 1969.

Bowlby, J. *Attachment and loss. Vol. 2.: Separation: Anxiety and anger.* New York: Basic Books, 1973.

Breger, L. *From instinct to identity: The development of personality.* Englewood Cliffs: Prentice Hall, 1974.

Brenman, M. On teasing and being teased and the problem of moral masochism. *The psychoanalytic study of the child, 7:* 264–285, New York: International Universities Press, 1952.

Brenner, C. The masochistic character. *Journal of the American Psychoanalytic Association,* 1959, *7:* 197–226.

Bromberg, N. Maternal influences in the development of moral masochism. *American Journal of Orthopsychiatry,* 1955, *25:* 802–809.

Bromberg, N. Stimulus-response cycles and ego development: With specific reference to the masochistic ego. *Journal of the American Psychoanalytic Association,* 1959, *7:* 227–247.

Brownmiller, S. *Against our will: Men, women and rape.* New York: Simon and Schuster, 1975.

Butler, S. *Conspiracy of silence: The trauma of incest.* New York: Bantam Books, 1978.

Bychowsky, G. Some aspects of masochistic involvement. *Journal of the American Psychoanalytic Association,* 1959, *7:* 248–273.

Chadwick, M. *The psychological problems in menstruation.* New York: Nervous and Mental Disease Publications, 1932.

Chasseguet-Smirgel, J. Transsexuality, paranoia and the repudiation of femininity. In *Psychosexual imperatives,* M. Coleman Nelson ed. New York: Human Sciences Press, 1979.

Chassel, J. Report of panel on psychotherapy. *Journal of the American Psychoanalytic Association,* 1953, *1:* 550–553.

Chessick, R. D. *How psychotherapy heals.* New York: Science House, 1969.

Chessick, R. D. *Why psychotherapists fail.* New York: Science House, 1971.

Chessick, R. D. *Intensive psychotherapy of the borderline patient.* New York: Jason Aronson, 1977.

Chessick, R. D. A practical approach to the psychotherapy of the borderline patient. *American Journal of Psychotherapy*, 1979, *33:* 531–546.

Cohen, M. B. Personal identity and sexual identity. *Psychiatry*, 1966, *29:* 1–14.

David, H. T. and Mendel, A. *The Bach reader, a life of Johann Sebastian Bach in letters and documents.* New York: W. W. Norton, 1945.

Davidson, T. *Conjugal crime.* New York: Hawthorne Books Inc, 1978.

Davoren, E. The role of the social worker. In *The battered child,* R. E. Helfer and C. H. Kempe eds. Chicago: University of Chicago Press, 1968.

Deluze, G. *Masochism.* New York: George Braziller, 1971.

De Monchy, R. Masochism as a pathological and as a normal phenomenon in the human mind. *International Journal for Psychoanalysis,* 1950. *31:* 95–97.

De Saint Exupéry, A. *The little prince.* K. Woods trans. New York: Harcourt, Brace and World, 1943.

Deutsch, H. *The psychology of women.* New York: Grune and Stratton, 1944.

Dinnerstein, D. *The mermaid and the minotaur: Sexual arrangements and human malaise.* New York: Harper and Row, 1976.

Domash, L. and Shapiro, R. Dysfunctional patterns of thinking in the borderline personality. *Journal of the American Academy of Psychoanalysis,* ——, *7:* 543–552.

Ehrhardt, A. A. and Joney, J. *Man and woman, boy and girl.* Baltimore: The John Hopkins Press, 1972.

Eibl - Eibesfeld, I. *Love and hate: The natural history of behavior patterns,* G. Strachen trans. New York: Holt, Rinehart and Winston, 1972.

Eidelberg, L. *A contribution to the study of masochism.* New York: Nervous and Mental Disease Series, 75, 1948.

Eidelberg, L. Humiliation in masochism. *Journal of the American Psychoanalytic Association,* 1959, *7:* 274–283.

Eisenbud, R. J. Masochism revisited. *Psychoanalytic Review,* 1967, *54:* 5–27.

Eissler, K. R. The effect of the structure of the ego on psychoanalytic technique. *Journal of the American Psychoanalytic Association,* 1953, *1:* 105–143.

Elkish, P. The psychological significance of the mirror. *Journal of the American Psychoanalytic Association,* 1959, *5:* 253–244.

Epstein, G. Healing and imagination. *The Academy Forum,* 1977, *21:* 4.

Epstein, G. The experience of the waking dream. In *Healing: Implications for psychotherapy,* P. Olsen and J. Fosshage eds. New York: Human Sciences Press, 1978.

Erikson, E. *Identity youth and crisis.* New York: W. W. Norton, 1968.

Fairbairn, W. R. D. *Psychoanalytic studies of the personality.* London: Tavistock Publications, 1952.

Fenichel, O. A critique of the death instinct. In *Collected papers, 1:* 363–373. New York: W. W. Norton, 1935.

Fenichel, O. *The psychoanalytic theory of neuroses.* New York: W. W. Norton, 1945.

Fineman, J. Psychoanalysis, bisexuality and the difference before the sexes. In *Psychosexual imperatives,* M. Coleman Nelson ed. New York: Human Sciences Press, 1979.

Fleming, J. Some observations on object constancy in the psychoanalysis of adults. *Journal of the American Psychoanalytic Association,* 1975, *23:* 743–760.

Forisha, B. L. *Sex roles and personal awareness.* Morristown, N.J.: Scott, Foreman & Co, 1978.

Forrest, T. The dreams and dynamics of obsessional women. In *Psychosexual imperatives,* M. Coleman Nelson ed. New York: Human Sciences Press, 1979.

Foucault, M. *The history of sexuality.* R. Hurley trans. New York: Pantheon Books, 1978.

French-Wixon, J. Differences between father-absent and father-present fifth-grade boys in political socialization. *Dissertation Abstracts International:* 37. Florida State Univeristy, 1977.

Freud, A. and Burlingham, D. *Infants without families: The case for and against residential nurseries.* New York: International Universities Press, 1943.

Freud, A. and Dann, S. An experiment in group upbringing. *Psychoanalytic study of the child, 6:* 127–168. New York: International Universities Press, 1951.

Freud, S. On the sexual theories of children. *Collected Papers, 2.* (1950) London: Hogarth Press, 1908.

Freud, S. Some characters met with in psychoanalytic work. *Collected Papers, 4.* (1950) London: Hogarth Press, 1915a.

Freud, S. Instincts and their vicissitudes. *Collected Papers, 4.* (1950) London: Hogarth Press, 1915b.

Freud, S. A child is being beaten: A contribution to the study of the origin of sexual perversions. *Collected Papers, 2.* (1950). London: Hogarth Press, 1919.

Freud, S. *Beyond the pleasure principle.* London: Hogarth Press, 1920.

Freud, S. *The ego and the id.* London: Hogarth Press, 1923.

Freud, S. The economic problem in masochism. *Collected Papers, 2.* (1950) London: Hogarth Press, 1924.

Freud, S. *An outline of psychoanalysis.* J. Strachey ed. New York: W. W. Norton, 1949.

Freud, S. The psychology of women. In *New introductory lectures on psychoanalysis*. New York: W. W. Norton, 1953.

Freud, S. Totem and Taboo. In *Standard Edition of the Complete Psychological Works of Sigmund Freud*. J. Strachey ed. *13:* 1–162. London: Hogarth Press, 1955.

Freud, S. Lines of advance in psychoanalytic therapy. In *Standard edition of the complete psychological works of Sigmund Freud, 17*. J. Strachey, ed. London: Hogarth Press, 1964a.

Freud, S. Three contributions to the theory of sexuality. In *Standard edition of the complete psychological works of Sigmund Freud, 17*. J. Strachey, ed. London: Hogarth Press, 1964b.

Freud, S. The taboo of virginity. In *Sexuality and the psychology of love*, P. Rieff, ed. New York: Collier Books, 1972a.

Freud, S. Some psychological consequences of the anatomical distinction between the sexes. In *Sexuality and the psychology of love*, R. Rieff, ed. New York: Collier Books, 1972b.

Friday, N. *My mother myself.* New York: Delacorte Press, 1977.

Frieze, I. H., Parsons, J. E., Johnson, P. B., Ruble, D. N., and Zellman, G. L. *Women and sex roles.* New York: W. W. Norton, 1978.

Fromm, E. Über Methode und Aufgabe einer analytischen Sozialpsychologie. *Zeitschrift für Sozialforschung, 1932a, 1–2:* 28–54.

Fromm, E. Die psychoanalytische Characterologie und ihre Bedeutung für die Sozialpsychologie. *Zeitschrift für Sozialforschung,* 1932b, *3:* 253–277.

Fromm, E. Sozialpsychologischer Teil. In *Studien Über Autorität und Familie*, M. Horkheimer, ed. Paris: Librairie Félix Alcan, 1936.

Fromm, E. *Escape from freedom.* New York: Holt, Rinehart and Winston, 1941.

Fromm, E. *The forgotten language.* New York: Grove Press, 1951.

Fromm, E. *The anatomy of human destructiveness.* New York: Fawcett Crest Books, 1973.

Gadpaille, W. Research into the physiology of maleness and femaleness. *Archives of General Psychiatry,* 1972, *26:* 193–206.

Galen, A. Rethinking Freud on female sexuality: A look at the new orthodox defense. *Psychoanalytic Review,* 1979, *66:* 173–186.

Gedo, J. H. and Goldberg, A. *Models of the mind.* Chicago: University of Chicago Press, 1973.

Gedo, J. H. Theory of object relations: A metapsychological assessment. *Journal of the American Psychoanalytic Association,* 1979, *27:* 361–373.

Gero, G. Sadism, masochism and aggression: Their role in symptom formation. *Psychoanalytic Quarterly,* 1962, *31:* 31–42.

Gil, D. G. *Violence against children*. Cambridge: Harvard University Press, 1970.

Gill, M. M. Ego psychology and psychotherapy. *Psychoanalytic Quarterly,* 1951, *20:* 62–71.

Gill, M. M. Psychoanalysis and exploratory psychotherapy. *Journal of the American Psychoanalytic Association,* 1954, *2:* 771–797.

Goodman, N. Eve, child of Adam. In *Psychosexual imperatives*, M. Coleman Nelson, ed. New York: Human Sciences Press, 1979.

Gordon, R. E., Kapostins, E. E. and Gordon, K. K. Factors in postpartum emotional adjustment. *Obstetrics and Gynecology,* 1967, *25:* 158–166.

Greene, G. and Greene, C. *S-M The last taboo*. New York: Ballantine Books, 1974.

Guntrip, H. *Personality structure and human interaction*. New York: International Universities Press, 1961.

Hallie, P. *The paradox of cruelty*. Middletown, Conn.: Wesleyan University Press, 1969.

Harris, H. Some linguistic considerations related to the issue of female orgasm. *Psychoanalytic Review,* 1979, *66:* 197–200.

Hartmann, H., Kris, E. and Lowenstein, R. Notes on the theory of aggression. *The psychoanalytic study of the child. 3–4*: 9–36. New York: International Universities Press, 1949.

Hartmann, H. *Essays on ego psychology*. New York: International Universities Press, 1964.

Hartmann, H. and Lowenstein, R. Notes on the superego. *The psychoanalytic study of the child, 17:* 42–81. New York: International Universities Press, 1962.

Hays, R. H. *The dangerous sex: The myth of feminine evil*. New York: G. P. Putnam and Sons, 1964.

Heimann, P. Comment on Dr. Kernberg's paper. *International Journal of Psychoanalysis,* 1966, *56:* 137–146.

Helfer, R. A. and Kempe, H. C., eds. *The battered child*. Chicago: University of Chicago Press, 1968.

Hentig, H. von *Der nekrotope Mensch*. Stuttgart: F. Enke Verlag, 1964.

Herman, J. and Hirshman, L. Father daughter incest. *Signs,* 1977, *2:* 735–756.

Hoch, P. H. Masochism: Clinical considerations. In *Individual and family dynamics*, J. Masserman ed. New York: Grune and Stratton, 1959.

Horney, K. *New ways in psychoanalysis*. New York: W. W. Norton, 1939.

Horney, K. *Feminine psychology*. New York: W. W. Norton, 1967.

Hull, D. Examination of three maternal characteristics in relationship to sex role development in father-present and father-absent children. *Dissertation Abstracts International,* 37. University of Washington, 1976.

Jackins, H. *The human side of human beings.* Seattle: Rational Island Publishers, 1964.

Jacobson, E. *Depression: Comparative studies of normal, neurotic and psychotic conditions.* New York: International Universities Press, 1971.

Jacobson, E. *The self and the object world.* New York: International Universities Press, 1973.

Justice, B. and Justice, R. *The broken taboo: Sex in the family.* New York: Human Sciences Press, 1979.

Kadison, C. *Structure and dynamics in sadistic and masochistic sexual fantasies.* Unpublished B.A. Thesis. State University of New York: College at Purchase, 1977.

Kadushin, C. *Why people go to psychiatrists.* New York: Atherton Press, 1969.

Kanzer, M. Object relation theory: An introduction. *Journal of the American Psychoanalytic Association,* 1979 *27:* 313–325.

Kardiner, A. *Psychological frontiers of society.* New York: Columbia University Press, 1945.

Kernberg, O. Early ego integration and object relations. *Annals of the New York Academy of Sciences,* 1972, *193:* 233–247.

Kernberg, O. *Borderline conditions and pathological narcissism.* New York: Jason Aronson, 1975.

Kernberg, O. *Object relations theory and clinical psychoanalysis.* New York: Jason Aronson, 1976.

Khan, M. M. R. *The privacy of the self.* New York: International Universities Press, 1974.

Khan, M. M. R. *Alienation in perversions.* New York: International Universities Press, 1979.

Kinsey, A., Pomeroy, W. B., Martin, C. E. and Gebhard, P. *Sexual behavior in the human female.* Philadelphia: Saunders and Co, 1953.

Klein, M. *Contributions to psychoanalysis.* London: Hogarth Press, 1940.

Klein, M. *Envy and gratitude.* London: Tavistock Publications, 1957.

Klein, V. *The feminine character: History of an ideology.* Chicago: University of Illinois Press, 1972.

Kohut, H. Forms and transformations of narcissism. *Journal of the American Psychoanalytic Association,* 1966, *14:* 243–272.

Kohut, H. *The analysis of the self.* New York: International Universities Press, 1971.

Kohut, H. *The restauration of the self.* New York: International Universities Press, 1977.

Lash, C. *The culture of narcissism.* New York: W. W. Norton, 1979.

Le Boit, J. and Capponi, L. eds. *Advances in psychotherapy of the borderline patient.* New York: Jason Aronson, 1979.

Lederer, W. *The fear of women.* New York: Harcourt, Brace Jovanovich, 1968.

Leites, N. *Depression and masochism.* New York: W. W. Norton, 1969.

Lesse, S. The status of violence against women: Past, present and future factors. *American Journal of Psychotherapy,* 1979, *33:* 190–200.

Lester, E. On the psychosexual development of the female child. *Journal of the American Academy of Psychoanalysis,* 1976, *4:* 515–529.

Lewis, H. Block *Shame and guilt in neuroses.* New York: International Universities Press, 1971.

Lewis, H. Block *Psychic war in men and women.* New York: New York University Press 1976.

Lichtenberg, J. D. Factors in the development of the sense of the object. *Journal of the American Psychoanalytic Association,* 1979, *27:* 375–386.

Loewald, H. W. On the therapeutic action of psychoanalysis. *The International Journal of Psychoanalysis,* 1960, *41:* 16–33.

Loewald, H. W. Instinct theory, object relations and psychic structure formation. *Journal of the American Psychoanalytic Association,* 1978, *26:* 493–506.

Lorand, S., ed. *Perversions: Psychodynamics and therapy.* New York: Random House, 1956.

Lorenz, K. *King Solomon's ring: New light on animal ways.* New York: Thomas Y. Crowell, 1952.

Lorenz, K. *On aggression.* New York: Harcourt, Brace and World, 1966.

Lowenstein, R. A contribution to the psychoanalytic theory in masochism. *Journal of the American Psychoanalytic Association.* 1957, *5:* 197–234.

Mc Devitt, J. B. and Settlage, C. S., eds. *Separation, individuation: Essays in honor of Margaret S. Mahler.* New York: International Universities Press, 1971.

Mc Devitt, J. B. The role of internalization in the development of object relations during the separation individuation phase. *Journal of the American Psychoanalytic Association,* 1979, *27:* 327–343.

Mahler, M. S. On human symbiosis and the vicissitudes of individuation. *Journal of the American Psychoanalytic Association,* 1967, *15:* 710–762.

Mahler, M. S. *On human symbiosis and the vicissitudes of individuation.* New York: International Universities Press, 1968.

Mahler, M. S., Pine, F. and Berman, A. *The psychological birth of the human infant.* New York: Basic Books, 1975.

Mailer, N. The prisoner of sex. *Harpers Magazine,* 1971, Vol. 242. No. 1450.

Malleus Maleficarum, Part I. Rev. Montague Summers, trans. London: The Pushkin Press, 1928.

Maslow, A. *Motivation and personality*. New York: Harper and Bros, 1954.

Martin, D. *Battered wives*. New York: Pocket Books, 1977.

Masserman, J. Masochism: A biodynamic summary. In *Individual and family dynamics*, J. Masserman ed. New York: Grune and Stratton, 1959.

Masterson, J. F. *Treatment of the borderline adolescent: A developmental approach*. New York: Wiley and Sons, 1972.

Masterson, J. F. *Psychotherapy of the borderline adult: A developmental approach*. New York: Brunner and Mazel, 1976.

Masterson, J. F., ed. *New perspectives on psychotherapy of the borderline adult*. New York: Bruner and Mazel, 1978.

Mead, M. *Male and female*. New York: William Morrow and Co, 1949.

Meissner, W. W. Notes on some conceptual aspects of borderline personality organization. *International Review of Psychoanalysis*, 1978a, *5:* 297–310.

Meissner, W. W. Theoretical assumptions of concepts of the borderline personality. *Journal of the American Psychoanalytic Association*, 1978b, *26:* 559–598.

Meissner, W. W. Internalizations and object relations. *Journal of the American Psychoanalytic Association*, 1979, *27:* 345–360.

Menaker, E. The masochistic factor in the psychoanalytic situation. *Psychoanalytic Quarterly*, 1942, *11:* 171–186.

Menaker, E. Masochism as a defense reaction. *Psychoanalytic Quarterly*, 1953, *22:* 205–220.

Menaker, E. *Masochism and the emergent ego*. New York: Human Sciences Press, 1979.

Menninger, K. *Man against himself*. New York: Harcourt and Brace, 1938.

Millet, J. A. Masochism: Psychogenesis and therapeutic principles. In *Individual and family dynamics*, J. Masserman, ed. New York: Grune and Stratton, 1959.

Millett, K. *Sexual politics*. Garden City, N.Y.: Doubleday and Co, 1970.

Mitscherlich, A. *The inability to mourn*. B. R. Placzek, trans. New York: Grove Press, 1975.

Modell, A. Primitive object relationships and the predisposition to schizophrenia. *International Journal of Psychoanalysis*, 1963, *44:* 282–292.

Modell, A. *Object love and reality*. New York: International Universities Press, 1968.

Modell, A. The ego and the id: Fifty years later. *International Journal of Psychoanalysis*, 1975a, *56:* 57–68.

Modell, A. A narcissistic defense against affect and the illusion of self-sufficiency. *International Journal of Psychoanalysis*, 1975b, *56:* 275–282.

Money, J. Gender role, gender identity, core gender identity: Usages and definition of terms. *Journal of the American Academy of Psychoanalysis*, 1953, *1:* 397–404.

Montagu, A. *Man and aggression.* Oxford: Oxford University Press, 1968a.

Montagu, A. *The natural superiority of women.* New York: Macmillan, 1968b.

Moser, T. *Years of apprenticeship on the couch.* New York: Urizen Books, 1977.

Murray, J. M. Narcissism and ego ideal. *Journal of the American Psychoanalytic Association*, 1964, *12:* 477–528.

Nunberg, H. *Principles of psychoanalysis.* New York: International Universities Press, 1955.

Nydes, J. The paranoid masochistic character. *Psychoanalytic Review*, 1963, *50:* 55–91.

Ostow, M. *Sexual deviation: Psychoanalytic insights.* New York: Quadrangle/The New York Times Book Co, 1974.

Panken, S. *The joy of suffering: The psychoanalytic theory of masochism.* New York: Jason Aronson, 1973.

Person, E. and Oversey, L. Transvestism: New perspectives. *The Journal of the American Academy of Psychoanalysis*, 1978, *6:* 301–323.

Piaget, J. and Inhelder, B. *The psychology of the child.* New York: Basic Books, 1966.

Piaget, J. *The child and reality.* New York: Penguin Books, 1976.

Rado, S. Fear of castration in women. *Psychoanalytic Quarterly*, 1953, *2:* 425–475.

Rangell, L. Lessons from watergate: A derivative for psychoanalysis. *Psychoanalytic Quarterly*, 1976, *45:* 37–61.

Rank, O. *Will therapy.* New York: W. W. Norton, 1978.

Reich, A. A contribution to the psychoanalysis of extreme submissiveness in women. *Psychoanalytic Quarterly*, 1940, *9:* 470–480.

Reich, W. *Character analysis.* New York: Orgone Institute Press, 1933.

Reik, T. *Masochism in modern man.* New York: Farrar and Strauss, 1941.

Reik, T. The creation of women. New York: Mc Graw Hill, 1960.

Reiter, R. R., ed. *Toward an anthropology of women.* New York: Monthly Review Press, 1975.

Restak, R. M. *From the brain: The last frontier.* New York: Doubleday and Co., 1979.

Robertiello, R. C. and Shadmi, R. M. Dynamics in female sexual problems. *Journal of Contemporary Psychotherapy*, 1968, *1:* 19–25.

Roberts, A. R. ed. *Self destructive behavior.* Springfield, Ill.: Charles C. Thomas, 1975.

Romm, M. E. The roots of masochism. In *Individual and family dynamics,* J. Masserman, ed. New York: Grune and Stratton, 1959.

Rubinfine, D. On beating fantasies. *International Journal of Psychoanalysis,* 1965, *46:* 315–322.

Sack, R. L. and Miller, W. Masochism: A clinical and theoretical overview. *Psychiatry,* 1975, *38:* 244–257.

Salzman, L. Masochism: A review of theory and therapy. In *Individual and family dynamics,* J. Masserman, ed. New York: Grune and Stratton, 1959.

Satran, G. Notes on loneliness. *The Journal of the American Academy of Psychoanalysis,* 1978, *6:* 281–300.

Schatzman, M. *Soul murder: Persecution in the family.* New York: Random House, 1973.

Schecter, D. E. Fear of success in women: A psychodynamic reconstruction. *Journal of the American Academy of Psychoanalysis,* 1979, *7:* 33–43.

Schilder, P. *Psychoanalysis, man, and society.* Arr. by L. Bender. New York: W. W. Norton, 1951.

Schimmel, J. L. The function of wit and humor in psychoanalysis. *The Journal of the American Academy of Psychoanalysis,* 1978, *6:* 359–379.

Schuker, E. Psychodynamics and treatment of sexual assault victims. *Journal of the American Academy of Psychoanalysis,* 1979, *7:* 553–574.

Schuster, D. B. Notes on a child is being beaten. *Psychoanalytic Quarterly,* 1966, *35:* 357–367.

Searles, H. *Collected papers on schizophrenia and related subjects.* New York: International Universities Press, 1965.

Seidenberg, R. Psychoanalysis and the feminist movement. In *Psychosexual imperatives,* M. Coleman Nelson ed. New York: Human Sciences Press, 1979.

Shainberg, D. Working with imagination in the treatment of borderline patients. *Journal of the American Academy of Psychoanalysis,* 1979, *7:* 419–435.

Shainess, N. Vulnerability to violence: Masochism as process. *American Journal of Psychotherapy,* 1979, *33:* 174–181.

Shengold, L. L. Child abuse and deprivation: Soul murder. *Journal of the American Psychoanalytic Association,* 1979, *27:* 535–559.

Sherman, J. *On the psychology of women: A survey of empirical studies.* Springfield, Ill.: Charles C. Thomas, 1971.

Shorr, J. E. *Psycho-imagination therapy.* New York: Intercontinental Book Corporation, 1972.

Smirnoff, V. N. The masochistic contract. *International Journal of Psychoanalysis,* 1969, *50:* 665–671.

Somers, B. Re-evaluation therapy: Theoretical framework. *Journal of Humanistic Psychology*, 1972, *1:* 72–92.

Spitz, R. A. *The genetic field theory of ego formation.* New York: International Universities Press, 1959.

Spitz, R. A. *The first year of life.* New York: International Universities Press, 1965.

Spotnitz, H. *Psychotherapy of preoedipal conditions: Schizophrenia and severe character disorders.* New York: Jason Aronson, 1976.

Spruiell, V. Object relations theory: Clinical perspectives. *Journal of the American Psychoanalytic Association,* 1976, *27:* 387–389.

Steele, B. F. and Pollack, C. B. A psychiatric study of parents who abuse infants and small children. In *The battered child,* R. E. Helfe and G. H. Kempe eds. Chicago: University of Chicago Press, 1968.

Stein, M. (Chairman) Panel on aggression. A. Nissier (Reporter) *International Journal of Psychoanalysis,* 1972, *53:* 13–20.

Steinmetz, S.K. *The cycle of violence.* New York: Holt, Rinehart and Winston, 1977.

Stern, A. Psychoanalytic investigation of and therapy in the borderline group of neuroses. *Psychoanalytic Quarterly,* 1938, *7:* 467–489.

Stern, A. Psychoanalytic therapy in borderline neuroses. *Psychoanalytic Quarterly,* 1945, *14:* 190–198.

Stoller, R. J. *Sex and gender Vol. 2.* New York: Jason Aronson, 1968.

Stoller, R. J. *Splitting: A case of female masculinity.* New York: Dell Publishing Co, 1973.

Stoller, R. J. *Perversion.* New York: Dell Publishing Co, 1975.

Stoller, R. J. Fathers of transsexual children. *Journal of the American Psychoanalytic Association,* 1979, *27:* 837–866.

Stolorow, A. D. and Lachman, M. *Psychoanalysis of developmental arrests.* New York: International Universities Press, 1980.

Stolz, R. *Father relations of war born children.* Stanford: Stanford University Press, 1954.

Stone, L. Psychoanalysis and brief psychotherapy. *Psychoanalytic Quarterly,* 1951, *20:* 215–235.

Stone, L. The widening scope of indications for psychoanalysis. *Journal of the American Psychoanalytic Association,* 1954, *2:* 567–594.

Stone, L. Reflections on the psychoanalytic concept of aggression. *Psychoanalytic Quarterly,* 1971, *40:* 195–244.

Stone, M. H. Psychodiagnosis and psychoanalytic psychotherapy. *Journal of the American Academy of Psychoanalysis,* 1979, *7:* 79–100.

Stone, M. H. *The borderline syndromes.* New York: Mc Graw Hill, 1980.

Storr, A. *Human destructiveness.* New York: W. Morrow and Co, 1972.

Symonds, A. Violence against women: The myth of masochism. *American Journal of Psychotherapy,* 1979, *33:* 161–173.

The New York Times. Fashion of the times: The way to dress. *The New York Times Magazine,* Part 2. Aug. 24, 1980.

Thomas, A. and Chess, S. *The dynamics of psychological development.* New York: Bruner and Mazel, 1980.

Thompson, C. The interpersonal approach to the clinical problems of masochism. In *Individual and family dynamics,* J. Masserman ed. New York: Grune and Stratton, 1959.

Toch, H. *Violent men: An inquiry into the psychology of violence.* Chicago: Aldine Publ. Co, 1969.

Tuttman, S. Regression: Is it necessary or desirable? *Journal of the American Academy of Psychoanalysis,* 1979, *7:* 111–133.

Vanggaard, T. *Phallós: A symbol and it's history in the male world.* New York: International Universities Press, 1972.

Vaillant, G. The natural history of male psychological health. In *The adult life cycle from 18–50.* Harvard: Seminars in Psychiatry, 1974.

Waelder, R. The principle of multiple function. *Psychoanalytic Quarterly,* 1936, *15:* 45–62.

Waelder, R. *Basic theory of psychoanalysis.* New York: Schocken Books, 1960.

Walters, D. R. *Physical and sexual abuse of children: Causes and treatment.* Bloomington: Indiana University Press, 1975.

Weil, A. P. Maturational variations and genetic dynamic issues. *Journal of the American Psychoanalytic Association,* 1978, *26:* 461–491.

Weinberg, K. S. *Incest behavior.* New York: Citadel Press, 1955.

Westhoff, C. F., Potter, R. G. Jr., and Sagi, P. C. *The third child.* Princeton, N.J.: Princeton University Press, 1963.

White, R. Competence and the psychosexual stages of development. In *Nebraska symposium on motivation,* M. R. Jones ed. Lincoln, Neb: University of Nebraska Press, 1960.

White, R. Ego and reality in psychoanalytic theory. *Psychological Issues,* 3. New York: International Universities Press, 1963.

Winnicott, D. W. Transitional objects and transitional phenomena. *International Journal of Psychoanalysis,* 1953, *34:* 89–97.

Winnicott, D. W. *The maturational processes and the facilitating environment.* New York: International Universities Press, 1965.

Winnicott, D. W. Mirror role of mother and family in child development. In *The predicament of the family*. P. Lomas ed. London: Hogarth Press, 1967.

Witenberg, E. G. The inevitability of uncertainty. *Journal of the American Academy of Psychoanalysis*, 1978, *6:* 275–279.

Wolberg, A. *The borderline patient*. New York: International Medical Book Corp, 1973.

Zetzel, E. and Meissner, W. *Basic concepts of psychoanalytic psychiatry*. New York: Basic Books, 1973.

Zetzel, E. A developmental approach to the borderline patient. *American Journal of Psychiatry*, 1971, *128:* 867–871.

Zilboorg, G. Sidelights on parent-child antagonism. *American Journal of Orthopsychiatry*, 1932, *2:* 35–43.

Zilboorg, G. Masculine and feminine. *Psychiatry*, 1944, 7: 257–296.

INDEX

INDEX